Praise for Lacrosse For Dummies

"I loved playing lacrosse and I'm still a huge fan. *Lacrosse For Dummies* has something for every lacrosse coach, player, and fan."

> — Brendan Shanahan, three-time Stanley Cup champion and former lacrosse star

"We've seen lacrosse grow so much in the last five years. As lacrosse gets more popular at all levels, more and more people want to find out what this game is all about. *Lacrosse For Dummies* helps people understand why lacrosse is the 'fastest game on two feet.'"

> — Larry Power, Ontario lacrosse historian

"Not only is *Lacrosse For Dummies* informative and entertaining for the newcomers to lacrosse, it's also a must-have reference for us so-called experts."

> — Brian Shanahan , five-time Mann Cup winner and television analyst for Sportnet's NLL coverage

"This book gives the inside edge to die-hard fans and newcomers to the sport."

> — Les Bartley, coach of the NLL's Toronto Rock and six-time NLL champion

"The toughness and physical aspect of lacrosse has definitely had an influence on my playing ability in hockey. This book is the bible for all lacrosse books, explaining in depth the intricacies of playing this game. Jim has called on his 40 years of experience to help produce an entertaining and informative guide to lacrosse fans, coaches, and players."

> — Gary Roberts, NHL all-star and former junior A Canadian lacrosse champion

"*Lacrosse For Dummies* has all the answers and more."

> — Wayne Colley, former coach of the NLL's Columbus Landsharks

"Jim Hinkson's passion and enthusiasm for lacrosse comes through on every page."

> — Joe Nieuwendyk, NHL all-star and MVP of the 1984 Minto Cup championship

Lacrosse For Dummies®

Tracking the Players: A Lacrosse Game Box Score

Ready to head out for a lacrosse game? Take this box score with you so that you can keep track of your favourite players — whether they be NLL players, NCAA players, or your daughter and her teammates. Be sure to make photocopies of this original so that you can use this handy tool during every game. And don't forget to take along the referee signal primer on the other side of this cheat sheet.

#	Player	G	A	Pts	PPG	SHG	Total shots	Shots on goal	Shots off goal	Penalties (#/min.)	Faceoffs (W-L)	LB

Key: ## = player's number; G = goals; A = assists; Pts = combined total of goals and assists; PFG = power-play goals; SHG = short-handed goals; LB = loose balls

...For Dummies®: Bestselling Book Series for Beginners

Lacrosse For Dummies®

Speaking Lacrosse Referee-ese

Lacrosse is enough of a fast-paced game to leave your head spinning and your eyes darting without having to worry about what each referee signal means. Next time you're at a game, take along a copy of this helpful reference so that you can tell your hand-ball from your butt-end — call, that is.

You can find these images in Chapter 4 of this book, along with a bit more detail about when each violation and penalty come into play. This cheat sheet places them all on one page so that you can take a copy with you to the arena.

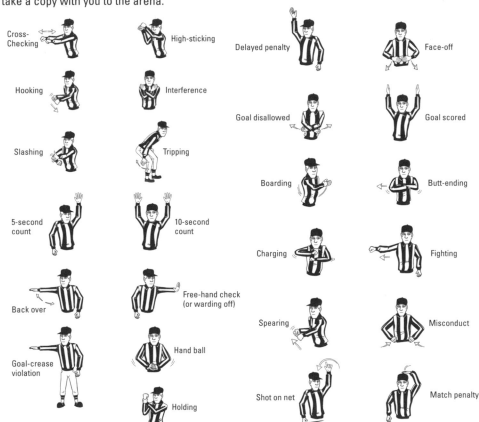

...For Dummies®: Bestselling Book Series for Beginners

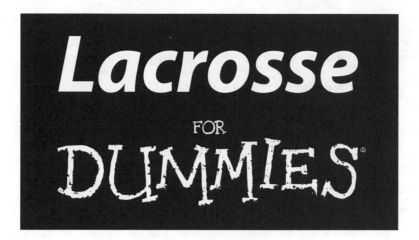

by Jim Hinkson, John Jiloty, and Robert Carpenter

Foreword by Brian Shanahan

John Wiley & Sons Canada, Ltd

Lacrosse For Dummies®

Published by
John Wiley & Sons
6045 Freemont Blvd.
Mississauga, ON L5R 4J3
www.wiley.ca

National Library of Canada Cataloguing in Publication

Hinkson, Jim

Lacrosse for dummies / Jim Hinkson, the editors of Inside lacrosse.

Includes index.
ISBN 1-894413-49-0

1. Lacrosse. I. Title.

GV989.H55 2003   796.34'7   C2003-900994-7

Printed in Canada

2 3 4 5 TRI 09 08 07 06

For general information on John Wiley & Sons Canada, Ltd., including all books published by Wiley Publishing, Inc., please call our warehouse, Tel 1-800-567-4797. For reseller information, including discounts and premium sales, please call our sales department, Tel 416-646-7992. For press review copies, author interviews, or other publicity information, please contact our marketing department, Tel: 416-646-4584, Fax 416-236-4448.

For authorization to photocopy items for corporate, personal, or educational use, please contact Cancopy, The Canadian Copyright Licensing Agency, One Yonge Street, Suite 1900, Toronto, ON, M5E 1E5 Tel 416-868-1620 Fax 416-868-1621; www.cancopy.com.

About the Authors

Jim Hinkson has been involved in the game of lacrosse since he was 19, his first season of play coming under the tutelage of legendary coach Jim Bishop in 1962. Hinkson played lacrosse for 11 more years, participating in 9 national minor championship games and winning 6 titles. He also played for a season in the 1970s version of the National Lacrosse League, and represented Canada as part of the national team competing in the 1974 World Lacrosse Championship in Melbourne, Australia.

Hinkson has coached at every level in lacrosse from house league to professional, participating in two Canadian junior championships, winning one. His coaching stints have included teams in Toronto, Whitby, and St. Catharines, Ontario; and the New York Saints and New Jersey Storm of today's National Lacrosse League. And he is the author of four books on lacrosse and coaching.

Hinkson grew up on a farm in Oshawa, Ontario, and he still lives in nearby Whitby, Ontario, with his wife Cynndy and their three children, to whom he dedicates this book. Lacrosse is an all-Hinkson family activity. Daughter Maggie, a first-year teacher in Whitby, played women's field lacrosse at the University of Western Ontario; daughter Kate attends Brock University in St. Catharines and plays for its women's field lacrosse team; and son James, who attends St. Thomas University in Fredericton, New Brunswick, has played box lacrosse for the Darlington Green Gaels, who just won the Founder's Cup emblematic of junior B lacrosse for Canada.

John Jiloty is the editor-in-chief of *Inside Lacrosse* magazine and a 2000 graduate of Syracuse University, where he covered men's lacrosse as the sports editor of *The Daily Orange*. John was recognized in *The Best American Sports Writing 2002* for a story he did in 2001 on fighting in the National Lacrosse League.

Robert Carpenter is the founder and publisher of *Inside Lacrosse* magazine. He played lacrosse at Duke University, from which he graduated in 1996. *Inside Lacrosse* is the sport's only media outlet that has been honored for coverage by both the men's and women's college coaches associations. *Inside Lacrosse* also publishes *Face-Off Yearbook,* an annual glossy preview of men's college lacrosse, and operates a lacrosse camp Web site called USLaxcamps.com.

Acknowledgements

Jim Hinkson: Thanks to my former teammates, players, and friends in lacrosse who have touched my life as I journeyed along my whirlwind lacrosse path. From Oshawa to Brooklin to Detroit to Peterborough to Windsor to Philadelphia to Rexdale to Whitby to St. Catharines to New York to Toronto and to New Jersey, it has been a great ride with lots of ups and downs.

I would like to thank the following NLL coaches and players for their contributions to the book: Coaches Les Bartley, Ed Comeau, and Derek Keenan of the Toronto Rock; Terry Sanderson of the Ottawa Rebel; and Wayne Colley of the Columbus Landsharks. Players Chris Driscoll and Gee Nash of the New York Saints; Steve Toll, Jim Veltman, and Bob Watson of the Toronto Rock; Derrick Suddons of the Columbus Landsharks; Brad MacArthur of the Calgary Roughnecks; Nick Trudeau and Cam Woods of the Albany Attack; Steve Fannell of the Ottawa Rebel; and Dallas Eliuk of the Philadelphia Wings.

I would like to thank the following people for their input in the book: Mark Brown on equipment, Stan Shillington and Larry Power for their help on the history of lacrosse in British Columbia and in Ontario, Paul Ravary for his expertise on refereeing, and Andy Glen and Josh Colley with the Darlington Green Gaels.

Publisher's Acknowledgments

We're proud of this book; please send us your comments at canadapt@wiley.com. Some of the people who helped bring this book to market include the following:

Acquisitions and Editorial

Executive Editor: Joan Whitman

Editor: Michael Kelly

Copy Editor: Pamela Erlichman

Cover and Interior Photography:
Karen Whylie

Interior Art: Shelley Lea, Rashell Smith,
Shelley Norris

Production

Publishing Services Director: Karen Bryan

Project Manager: Elizabeth McCurdy

Project Coordinator: Abigail Brown

Layout and Graphics: Kim Monteforte,
Heidy Lawrance Associates

Proofreader: Susan Gaines

Indexer: Belle Wong

John Wiley & Sons Canada, Ltd

Bill Zerter, Chief Operating Officer

Robert Harris, Publisher, Professional and Trade Division

Publishing and Editorial for Consumer Dummies

Diane Graves Steele, Vice President and Publisher, Consumer Dummies

Joyce Pepple, Acquisitions Director, Consumer Dummies

Kristin A. Cocks, Product Development Director, Consumer Dummies

Michael Spring, Vice President and Publisher, Travel

Suzanne Jannetta, Editorial Director, Travel

Publishing for Technology Dummies

Andy Cummings, Acquisitions Director

Composition Services

Gerry Fahey, Executive Director of Production Services

Debbie Stailey, Director of Composition Services

Contents at a Glance

Table of Contents

Foreword

· ·

An old lacrosse coach of mine used to say that lacrosse is not a sport; it's an incurable disease. Once you get it in your blood, you can't get it out of your system. I don't like describing something that I love as a "disease," but there is definitely something addictive about lacrosse. It's a magical feeling when you pick up your first lacrosse stick. And all you need is a stick, a ball, and a wall to get started. Add some imagination and who knows how far you'll go.

Through my years involved in lacrosse I was lucky enough to see some of the greatest legends of the game up close, as teammates or opponents. John Tavares, Paul and Gary Gait, John Grant (Junior and Senior) are just some of the superstars that graced the game over the last 30 years. I also got to know some of the legends of earlier eras, such as Bobby Allan and the late Jack Bionda and Gaylord Powless. Besides their athletic ability, what I found most interesting is their ability to play the game with great imagination. When John Tavares started scoring from behind the net as a 14-year-old, I saw referees and opposing coaches scrambling for rulebooks to find out whether his moves were legal. The first time I played against the Gait brothers, I was amazed to see how they could shoot so hard and accurately right-handed, left-handed, one-handed, and even between the legs. Imagine the amazement that players and fans felt the first time they watched Bobby Allan whip a shot from behind his back 40 years ago. He was so well known for this shot that it's still known in Mimico, Ontario, as the "Bobby Allan shot."

When you talk to any of the greats of the game, you'll find that they spent much of their youth with a lacrosse stick in their hands, either at an outdoor rink or throwing against a schoolyard wall. Did they do it simply for practise? No, they did it because it was fun — fun to invent and practise new fakes and shots. The next time you see Colin Doyle, John Tavares, or Gary Gait bring a crowd to its feet by scoring a beautiful goal after a dazzling fake, remember that that move was probably rehearsed a thousand times before in a quiet schoolyard on a hot summer afternoon. If you are a new lacrosse player or parent of a lacrosse player, *Lacrosse For Dummies* will help introduce you to our traditional game. But if you want to become a real player, just take your stick and ball and find a nice large wall. Who knows — maybe someday you'll be thrilling the crowds with a shot you perfected in your backyard.

— Brian Shanahan
   Television analyst, Sportsnet national lacrosse telecasts
   Played with five Mann Cup championship teams
   Past President, Mimico Minor Lacrosse Association

Introduction

· ·

*W*elcome to *Lacrosse For Dummies*. Now, don't get me wrong about this title, because I know a lot of you who are reading this book are very knowledgeable people or even students of the game. I wrote this book for readers at every level of lacrosse, from the "peanut" player (four or five years old) to the old-timer, from the new fan to the fanatic, from the beginning coach to the experienced coach, from the parent who's a novice to the parent who has been through the "wars" of lacrosse.

Lacrosse is the fastest growing sport in North America, thanks to the influence of the National Lacrosse League (NLL). Lacrosse has had a hectic history of ups and downs, probably more than any other sport, including a probably deserved bad reputation for its physical contact, violence, and brutality. But now players are playing the game at a higher speed than ever — still physical, but less violent — and fans are appreciating the finesse and skill that it takes to play this fast-paced game.

I believe that lacrosse is the greatest game ever invented. It contains the physical hitting of football, the speed and quickness of hockey, and the passing and shooting ability of basketball. Anybody can play this game, from the little guy who has speed and quickness to the bigger guy who has strength and power. Make no mistake that once you have thrown a lacrosse ball with a lacrosse stick, the game has got you!

About This Book

This is a book that tells you everything you wanted to know about lacrosse but were afraid to ask — and even what you don't know to ask. I want this book to satisfy everyone who is involved or not involved in lacrosse — from the person who knows nothing about the sport to the hard-core fan who knows everything. You will find a lot of information about lacrosse that you can't find anywhere else, whether it's discovering the roots of lacrosse, browsing through a group of diverse top ten lists, or picking up some tips from the pros.

The beauty of . . . *For Dummies* books is that they are so easy to use to find what you need to know. Just pick the book up and start reading anywhere you wish. You can choose to read it from front to back, but you don't have to — you can read each chapter on its own.

Beginners and fans may want to turn to Appendix A for a glossary of lacrosse terms and their definitions. Or you may want to start with the fundamentals of the game (in Chapters 2 and 3). If you're a parent and new to the sport, turn to Chapter 19 and read about youth lacrosse and coaching. If you're a spectator, Chapter 5 is a great beginning on how to watch lacrosse. Chapter 4 can help you to understand the rules of the game. If you are a coach, you may want to start with Part IV. Or if you've already played for a few years and want to pick up some new tips, you can start with Part III. Finally, the Part of Tens of any . . . *For Dummies* book appeals to just about everybody. So sit down and select a chapter to help you understand and appreciate lacrosse.

Also, note that in explaining the game, this book includes photos, diagrams, and tips from NLL players. To make it easier to go back over something that you have already read or to find out something on a related topic, this book is filled with cross-references that help you navigate quickly from one chapter to another.

By the way, it's a good idea to keep a stick and ball close by — if you're reading about fundamentals and want to try something new, you can experiment with the stick and ball.

Conventions Used in This Book

Lacrosse is made up of terms not found in other sports, such as Indian-rubber ball, cradling, shooting strings, scoop pick-up, Indian pick-up, underhand shot, sidearm shot, back-hand shot, over-the-shoulder shot, the hook, hidden-ball trick, cocking the stick, winding up, clamp, draw, rake, up-and-over draw, bounce shot, man short, diamond man short, box man short, pointman, cornerman, and creaseman. Whew. For a full glossary of lacrosse terms, see Appendix A.

Box lacrosse player positions (and some field lacrosse player positions) are still universally male in gender: attackman, cornerman, creaseman, defenseman, and pointman. Despite these male-oriented names, most of the information found in this book applies to all lacrosse players, male and female.

This book uses box lacrosse floor markings to describe lacrosse terminology, as well as, of course, the favourite pastime of most coaches, *X*s and *O*s, to show formations, plays, and player movement. Here are the symbols and what they mean so that you will understand what I'm talking about when discussing strategy and drills:

Symbol	What It Means
○	Offensive player
●	Ballcarrier
ⓡ	Right-shot player
ⓛ	Left-shot player
X	Defensive player
G	Goalie
————	Offensive and defensive player path
wwwwww	Ballcarrier's path
- - - - - - - -	Ball path

Foolish Assumptions

The game of lacrosse can be played in different environments — on a field or in an arena; with flat sticks or deep-pocketed sticks; with a variety of equipment and a variety of rules; by men or by women; and at one time, even with different balls, one for the field game and one for the box game.

Lacrosse is a diverse game, and many of you are coming to this book for diverse reasons. Rest assured, this book gives you the information you are looking for, whether you are a lacrosse fan, parent, player, or coach. It doesn't matter whether you know very little about the game or are an expert, this book has something for everyone. Here are a few possible scenarios where this book will help:

- ✔ You know how to play lacrosse but very little about the history of the game.

- ✔ You are a parent who wants to know what to expect from a minor coach who is coaching your son or daughter.

- ✔ You want to become a better player and read the little things that NLL players do to improve their game.

- ✔ You just want to know more about lacrosse than you do right now.

Why You Need This Book

No other book about lacrosse has been written like this one. This book contains information for everybody involved in the game of box lacrosse — the coach, the player, the fan, and the parent. I don't think I have left anybody out, but if I have, this book is for them too.

As a spectator, you'll appreciate lacrosse's finer points discussed in this book and have an easier time watching and understanding the game. You will know what the players are trying to accomplish on the floor even if they don't execute a play and why what they are doing is all part of the strategy of the game. You'll also have a better grasp of the rules of the game, as well as the basic elements of the game, such as player roles and positions, how to get dressed and what equipment to use, and the basics of playing the game.

As a beginning lacrosse player, you need this book because its emphasis on fundamentals will help you understand the basics that you need to play the game at a high level. Do you know how to take a good position to play defence? Do you know how to hold the stick properly to pass the ball? Do you know how to get in the clear to receive a pass? All these fundamental techniques are discussed. Do you know what equipment to use or how to put it on so that it both protects properly and fits loosely and at the same time doesn't hinder your play? Do you know how to train to get in shape for training camp? Do you know the NLL teams? Do you know what the pros do to get ready to play? This book answers all these questions and more.

Lacrosse For Dummies also helps seasoned veterans understand the game better, whether from a historical view, a technical view, a statistical view, or a strategic view. The experienced player, who could be a Pee Wee player in this day and age, can find veteran advice in my discussion of fundamentals and team strategies in Part III.

I believe it is important that the true lacrosse player becomes a student of the game — understanding how the game came about, knowing the greats of the game, knowing where to get more information on different leagues, and using the little hints from the pros on how to play the game a little bit better.

I also believe the true player should give back to the game that he plays and loves. How? By volunteering to help in minor lacrosse, by helping out as a coach or an assistant coach, and by not hogging his ideas on how to play the game. As lacrosse people, we have to learn to exchange ideas to make all of us a little bit better. Besides having great talent, great players have a great passion for the game.

I hope you find this book to be an instructional journal, a philosophical journal, a statistical journal, a parenting journal, a coaching journal, a historical journal, a rules and regulations journal, a journal of lists, a conditioning journal, and a mental preparation journal all rolled up into one. No matter at what level you are — player, coach, fan, parent — you will find something in this book to make you play or understand the game better.

Finally, this book can help you answer some of the burning questions of the day — or at least by the time you've read this book, they'll be burning questions:

- Why do they line up at centre for the faceoff?
- Is there an offsides violation?
- Why does a whistle start the play?
- Why are players allowed to slash an opponent and not get a penalty?
- Does all that hitting on the body hurt?

How This Book Is Organized

Lacrosse For Dummies is presented in five parts, starting with the basics of the game (such as the ball and stick, the number of players, the equipment used, and the way the game is played). The rest of the book moves through how to watch the game (specifically, the NLL), how to become a player, and how to coach lacrosse. So this book can be whatever you want it to be to you, simple basic reading or in-depth reading.

Part I: Essential Lacrosse

This part gives you a good idea of what the basic game of lacrosse is all about, breaking the game down into simple terms about the different player roles and positions on the floor and some particulars about how the game is played. This part also discusses lacrosse equipment and how to get dressed so that you are well protected — a necessity in lacrosse!

This part also covers the fundamentals for minor players, including basic passing, basic defence, and basic goaltending. Game plans are talked about from a simple offensive philosophy to a simple defence philosophy. And thanks to the help of National Lacrosse League referee Paul Ravary, Chapter 4 describes the rules of the game.

Part II: Following Lacrosse: The Fan's Point of View

Of course, when I refer to fans, I mean everybody involved in lacrosse from player to parent. This part explains how to watch the intricacies of the game, the little things that make great plays; the different formations that are used on defence, on offence, and on the specialty teams; and the power play and the man short. You can find out about the National Lacrosse League, the best lacrosse league in the world. Read about its 12 teams, the set-up of league games, and other tidbits, including where you can watch the league on TV. Finally, I talk about the other leagues in lacrosse from women's lacrosse to minor lacrosse to NCAA.

Part III: Playing Lacrosse: What You Need to Know to Succeed

This part is the meat-and-potatoes of the book where you find out how to play the game. A player can participate in lacrosse without solid fundamentals, but he won't enjoy the game as much. The game may look easy to you, but it is very difficult to throw a ball straight, right into a teammate's stick. In this part, I want to help you improve every facet of your game — how to beat a defender, how to stop an offensive player, how to hit that little open spot with a shot, how to get that all-important loose ball, how to pass and catch. All these fundamentals take practice and the proper technique to execute.

In this part, I also discuss the toughest position to play in lacrosse: goaltender. All the basics of goaltending will be covered thanks to the help of some of the top goalies in the NLL. (In this part, you'll find tips from many NLL players.) You also find out about the offensive and defensive systems of lacrosse. Lastly, I offer some tips on how to become a better lacrosse player, from physical conditioning to mental preparation.

Part IV: Coaching Lacrosse: Winning Strategies

In this part, you find out how a coach prepares for a game, from scouting to using statistics, from setting up practices to motivating the team. You also discover how a coach "game coaches," from setting up an offensive system to establishing a defensive system and then applying these systems to certain situations in a game. Knowing how teams get ready to play in the NLL is another interesting topic, including setting team behaviour goals, performance goals, and pre-game talks.

Finally, I include a great chapter on minor coaching, a sore point for many of us. This part gives you some ideas on what to expect in a minor coach, how a minor coach should deal with young people, and how a minor coach should deal with parents.

Part V: The Part of Tens

This essential part of every . . . *For Dummies* book is fun because it includes my list of the top NLL players of all time, which can start great arguments, er, discussions. This part also discusses the magical elements of the game that make it such a fan favourite and directs you to newspapers, magazines, Web sites, and lacrosse organizations that you can use to keep informed about lacrosse.

Appendixes

In the back of this book, I've included a few appendixes to share some of the nuts and bolts of lacrosse with you. To understand the game you have to understand the language of lacrosse, so I've included a glossary of lacrosse vocabulary in Appendix A. And Appendix B offers some resources that you can use to establish relationships with coaches, parents, or players.

Icons Used in This Book

In every . . . *For Dummies* book, icons in the margins of the pages bring attention to important tidbits and valuable advice. *Lacrosse For Dummies* uses the following icons:

This icon points you to what some of the best NLL players have to say about the game and how they play it. You'll also find suggestions that help improve your play.

This icon provides tips for coaches. I also throw my two cents' worth in about what I have found to be successful in my 25 years of coaching.

This icon points out important information that is helpful to remember, whether as a player, coach, parent, or fan.

This icon offers some cautionary words about potential safety concerns and other dangers that may come into play when playing and coaching lacrosse.

Need to know why something happens the way it does in lacrosse? This icon alerts you to some technical information that you can choose to read — or not.

Like it or not, some differences exist between the game of box lacrosse (indoors) and the game of field lacrosse (outdoors). This icon helps you sort out the details.

Where to Go from Here

If you are just getting started in lacrosse — as a player, coach, parent, or fan — you can turn to any chapter you want; but to me, the most important chapters deal with the fundamentals (Chapters 2 and 3), because that is where everything begins. As a fan, you'll appreciate the execution of the skills more and understand how hard it is to play this game. As a parent, you may wish to start with Chapter 19, where you'll understand how to handle your child while he goes through his or her minor lacrosse years and how important it is to help and support but not to interfere — easy to say and hard to do! As a coach, beginner or experienced, reading what the pros do in practices and games gives you another perspective of the game, so any of the chapters in Part IV are a good place to start. And finally as a player, soak up all the tips and suggestions given by the pro players to help make you a better player and thereby enjoy the game more (Part III).

In this book, I share information that comes from being beaten badly in games, winning the close games, winning championships, and coaching at every level from house-league to the pros.

Part I
Essential Lacrosse

The 5th Wave   By Rich Tennant

"This is great! It even comes with a jar of tooth-black for that 'just checked' look."

In this part . . .

Every lacrosse game starts with a faceoff; this part begins play for you with this book. In these chapters, you'll discover the basics of the game, what you need to get a head start toward understanding how to play the game and how the game is played. You'll find out how to break the game down to its most fundamental elements, including passing, catching, shooting, defending, coaching, and understanding the rules of the game.

Chapter 1

The Faceoff: Getting Started

*U*nlike individual sports, team games need a starting-off point. The place-kicker can't just sidle up to the 35-yard-line as if he's approaching the first tee; football needs its kickoff. The point guard doesn't just start dribbling toward the basket as if she's trying for a strike in the first frame; basketball needs its tipoff. The centre can't just set out for the goal on a breakaway as if he's setting out to attempt a triple axle; hockey needs its faceoff.

Lacrosse, too, needs a faceoff to get things started; and this chapter serves as the faceoff for this book. Grab your stick and get ready for the basics.

Why Would Anyone Want to Play Lacrosse?

That's easy: Most kids — including big kids — love to kick, throw, catch, bounce, and shoot a ball. One of the best feelings in the world is to throw a ball and have it go where you want it to go. With lacrosse, throwing the ball — accurately — is the name of the game; the difference is that you have to throw the ball from a stick, not from your hand. Although it's not all that easy to do, with good instruction, good feedback, and lots of practice, in a short time anybody can master this basic lacrosse skill.

Survival of the fittest — from the game's origins

Lacrosse's reliance on players who are fit, quick, and can endure constant movement developed because of the game's origins. It was first played by Native peoples in North America, usually as a way to settle intra-tribal disputes or to celebrate and honour religious rituals. In these early contests, the field of play could stretch for hundreds and hundreds of metres with no boundaries to speak of. And the game itself could last for several days. In this setting, the small, speedy, and healthy players would have been the earliest stars of the game.

Kids — including big kids — also like to push people around. In box lacrosse, they can do this legally and not get into trouble. Although parents may shudder at all the contact in the game, if players wear the proper equipment and learn the proper way to receive a hit, kids will probably not get hurt, at least not while playing lacrosse.

Lacrosse is a game of running, dodging, spinning, cutting, and faking, all of which kids also love to do — well, perhaps maybe not the big kids. Lacrosse offers thrills by the bundle, from running full-bore down the floor on a fast break, to out-running an opponent for a breakaway goal. You can take on a player who thinks he has you lined up for a cross-check and fake him out of position, or better yet, make him lunge at the point on the floor where you used to be, missing you and looking like a fool while you go around him.

All this and more awaits the lacrosse player. And unlike many other team sports where size (300-pounds-plus football players), height (7-foot-tall basketball players), and strength (driving a golf ball over 300 yards) matter, lacrosse rewards the small, the short, and the speedy. Small players can excel in lacrosse because of their quickness, intelligence, aggressiveness, and stick skills: they can play with the best of them.

The Tools of the Trade — the Ball and the Stick

In the early playing days of lacrosse, the ball had no standard size, although most were about the size of a tennis ball. Most lacrosse balls had an outside cover of rawhide or deerskin and were stuffed with deer hair. Or they were just plain round wood wrapped with rawhide. In 1867, Dr. George Beers, a Canadian dentist considered by many to be the father of lacrosse because he created the first set of rules, replaced the hair-stuffed deerskin ball with a hard rubber ball.

Today, the so-called *Indian-rubber ball* is standard for all lacrosse play. The ball, which can be white, yellow, or orange, generally measures just less than 8 inches in diameter and weighs a little over 5 ounces.

The stick first used by Native players was about 3 feet long with a circular net at one end, laced with thongs to hold the ball in place. This netted pocket at the end of the stick was very deep in order to carry the ball. The deep pocket of the stick made it difficult to throw the ball, so the early game had little passing — it was more a game of strength and endurance than a game of skill.

In the 1880s, the stick changed. Its handle (or shaft) was curved at the end and a large flat triangular surface of webbing extended from the top down about two-thirds the length of the handle. The deep-pocket stick used by the Native players required less skill. This new flat stick increased dodging and led to more passing, which sped up the game.

In the old days, all lacrosse players played with sticks that had handmade hickory handles that were hooked on top. The primary netting was either all leather or leather runners and linen cord, and the side barriers were made of catgut. Native players such as Frank Benedict from Cornwall, Ontario; Matthew Etienne from Oka, Quebec; Billy Squire and Joe Logan from Six Nations, Ontario; and Wes Patterson from Tuscarora, New York, were among those who made these wooden sticks and proudly put their names on them.

Today, lacrosse players play with aluminum- or titanium-handled sticks with plastic heads. The stick, or the *crosse,* still has a net pocket at the end, but the depth is much shallower than it was in the game's beginnings, about the diameter of one ball or slightly less. The width of the pocket should be between 4½ and 8 inches. The stick's length should be between 42 and 46 inches. (In Pee Wee leagues, the minimum stick length drops down to 36 inches.) The goaltender's stick has no minimum or maximum length, but the pocket can be no more than 15 inches wide.

For best results, the depth of the stick — that is, how deep the *pocket* is — should be the diameter of one ball or slightly less, though box lacrosse has no specific rule that defines how deep the pocket should be. And most pockets today include two to three shooting strings to improve shot control. Figure 1-1 shows the parts of a lacrosse stick's pocket. For more information about customizing the pocket of your lacrosse stick, see Chapter 2.

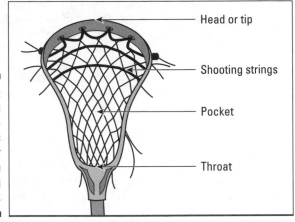

Head or tip

Shooting strings

Pocket

Throat

Figure 1-1:
Today's
lacrosse
stick is
designed for
maximum
shot-making
efficiency.

Field lacrosse offers the opportunity for a bit more individuality for players in terms of stick preference. In fact, sticks for defensive players (as well as one midfielder) can measure from 52 to 72 inches. (That's 6 feet — likely as long as, or longer than, most players on the field.) The longer sticks are designed for defence, making it harder for opposing offensive players to score, but they also limit field defencemen from getting involved offensively because of the decreased stick-handling ability that comes from carrying around 10 to 20 additional inches of stick. However, standard length for sticks in field lacrosse is between 40 and 42 inches, similar to the box game. The width of the pocket in a field lacrosse stick should be between 6½ and 10 inches. And by rule, the pocket must be shallow enough to see a portion of the ball over the frame. A goalie's stick head must measure between 10 and 12 inches, with the length of the shaft varying between 40 and 72 inches. And the NCAA (National Collegiate Athletic Association — the governing arm of U.S. collegiate sports) recently approved the use of a lime-green-coloured ball, though you're not likely to see it in wide use anytime soon. There's no truth to the rumour that the NCAA is considering applying a lime dye to the lacrosse-field grass to really spice up the game.

The stick is everything. As a player, you have to have confidence in your stick. If you don't, you won't have confidence in your shot or your game.

Introducing the Box Lacrosse Players

Whether you're playing the game, coaching the game, or just catching a National Lacrosse League (NLL) game on TV, you need to know the players and their roles. Throughout this book — and especially in Part III — I offer more details about what players should do in certain game situations. For now, this section gives a game-time introduction to the players on the floor — minus the public-address announcer.

Which side of the floor do you play on?

At the youth level of lacrosse, inexperienced players sometimes play both sides of the floor, not knowing a specific role except just to run around, go after every loose ball (youth lacrosse has a lot of those), and try to hit anybody who moves. However, where players position themselves on the floor is important for both offensive and defensive strategy.

For example, the cross-check is a defensive manoeuvre to stop or slow down the ballcarrier, and with the cross-check, players are getting hit on the side of the arm while carrying the ball. (A similar defensive tactic is the *poke-check*, discussed further in Chapter 10.) If the ballcarrier goes down the wrong side of the floor, that is, a left-shot creaseman goes down the left side of the floor, an incoming cross-check would force him to turn his body away from the cross-check to protect the ball and thereby turn his back to the play. But if that same ballcarrier goes down the proper side of the floor, that is, a left-shot creaseman goes down the right side of the floor, he can still turn sideways to protect the ball from an incoming cross-check, but he won't be forced to turn completely away from the play, thereby continuing to face the play to either see who is open or see the net.

Where does the winger play?

One problem with coaching lacrosse in Canada — not a big one, but one that does affect the game — is that a lot of lacrosse coaches also coach hockey. And, of course, a lot of young lacrosse players are also young hockey players. This issue is especially challenging when it comes to referring to lacrosse players, on both the offensive and defensive side of the ball.

In hockey, a right-winger is usually a right-shot — that is, a player that shoots from the right side of the body — who plays on the right side of the ice. But in lacrosse, the right-shot players play on the left side of the floor and are called *left creasemen* or *left cornermen.* And the *right creasemen* or *right cornermen* play on the right side of the floor, but are left-shot players. It all comes down to getting the best angle on the shot and protecting the stick with your body.

Box lacrosse coaches who come out of hockey still often call their offensive players wingers or centres, which is okay, but not great. However, it's not okay to call the backcourt players (or the last players to come up the floor on offence) defencemen. If they are called defencemen, they may develop a tendency to stay out of the regular flow of the offence, just as in hockey. Defencemen in hockey stay at the blue line and very seldom leave that area. If a lacrosse defender stays near the centre line without getting into the regular flow of the offence, the team ends up with three offensive players against five defenders. To avoid this tendency, coaches have to think more like basketball coaches: When your team has the ball, every player is an offensive player, and when your team doesn't have the ball, every player is a defensive player.

Naming the players: They are the eggmen; I am the walrus

To make up a *line* — a group of five players who go on the floor together — you need two creasemen (right and left), two cornermen (also right and left), and a pointman. When transitioning from defence to offence, the pointman can come up either side of the floor or up the middle of the floor. Oh yes, and don't forget the arguably most important player on the team, the goaltender.

In this day of political correctness, box lacrosse player positions remain decidedly one-sided. Unlike the occasional gender-neutral designations in field lacrosse (see "Introducing the Field Lacrosse Players" later in this chapter), box lacrosse designations reflect the decidedly one-sided nature of who actually plays box lacrosse, which remains a predominantly male game.

Hanging out with the goalie: The creasemen

The two creasemen are generally good goal scorers and usually play at the front of any *fast break*. A fast break is an offensive situation that sees players moving quickly up the floor from the defensive to the offensive end, often as a result of forcing a turnover on defence, such as stealing the ball, and usually with at least one more offensive player than defender. Once they get into the offensive end, and the fast break or odd-man situation has been successfully defended, the creasemen have a number of offensive options:

- **Cut to the ball:** From their floor position, which is usually in the area around the crease of the goal area (from centre left or right out to the sideboards), creasemen can move toward the ballcarrier in anticipation of a pass.

- **Pop out in the crease area:** By stepping out to receive a ball in the crease area of the floor, a creaseman can look for a one-on-one opportunity against the goalie or against a defender to get to the goalie.

✓ **Set a pick:** A creaseman can assist a teammate, either the ballcarrier or another offensive player, by setting a pick — that is, stepping in the path of his teammate's defender. This move may allow the ballcarrier to work away from his defender to get an open look to the goal for a shot, or it may allow an offensive teammate to work away from his defender to become open for a pass.

In fact, the best creasemen in the NLL are great at setting picks; the pick may often lead to a pass to the creaseman for a possible short shot on goal, an offensive set play known as the *pick-and-roll.* (For more about this and other offensive set plays, turn to Chapter 14.)

Creasemen are also very adept at going one-on-one against their defender when close around the goal. They should also be good loose-ball players, as one of their primary roles is to go after every loose ball in the near-goal corner on a missed shot at the goal or on an errant pass to a teammate. The critical qualities required in a good creaseman include stick skill, intelligence, mobility, quickness, and vision of the floor.

On defence, creasemen are usually not the bigger (and better) defenders who would play against the better offensive players on the opposition, but they still should play good defence, usually defending the offensive players nearest the centre line. This defensive positioning allows the creasemen to get a quick start on any fast-break opportunity.

Cutting corners: The cornermen

When transitioning from defence to offence, the two cornermen run up the floor behind the creasemen, often carrying the ball to try to create a fast-break opportunity. In an offensive set — that is, after a fast-break or odd-man situation is over — cornermen have the following options:

✓ **Shoot long:** With their typical positioning around the centre of the offensive zone, cornermen look for most of their shots from long range.

✓ **Look to go one-on-one:** With the ball, a quick-footed cornerman can look for opportunities to take on his defender, trying to shake him free for either an open shot on goal or a pass to a teammate. Also, taking advantage of a defender's slip, cornermen can quickly move toward the goal and take on another defender one-on-one. More often than not, this situation leads to a quick pass to a creaseman or other cornerman, whose defender has moved to help out his beaten teammate.

✓ **Look for a cutter:** When carrying the ball, a cornerman faces the play, waiting for a teammate (usually a creaseman) to shake free a bit from his defender and cut toward the ball. A good pass from the cornerman to a cutter can then set up an open shot on goal.

✔ **Wait for a pick:** On a pick-and-roll play, the cornerman's defender is usually the recipient of the pick. With his defender knocked off by his teammate's pick, a cornerman can look to score or look to pass to the creaseman who set the pick.

On offence, the cornermen help create action by passing the ball, either across the floor or down into the crease area. This skill is especially critical when the defence is preventing a lot of player movement on the offensive end of the floor. On defence, cornermen are usually the better defenders on a team, the players through whom the opposing offence must go.

Directing floor activity: The pointman

The pointman's responsibilities are similar to the cornermen's responsibilities. He can move up the floor behind a cornerman or run up the middle of the floor. He has all the qualities of a cornerman:

✔ **Good long-ball shooter:** His primary position in the offensive zone is in the top area of the floor, closest to the centre line.

✔ **Good at going one-on-one:** Being able to create some distance from himself and his defender, the pointman can more easily look to pass to a teammate closer to the goal.

✔ **Smart with the ball:** The pointman should develop the ability to read his own teammates' energy level so that he can determine which side of the floor to pass to create the best scoring opportunity.

His biggest asset is his ability to make good plays, that is, to initiate the action on an offensive set play, and still be a threat to score.

In this position, you can afford to have a bigger, slower player who is not usually a great scorer. He should, however, make up for this lack of speed with a great sense of the action on the floor, an awareness to anticipate where the ball goes and when the ball doesn't go where it's supposed to, and an ability to get back quickly on defence.

Defending the net: The goaltender

The goaltender's job is to stop the ball from going into the net. Sounds pretty simple, but it is the hardest position to play. Goalies are the backbone of the team. A successful team must have good goaltending! Goalies have to know how to play the angles, how to take away corner shots, and how to move around the crease area to get in good position to stop the ball.

But good goaltenders should be able to do more than just stop the ball; they must also be able to initiate a fast break or breakout. A good goalie is a real threat if he can send a deep pass to a player breaking out down the floor or even an accurate short pass to a teammate to run the ball up the floor. The better the goalie, the better the team.

Goalies tend to be a little different — as the saying goes, they walk to the beat of a different drummer — and that is probably one of the reasons why so many of them are so good.

Defending the floor: The defensive players

All offensive players — creasemen, cornermen, and pointmen — are also defensive players. Lacrosse is similar to basketball in this — when the player has the ball, he is on offence, and when he doesn't have the ball, he is on defence. (In the NLL, however, most positions are now specialized; offensive players play strictly on offence, and defensive players play defence.)

Unlike offence, defensive players have no set positions. Usually, a line sent out to the floor includes two or three players whose strength is playing defence rather than scoring. These players pick up the better offensive players on the opposing team to defend. The players on a line whose skills are primarily offensive usually end up defending the weaker offensive opponents when on defence.

It is usually a luxury to have several players on a line who can play both offence and defence well. There is nothing better than having a defensive player who is also a threat to score, breaking out to the offensive end of the floor. However, many lacrosse teams today tend to go with a so-called *offence–defence* system. This system allows players who excel on one end of the floor or the other to run on and off the floor depending on which team has possession of the ball. A solid defender, for example, will be on the floor to play defence when his team does not have the ball; when his team takes possession, he will head for his team's bench to be replaced by a more offensive-minded player.

Introducing the Field Lacrosse Players

While the box game is played mainly in Canada, an outdoor version of lacrosse is more popular in the United States. *Field lacrosse* is most popular in the northeastern U.S. (though since the 1980s, the game has spread throughout the U.S.) and differs from its box brother in many ways.

Though a summertime professional outdoor league called Major League Lacrosse (MLL) started in 2000, the most popular form of field lacrosse has always been played in the National Collegiate Athletic Association (NCAA). The collegiate field season starts in late February and runs through May. It is played by roughly 250 U.S. colleges and universities, spanning the Division I, II, III, and junior college varsity levels. The International Lacrosse Federation (ILF) sponsors a World Lacrosse Championship once every four years between countries throughout the world. (See Chapter 7 for more details about the university and international game.)

Because of the significantly larger playing field (110 by 60 yards), a field lacrosse team, well, fields a few more players than a box lacrosse team. (For more about the dimensions of the box lacrosse playing area see Chapter 14.) A men's field lacrosse team includes nine players, plus the goaltender; a women's team has eleven players, plus the goalie. This section introduces you to field participants and the roles they play (see Figure 1-2).

Figure 1-2:
Field
lacrosse
players in
action.

(Photo: Joe Apaestegui/Inside Lacrosse)

Though field lacrosse teams have more players on the field at once, each team is allowed a maximum of six players (plus the goalie) on one-half of the field at any one time. That is, when in their offensive zone, a men's field lacrosse team must keep three players (plus the goalie) behind the midfield line. Of course, it's not six on ten for them, as their opponent can only have seven players defending the zone (including the goalie) at the same time.

This so-called *split field* in outdoor lacrosse forces more specialization in playing positions. The four main positions are attackmen, midfielders, defencemen, and goalies, though each position includes even more specific roles. Teams employ lines of three attackmen, three midfielders, and three defencemen.

FIELD TIP

A look at women's field lacrosse

Women's field lacrosse at the U.S. collegiate level is just about the fastest growing sector of the sport. In part, this growth is thanks to Title IX, a U.S. federal regulation specifying that the athletic participation of every NCAA institution must mirror the gender ratio of its student body. Major universities outside the U.S. northeast, such as Vanderbilt, Northwestern, and Stanford, have established varsity women's lacrosse programs over the past decade. Following this trend, youth programs and club teams have dramatically expanded and advanced, introducing more young girls to the sport.

Although women's lacrosse is similar to the men's game in overall excitement, appearance, and geographic hotbeds, the two games have some significant differences. The major one is the lack of contact in the women's game.

✔ Women do not wear padding or helmets (except for goalies), so full checking is not allowed.

✔ Sticks cannot enter an imaginary 7-inch bubble around any player's head, and stick checks must be made away from the offensive player's body, so the women's game has much more emphasis on defensive footwork and positioning.

✔ Stick shafts are narrower and pockets are much shallower, making passing and catching vastly different from the men's game.

✔ Women's games have 12 players per team on the field (including a goalie), as opposed to 10 for men.

✔ Field sizes are recommended to be 120 by 70 yards, 10 yards longer and wider than the men's specifications.

✔ The offensive end, which can hold only seven offensive players and eight defensive players (including a goalie), is set off by a restraining line located 30 yards from the endline.

✔ Penalties for fouls are *free position shots*, taken from either an 8-metre (for a major penalty) or 12-metre arc (for a minor penalty) around the goal. Offending players must stand 4 metres behind (major foul) or to the side (minor foul), while the offensive player takes a free position shot.

✔ Faceoffs, called *draws* in the women's game, begin with the ball pinched between the backs of the opposing players' stick heads, which are held waist-high.

✔ **Attacking the goal:** The *attackmen* are the primary offensive weapons looking to feed and score. They create most of the offence and generally do not play defence, serving as the three players kept on the opposite side of the midline while the ball is at the other end. It's not uncommon for the attackmen to stay on the field the whole game. Many attackmen have the ability to both feed and score, but some focus on only one of those offensive elements.

- ✔ **Playing both ways:** *Midfielders* play offence and defence, following the flow of the game and getting involved at both ends of the field. Midfielders, or "middies," are crucial to a team's transition offence and defence. Teams generally run three lines consisting of three midfielders each. For example, some midfielders may be defensive specialists, coming on the field only in certain situations, while others may only play faceoffs and then run off the field. However, many midfielders also run regular midfield shifts, and a select few are dangerous offensive weapons. Although the three field players with longer sticks play defence, a fourth long stick can be used in the midfield.

- ✔ **Creating a first line of defence:** The *defencemen* generally stay on their half of the field while their team is on offence, though they are allowed to cross the midline in transition as long as an equal number of midfielders stays back. The role of the defencemen is generally to stop the opposing attackmen from scoring or creating offence. Occasionally, they will be dispatched to cover a dominant opposing midfielder.

- ✔ **Keeping the ball in play:** *Goalies* in field lacrosse have to be more athletic than those in box lacrosse because of the larger goal (6 by 6 feet, as opposed to 4¾ by 4 feet in box lacrosse). Goalies play with their sticks held upright and the head pointing skyward, unlike the hockey style used in box lacrosse. In addition to stopping shots and getting the ball out of the defensive end, goalies are also responsible for directing the defence.

Knowing How the Game Is Played

Earlier in this chapter, I introduced the number of players who are on the floor or field at any one time during a lacrosse game. Here are a few more technical details about how the game is played to help you develop an understanding of this unique and exciting game.

Really, the team that ends the game with the most goals, wins. It's that simple. A game clock dictates the length of the game, and scoring goals is the sole determiner of who wins and who loses. The following list offers a few of the technical essentials that you need to know to better understand the game:

- ✔ **Four quarters equals a game:** The length of a box or field lacrosse game is 60 minutes, with 4 quarters lasting 15 minutes each. Unless . . .

- ✔ **Two halves do make a whole (game):** Depending on the age and/or gender of the teams playing, variations on the length of a lacrosse game do exist. Women's lacrosse matches are divided into halves instead of quarters, and can range in length from 50 to 60 minutes. Minor league lacrosse games offer a wide variety of lengths and divisions, from 8- or 12-minute quarters to three 20-minute periods, much like a hockey contest. High-school field games have 12-minute quarters.

Whatever the length of the game, remember that any individual contest will include at least one intermission. There's a lot of running and bumping and hitting and missing to recuperate from.

✔ **Facing down the opposition:** A faceoff at the centre circle starts each game and each quarter, and it begins play after every goal scored.

A *faceoff* is another area where lacrosse resembles both hockey (the only other sport with faceoffs) and basketball (with its jump-ball set-up at the beginning of games). In a box lacrosse faceoff, the teams surround one of the lined circles on the floor, with two players in the centre of the circle awaiting the referee's whistle to begin play and go for the ball. Essentially, a faceoff is an organized, if sometimes frenetic, way to initiate play at the beginning of a game, or to restart play that has been stopped for some reason (opening a new playing period, after a scored goal, in a dead-ball situation, and so on). Any game can present many faceoff opportunities, so you better be pretty good at it to have a chance of controlling the ball and therefore giving your team more scoring opportunities. (For a more detailed discussion of faceoff strategy, see Chapter 16.)

Faceoffs in field lacrosse come at the start of each quarter and after each goal. They consist of two players at the centre X and two players from each team perched on the wing area lines (20 yards from the middle of the field and 20 yards long, parallel with the sideline). Once possession is gained by one of these eight players, the rest of the players can cross the restraining lines that are perpendicular to the sideline and 20 yards from the midline.

✔ **Games don't end in ties:** Well, at least not generally. Except for minor lacrosse, when games end regulation play with the two teams tied, a sudden-death overtime period determines the winner. In sudden death, the first team to score a goal wins. Minor lacrosse leagues typically allow a single sudden-death overtime period; however, if the game is still tied at the end of the period, the game is called a tie.

✔ **Stay out of the crease:** Offensive players must stay out of the crease area in front of the goal. The crease is a 9-foot semicircle that arcs from goalpost to goalpost.

The crease in field lacrosse is a 9-foot radius, and it sits farther away from the endline (15 yards to the goal) than in the box game. Much of a team's offence starts behind the goal, so management of the crease from defensive as well as offensive standpoints is tremendously important. Players are not allowed to step into or land in the crease, unless they are forced in by a defender. If this violation occurs, goals are waived off and possession is given to the defence.

- ✔ **Use steam for the sharpest crease:** When pressing your pants, make sure that your iron is set to steam to ensure a high-quality crease.

- ✔ **Stay in your own backyard:** Field lacrosse defenders always stay in the opposition's offensive zone, and the offensive players always stay in their own offensive zone. Only midfielders can run the entire field without restriction.

- ✔ **Penalties regulate the game's physical tendencies:** Referees monitor the physical play to help prevent injuries and out-and-out brawls. See Chapter 4 for a discussion of the game's penalties.

Chapter 2

Fundamentals of Playing Lacrosse

- -

In This Chapter

▶ Creating scoring chances on offence

▶ Preventing scoring chances on defence

▶ Serving as the last line of defence in goal

▶ Looking the part: Lacrosse equipment

- -

*E*very coach in any sport will tell you that the team that knows and sticks to the fundamentals is the team that has the best chance to win. The same goes for lacrosse. Mastering the basic skills of lacrosse takes practice, concentration, and diligence. Great players are great not only because they have the ability to make spectacular plays or to take control of a close game or to make their teammates look good, but also because they know that success starts with mastering the fundamentals.

This chapter covers the very basic of the basics — what you need to know to have a head start in understanding and playing this game with success. In addition to goaltending fundamentals, you can find out about the simple skills necessary to achieve success on the offensive or defensive side of the playing surface. You can also find out about the lacrosse player's required equipment needs.

Even though many box lacrosse teams play an offence–defence system — that is, offensive and defensive specialists are rotated in and out of the game based on who has control of the ball — you still need to be comfortable with the skills required on both ends of the floor. And field lacrosse players generally play both ways, so offensive and defensive fundamentals are critical for you as well.

Carrying the Offence: Keys for the Offensive Player

The ability to handle the ball — that is to pass, catch, cradle, and shoot with great skill — gives you and your team a tremendous advantage in a lacrosse game. But you also need to make use of certain offensive skills when you aren't carrying the ball. On offence, you must be able to beat a defender, whether you're with the ball or without the ball. And you should never take your eyes off the ball; you have to know where the ball is at all times.

This section offers the basics that you need to start with to gain success on the offensive end of the floor. Chapters 8 and 9 in this book go into greater detail on developing your offensive skills.

Practising efficient ball handling

Ball handling, of course, isn't really true "hand-ling"; you don't use your hand at all. Rather, efficient ball handling requires great skill with handling the lacrosse stick (see Figure 2-1). And the best ball handlers can work wonders with the ball and stick, whether catching, cradling, passing, or scoring.

Figure 2-1: How you hold the stick will prepare you for any offensive manoeuvre.

To become a great ballhandler — or at least to master the fundamentals of ball handling — you must practise, practise, practise. Walk to school while cradling a ball, spend Saturday mornings in the off-season throwing and catching off an outdoor wall (windowless, preferably), or set up a goal-shaped target to practise shooting against. Take the time to become comfortable with the basics of each of these ball-handling skills.

- **Catching:** Make sure that you're facing the direction that the pass is coming from, and allow your stick to give a little as it receives the ball. With these two reminders, you should have little trouble with any pass sent your way. Your best chance for catching a pass in your direction is to make sure that you're facing the passer and can see the path that the ball is taking toward your stick. Once the ball reaches your stick, give a little — that is, drop the stick back slightly as the ball hits the pocket to minimize the risk of the ball popping back out.

- **Cradling:** Efficiency at cradling — that is, holding the ball in your stick's pocket while you decide whether to shoot or pass — allows you to scan your options on the playing surface without having to look constantly at your stick to make sure you still have the ball. With different styles of cradling depending on the game situation, your goal is to protect the ball from a defender, hold on to the ball while you watch for a teammate to cut for a pass or for an opening for a shot on goal, and always be ready to release the ball.

- **Passing:** Just as you need to be in the proper position to catch a pass, positioning is critical to make a pass. However, facing the receiver directly is not usually the best bet; rather, have a slightly sideways stance because you're also likely to be keeping the ball away from a defender at the same time that you're passing it. Also, make sure that you've made eye contact with the receiver before you send a crisp two-handed pass her way.

- **Shooting:** Shooting is just like passing, except to a smaller target that doesn't move but has a large padded object in the way trying to "catch" your pass. The four most effective shot styles to work on are the over-hand long shot, the underhand long shot, the sidearm long shot, and the backhand shot that's usually from close in.

Moving — with and without the ball

Lacrosse is a game of constant movement. If you have the ball, you're working around the offensive zone trying to find an open teammate or trying to find an opening through which you can take a shot. If you don't have the ball, you're moving and running and picking and shifting and trying to shake free an opponent so that you can be in position to take a pass or pick up a loose ball.

Moving with the ball takes a combination of quickness, anticipation, and vision. Quick, darting moves may help you get past a defender so that you can break for the goal or pass to an open teammate. Anticipating when and from where a cross-check is coming may create yet another opening for a scoring opportunity. Keeping both eyes on the activity in the rest of the offensive zone, while your third and fourth eyes are looking out for defenders, takes particularly sharp concentration while you're also moving around the playing surface. (Some of the best playmakers in the game — or in any game, for that matter — do seem to have a third or fourth eye in the back of their heads; it's not actually a requirement for you.)

Moving without the ball helps you beat a defender and get open for a pass. The most basic play and most effective move without the ball is to just speed past your defender on the off-ball side. You can use quickness and deception, you can slash at your defender's stick to knock it down and go, or you can just cross-check your defender and push off.

Knowing where the ball is at all times

Having floor vision — an ability to see what's happening on the playing surface at all times — is a tremendous asset to successful lacrosse. The best players can see what their teammates are doing, anticipate where their teammates are going, know where the defensive players are and what they are likely to do, and still be able to keep an eye on where the ball is in the zone.

It will likely take you some time to be able to have the kind of floor vision that the best players have, so for now, work on making sure you know where the ball is. If you know which of your teammates has the ball, you can then quickly look around the floor for an opening or for an opportunity to set a pick or to anticipate a shot on goal and a possible loose ball.

Focusing on Defence: Keys for the Defensive Player

Half the battle of playing defence is good floor position. Of course, you need to know technically how to stop a man with the ball and without the ball, but good position saves you a lot of unnecessary work. How you use your stick on defence is also important, whether you use it as a slash, poke-check, or a cross-check. And sometimes you have to just use your body to compensate for making wrong decisions.

This section offers the basics that you need to start with to gain success on the defensive end of the floor. Chapter 10 in this book goes into greater detail on developing your defensive skills.

Establishing your position

Defensive positioning is a matter of how you play your opponent in relation to the rest of the defensive zone. Depending on game situations, you may choose to defend an offensive player by forcing him toward the sideboards or sidelines or by trying to get him to go higher up in the zone. Making the correct floor-position decision — knowing where on the floor is being in the right place at the right time defensively — is half the battle of playing solid defence.

Floor positioning also requires some understanding of how your teammates defend. By keeping yourself in a positive defensive position — such as between your opponent and the goal or between your opponent and the centre of the zone — you can be in a more ideal position to help out a teammate who has been beaten or to double-team a cutting ballcarrier.

Using (or not using) the stick

In box lacrosse, stick-checking is a legal defensive tactic. At one time, the thinking was that you should use your stick on defence only as an emergency measure or as an accessory to a cross-check. In the NLL today, however, stick-checking on the ballcarrier's gloves is one of the main tactics for stopping a ballcarrier. But this tactic remains illegal in minor lacrosse.

When you try to stick-check a player, you're trying to stop the momentum of a usually running, often-rather-large opponent with a piece of aluminum or wood. It's a bit like trying to block a 300-pound defensive lineman in football with a 170-pound placekicker. What you should be stopping your opponent's momentum with, is your body and a legal cross-check. In this better scenario, you hold the stick with both hands across your body as additional leverage for the check (see Figure 2-2). With this position, you're also keeping your hands on the stick so that you can quickly move to pick up a loose ball or intercept a pass.

In field lacrosse, stick-checking is more of an integral part of playing defence. In the field game, where sticks can be up to 72 inches long, stick-checks make up for roughly 85 percent of the defensive tactics. Footwork is crucial for a stick-check in order to keep yourself in good position to make a check or use the body. Stick-checks are effective in causing turnovers — deflecting passes or shots, stripping the ball from the opponent's crosse, and forcing a player into throwing an errant pass or shot. If an offensive player loses the ball, a defensive player's stick-check likely caused it. Field defenders use physical pressure with the body to keep an offensive player from dodging and putting himself in a good spot to shoot or pass.

Figure 2-2:
Using the stick on defence.

Defending with the cross-check

This defensive fundamental calls for keeping your body position low to the ground — knees bent, back straight, and eyes on your opponent and not on the ball or his stick — and maintaining your balance so that you can easily and quickly respond to an opponent's moves.

With this kind of proper body positioning, you're in good shape to take on your opponent with a well-timed cross-check.

Defending the Goal: Keys for the Goaltender

The position that most coaches either ignore or just don't know about is the goalie slot. The goalie is so often just left alone in practice to work on his own game by himself. "Go keep yourself busy until the next drill" is said by a lot of coaches. So when left to your own devices, what should you do to work on improving your goaltending skills? This section offers a few of the most basic tips (see Chapter 11 for more): goal positioning, the types of saves you can make, and communicating.

Taking your optimum goal position

The so-called *ready stance* is a balanced and relaxed position in the crease, ready to react forward, backward, or sideways, depending on the location of the ball. With your knees bent, your back straight, and your positioning square to the ball, this body positioning in front of the goal puts you in the best shape to take on any and all comers.

Use the goalposts to help you centre your stance, even grabbing both goalposts to help you guide yourself to the best goal-saving position. Once in position, hold your stick firmly between and in front of your feet so that it doesn't turn in your hand on a particularly hard shot.

Building up your save repertoire

Lacrosse goaltending comes down to two basic styles of saves: reflex saves and angle saves. Reflex saves refer to the kinds of saves that you make as a response to a shot, for example, a leg save that kicks away a low-flying shot, a body save that deflects a high shot, or a stick save that knocks away a bounce shot (see Figure 2-3).

Figure 2-3:
Types of goal saves include (clockwise from upper left) stick saves, glove saves, body saves, and leg saves.

Angle saves refer to how you position your body in goal in anticipation of a shot. With good body positioning in goal, you're effectively reducing the number of potential angles that an offensive player has for a shot on goal.

Field goalies may not need as much variety in their bag o' saves, but they do have to defend a larger net (6 by 6 feet). About 95 percent of a field goalie's saves are stick saves. Generally, field goalies use their bodies to save only when the ball gets by the stick and hits them in the chest.

Starting the offence

Possibly the most underappreciated skill that a lacrosse goalie can have is his ability to jump-start the offence with a well-timed and perfectly executed breakout pass. After stopping a shot, a goalie's quick-release pass to a teammate streaking toward the offensive zone can lead to a fast-break, two-on-one (or three-on-two) scoring opportunity.

Passing quickly and accurately is a highly specialized skill, especially with the bulky equipment that goalies wear today (see "Outfitting the goaltender" later in this chapter). Use your team's practice time to work on your passing; it's a good exercise when your coach has the rest of the team running drills at the other end of the floor.

From Head to Toe: Putting on the Equipment

With the advent and use of the plastic stick and aluminum handle, the game has moved in a new direction. In the old days, if you got hit, cross-checked, or slashed with a hickory wooden lacrosse stick, you felt the hardness of the wood and the result was pain or a bruise. Players used to pad up along their arms to prevent any unnecessary injuries. In today's game, however, the philosophy about equipment seems to be "less is better." Players in the NLL are dressing down with equipment that gives them more flexibility and less bulkiness. And as with any sports league, what the pros are doing soon trickles down to the minors and juniors and kids.

Injuries are still a concern but not as much as with the hickory stick. The key in minor lacrosse is to be well protected but have enough flexibility to handle the stick. However, if you face a dilemma of too much protection versus too little in order to get more movement, go with the protection first.

For a list of lacrosse equipment manufacturers, see Chapter 21.

Outfitting the players

Having the proper attire for lacrosse is more than just having the right look with the latest cool jersey design (though that's always nice to see, as long as it covers all your upper-body equipment). Equipping yourself for lacrosse is really more about making sure that you have all the accessories that will help keep you safe and healthy, as well as suiting yourself up to play the best possible lacrosse (see Figure 2-4). The required equipment discussed in this section will set you back approximately US$500–$600.

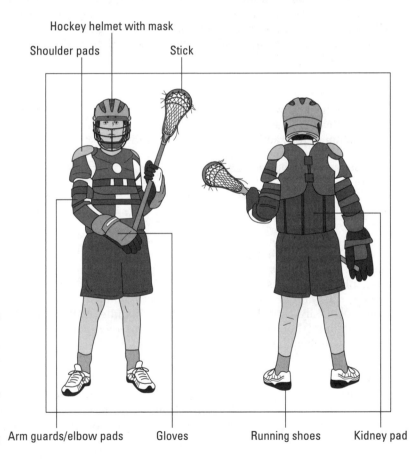

Hockey helmet with mask

Shoulder pads   Stick

Arm guards/elbow pads   Gloves   Running shoes   Kidney pad

Figure 2-4:
A fully equipped lacrosse player — front and back.

Stick head

Most lacrosse stick heads come flat when you buy them, that is, they have no pockets. You have to create (and then re-string) the pocket yourself. Try not to make your pocket right at the throat of the stick; you want it more toward the centre of the mesh. You may be able to ask your local sporting goods store to go ahead and create the pocket for you before you take your new stick home.

Beginning box players should start with a softer mesh, rather than the hard mesh that is preferred by field players. (More experienced players may want to go ahead and try a pocket with a medium-hard mesh.) Young players should also start with a wider face or more open head so that it is easier to catch the ball. Stay away from the more popular "pinched head" variety until you are proficient at passing and catching. And don't try to pinch the heads yourself; manufacturers today offer a good variety of "pinched head" sticks, especially for the box lacrosse game.

Introduced in the mid-1990s, *offset heads* (with the head set back from the shaft) are tremendously popular with players of all levels — youth to professional, box and field. An offset head allows the pocket to be deeper while still releasing the ball with a high trajectory, thereby enabling the shooter to increase the velocity of the shot while still adding torque to the cradle and making it harder for the ball to come out.

Stick handle

Unlike hockey players, lacrosse players don't use left-handed or right-handed sticks. Sticks are made *neutral,* which means that the middle of the tip of the head is lined up exactly in line with the handle.

The best way to pick a stick is to feel it in your hands. Some sticks just feel better than others, and you'll have to make that decision. Try out a few sticks before you buy. As you play more, you'll get a better idea of the kind of stick you like by trial and error with your own stick as well as by trying out other players' sticks.

Minor lacrosse players use the little junior stick, which has a thin aluminum handle. Junior sticks are fine for smaller players (from ages 4 to 8). But once players hit ages 9 to 12, they have to start getting into full-size handles because they are too strong for junior sticks, and the aluminum handle can bend too easily, especially when it is a thin handle. At this stage, they can still use aluminum, but most players use titanium, titanium alloy, or even a wooden handle, which is the cheapest.

Stick length

The rule for the length of the stick, from the end of the head to the end of the handle, is 36 inches or less for players up to 12 years of age in minor lacrosse. You should use a legal length that suits you. If you're choking up on the grip, the stick is too long for you.

As with the stick handle, look for a length that is comfortable for you. If you're handling the stick properly, there's no need to cut it off to make it shorter. If you cut your stick off short, then by the time you've grown, you may have to have to buy a new handle or another stick before another season begins. (Don't cut your stick too short, though; referees will check for legal stick length and may assess a minor penalty to a player with an illegal stick. In the 2002 World Lacrosse Championship, a U.S. player received this penalty during the championship game against Canada, though the U.S. went on to win the game.)

Talk with your coach and with other players for some ideas about which stick manufacturer to go with. And remember that if you're playing both box and field lacrosse, legal stick lengths for the outdoor game are different than for the indoor game; the box stick is smaller, shorter, and narrower (see Chapter 4).

Gloves

If you're just trying your hand at lacrosse and are not necessarily sure that it's something you'll want to continue, you can save a little money by using your hockey gloves rather than buying a new set of lacrosse gloves; if you're a hockey player, that is. If you don't play hockey either, the differences between lacrosse and hockey gloves are big enough to warrant buying lacrosse gloves. Lacrosse gloves have a lot more flexibility than hockey gloves and, as a result, increase your ability to handle the stick properly.

What do you look for in a lacrosse glove? Basically, you look for a good fit. Some less expensive gloves have a little more nylon on the top; the more expensive ones have a leather top. Both styles give adequate protection, but leather tends to last longer. Manufacturers put mesh in the palms so that the gloves can breathe a lot more, last a lot longer, and give you a better feel of the handle. The breathability is especially critical for box lacrosse played in hot arenas.

Shoulder pads, arm guards, and elbow pads

If you're making the transition from hockey to lacrosse, an inexpensive way to pad up is to use your hockey shoulder pads, and then tape a plastic shin guard from your hockey pants onto your upper arm where you're likely to feel the brunt of cross-checks. Keep in mind, however, that hockey shoulder pads are designed to keep your arms down (you're holding the stick down toward the ice); but in lacrosse, your arms are usually up in the air. If your hockey shoulder pads are light, you can definitely use them for lacrosse, but try to stay away from the bulkier, higher-end hockey shoulder pads.

Most lacrosse shoulder pads are fairly skimpy, but that comes in handy for today's "less-dressed" lacrosse player. The biggest function of lacrosse shoulder pads is to hold your arm guards on so that your arms don't get banged up. A three-piece pad comes all connected, with curved fibreglass to protect forearms, elbows, and biceps. With a properly fitted three-piece pad, you don't need extra elbow pads.

Some box lacrosse players use slash guards that are more in vogue for field lacrosse. This pull-on slash-guard goes from the middle of your arm to the top of your glove. Then you can put a padded arm guard over the top of the slash-guard (Velcro works well) to protect your biceps. This combination is fine, but it seems to leave a lot of space above the glove where your arms can get hit. Jim Veltman of the Toronto Rock says about equipment: "I wear as much light yet comfortable equipment as I can. I protect the areas where I tend to bruise a lot, especially my forearms."

Kidney pad

The single most important thing a minor player can wear is the kidney pad. You can play a game of lacrosse without a jock, but you can't play without a kidney pad, as you are always being hit in the back and the sides. The kidney pad is a one-piece unit that typically fits over the shoulders like suspenders and wraps around your stomach and lower and middle back for protection.

By the way, you *do* want to wear a jock while playing lacrosse.

Helmet

The lacrosse helmet should fit properly and not move or flop around. Most box players wear a cage over their face, not a full-face visor, because the visor is too hot for summer wear (though all field players wear visors). And for minor players, chinstraps are required (recommended for all players).

Many players today wear a helmet with a mask that is much like an old goalie hockey mask, with wider spaces in the mask for better vision. Whatever helmet and mask you choose, make sure that it's approved for use by your league or association; they may even have a list of approved equipment from which to choose. Helmets and masks are typically approved for ice hockey as well.

Mouth guard

Mouth guards are mandatory in minor lacrosse. You can get your dentist to make you a guard or you can buy a pre-made one that is a bit cheaper but will do the job effectively. The biggest difference between the two is that the dental mouth guard is built from a mold taken of your teeth, so it tends to stay on your teeth a little more comfortably and leads to less gagging.

The mouth guard not only protects your teeth from getting chipped and cracked but also helps prevent concussions by keeping your teeth from jamming together. The contact of the upper and lower jaw can cause a shock wave that may lead to a concussion. Having this cushion in your mouth will help to prevent that.

Running shoes

Look for three-quarter-cut or high-top shoes rather than low-cut shoes. The higher-cut shoes are better to absorb all the cutting and picking and rolling in lacrosse. Also, keep your lacrosse shoes separate from your everyday shoes. Wearing your lacrosse shoes daily will break down the soles, causing you to slip and slide in a game.

Make sure your shoes are a good fit; shoes that are too big will cause blisters. Some players wear two pairs of thick socks for absorption and protection of their feet. Others wear ankle socks for looks and comfort. Just make sure your socks are smooth when you put them on because any wrinkle can also cause blisters.

Dressing for the game

Unless you have some kind of personal superstitious ritual that requires you to get dressed with your gloves on, suiting up for a game is straightforward and simple.

✔ Start with your cup, uniform shorts, T-shirt, socks, and shoes.

✔ Your kidney pads should be the first protective equipment you put on (after your cup, of course) so that the other layers of equipment and clothing will help keep the shoulder straps in place. You may wish to tape the straps together to make sure that they stay on.

✔ Your shoulder pads and slash-guards will be attached, so you can put them on together.

✔ Your sweater should be big enough to go over your equipment, but not so big that you get lost in it and not so small that it is too tight.

✔ Finally, your helmet and gloves go on.

Also, make sure that you keep up maintenance on your equipment, such as tightening screws and replacing straps. After every game, air out your equipment so that it won't be wet when you play the next game and it won't mildew.

In 1968, Converse made the first leather running shoe for the Detroit Olympics of the National Lacrosse Association. It was a red-and-white high-top version of the Chuck Taylor Converse All-Star.

Outfitting the goaltender

The general rule for goalies is that if you get hurt somewhere on your body, fix your equipment up with some padding. That's basically how the improvements in goaltending equipment have evolved. This section shows you what you need to protect yourself (see Figure 2-5) while you're protecting your team (on the scoreboard, that is). To complete your goaltender outfit, you'll need to spend about US$700–$800.

Make sure that your equipment fits comfortably and gives you plenty of protection, but it also needs to be flexible enough to allow you to reach for shots or defend a player behind the goal or dive for a loose ball in front of the crease. As a parent, I know that we want to overprotect the child tending goal. Remember, though, that today's equipment is specially designed to withstand the toughest punishment that lacrosse can offer.

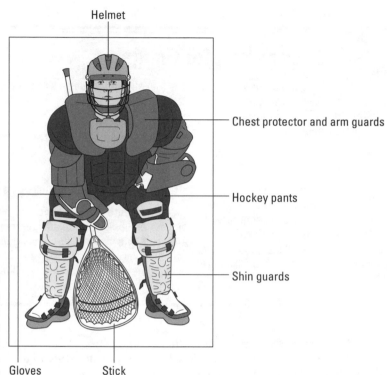

Helmet

Chest protector and arm guards

Hockey pants

Shin guards

Figure 2-5:
What
goalies
wear in the
crease.

Gloves   Stick

Goalie stick

The plastic field-type goalie stick is the most common stick used in lacrosse these days. The approved width for the stick's pocket is 15 inches. A wooden stick may be more efficient because it covers more of the net, but it is harder to buy now, harder to pass with because of its size, and is illegal in the NLL.

Gee Nash, an all-star goalie with the NLL's New York Saints recommends a durable, lightweight stick for younger players: "I also recommend having the pocket in the upper-middle part of the stick because it allows for a quicker ball release, which is very important when starting the fast break. Try to make the pocket deep enough so that the ball does not bounce out easily on a shot allowing for unneeded rebounds. Make sure the pocket is not so deep that the ball hooks upon release."

Goalie shin guards and pants

Shin guards protect the goalie's lower legs and ankles. All manufacturers offer good shin guards that are usually made of hard plastic. Lacrosse rules say that goalie pads have to form to the goalie's body. These pads start above the knee and cover all the way down to the tops of the feet, not unlike a baseball catcher's leg pads. They strap to the lower legs so that your knees, ankles, and feet are not restricted in movement. As with other goalie equipment today, these are big and bulky — the bigger the better.

The goalie's pants (shorts, really) provide protection for your waist and thighs.

Goalie gloves

While a hockey goalie's equipment includes a mitt used to catch shot pucks out of mid-air, lacrosse goalies rely on their stick's pocket to catch shots on goal. A goalie's gloves are used to protect the hands and wrists. Look for gloves that can both protect your hands and be flexible enough to grasp and manoeuvre your stick with ease. Make sure that your gloves have enough flexibility in the thumbs; opposable thumbs are especially handy for grasping lacrosse sticks.

You may find that higher-end hockey gloves will do the trick. However, they don't have the protective backing that lacrosse goalie gloves provide. If you use your old hockey gloves, make sure to attach or insert a hard cover to the back of them for protection.

Goalie chest protector and arm guard

Most of these come in a one-piece chest-arm combination that fits over your shoulders and chest like a football player's shoulder pads. They're designed to protect your shoulders, chest, and arms. As with all your other equipment, you'll want to look for a protector that gives you a bit of freedom and flexibility to move around in the crease. And, like the jerseys of your teammates, your jersey must cover all your protective equipment.

Chest protectors and arm guards and other protective equipment are just that — protective equipment. Don't get in the habit of relying on what you wear to stop shots. Continue to develop your skills so that you're making stick saves or hand saves or leg saves rather than bodying up to a shot on goal. All-star goaltender Dallas Eliuk of the Philadelphia Wings of the NLL says: "I don't use padding for bulk as I feel it will hinder a goaltender from developing his skills. Most goaltenders rely on padding rather than on ability in stopping the ball."

In addition to his chest protector and arm guards, Bob Watson of the Toronto Rock wears elbow pads, which help prevent turf burn from the NLL's indoor Astroturf carpets.

Chest protectors for field goalies do not include arm guards. In fact, field goalies rarely wear arm guards at all.

Goalie helmet

You can wear a hockey goaltender mask, a regular hockey helmet with a cage, or a field lacrosse helmet (also with a cage). Field helmets may be a little trickier to work with because the front of the helmet comes to a peak, but its mask is better because of its heavier cage. The pros tend to use a fibreglass goalie mask or a field helmet for its heavier and stronger cage structure. Make sure the helmet fits snugly as you don't want the helmet to fall down in front of your eyes or move to the side on a shot.

The throat protector is an essential (in fact, mandatory for minor leagues) accessory. It's simply a piece of flat fibreglass that hangs down from the bottom of the cage so that a ball doesn't bounce up and hit you in the throat.

Chapter 3

Fundamentals of Coaching Lacrosse

● ●

In This Chapter

▶ Finding a game plan to match your players

▶ Finding the players to achieve your game plan

▶ Assembling your game plan

▶ Mastering the great equalizer: Coaching specialty teams

▶ Understanding what it takes to coach kids

● ●

Successful coaches in any sport have been motivators, taskmasters, disciplinarians, sympathizers (so-called "players' coaches"), virtuosos of the *X*s and *O*s (great game planners), delegators, or micromanagers. However, unsuccessful coaches in any sport have also had all of these traits. What sets the successful coaches apart from their peers is the ability to match the personnel on their team to a style of play that gives their team the best opportunity to win.

This chapter introduces the fundamentals of coaching as simply that: selecting the best players available and creating a system that will take the fullest advantage of their skills. In addition, I offer a few tips about coaching kids, as well as developing specialty teams, one of the lesser-known keys to successful coaching. For a more detailed discussion about coaching, check out Part IV of this book.

Determining Your Team's Style of Play

What style of play do you want your team to play? Should you run or should you slow the game down? Should you play a tough physical style or a quick finesse style? Do you need to score a lot of goals or can you keep the score in a game low? These are some of the questions you have to have answers for to succeed as a coach. By knowing your style, you can then look for players to complement that style, and this will help you to develop your team quicker.

You may not have the luxury of selecting players that fit your system, however. You may have to take whoever shows up, plus run around town looking for other players who may fit into your system and convince them that lacrosse is a great sport to play.

No matter how you build your team, you still need a style of play so that every player is playing from the same page of your playbook. You may have to try to fit misfits into your system: for example, you may want your team to run but have slow players, and your best hope is that your slowest player can outrun your opponent's slowest player. Or you may have to take advantage of your players' strengths and adapt your system to your players: for example, you may not have the biggest team in the league, but you do have the smartest, and your "overpower-them" strategy quickly becomes your "outwit-them" strategy. The art of coaching comes down to this: Put the players you have into a style of play that brings out the most in all of them.

Building Your Team

After you decide the type of system you'd like to try to run, you need to start looking for players who will best fit into that system. You look for players who have the skills necessary to achieve success in your style of play, as well as the game sense to recognize opportunities to both press forward and hold back with that style of play.

Regardless of what style of play your team focuses on, you should also try to build a team that has some overall balance. If you're coaching a quick, fast-breaking team, you still need to have a few bigger players who can counteract those opponents who play a tough, hard-hitting, grind-it-out kind of game. If your top goal scorer is a right-shot player, try to add a couple of decent left-shot players so that you can run plays that offer scoring opportunities from both sides of the goal.

Finally, remember that players who have won before are more likely to win again. These players have experienced both the ecstasy of winning and the pressure to get there. And they can serve as surrogate coaches for you, by helping less experienced players understand what it takes to be successful.

When selecting your players, think about building your team in stages. If you are allowed 15 players on your team, decide first — based on your style of play — what skills you must have from your top 5 players, how your middle 5 players will support your best players, and how your last 5 players will contribute.

✔ **Finding the cream of the crop:** Usually your top players are going to carry the team offensively. They will be responsible for at least 80 percent of your scoring and will need to be quick enough to stay away from disruptive cross-checks, wily enough to anticipate defensive tendencies, and have the floor vision to spot an open teammate.

✔ **Finding players who love the dirty work:** Doing the dirty work doesn't (necessarily) mean taking on an opponent physically. Your middle group of players needs to have strong fundamental skills that will support your top players. These players should be able to play well on both ends of the floor. You're looking for solid, if not great, defenders, occasional goal scorers, and players with size and defensive quickness who are willing to take one for the team to get a loose ball or to slow down an opponent.

✔ **Finding the right blend to complement your best:** This last group is usually the toughest group to pick because the traits you should look for are often hard to spot. But based on your team's style of play, you'll need a few players who have a great work ethic and attitude to encourage your best players to stay within the system. This group is also where you'll place any role players or specialists, such as a player who gives your team the best chance to win any faceoff. Or you may want to use this group to add players who are athletic enough to play any position on the team, giving you a bit of flexibility should you lose a player or two to injury.

Developing a Game Plan

The goal of any game is very simple: to play to the best of your ability and try to win the game. Coming up with a plan to achieve that goal, however, takes a bit more time and creativity.

Understanding your opponent

Find out everything you can about your upcoming opponent. Who are their biggest offensive threats? What are the weaknesses of their defenders? What are the tendencies of their goaltender, that is, is he more likely to save with his stick or with his body? Under what style of play are they most effective? By understanding what an opposing team is likely to do during a game, you can build your game plan to match or overcome their strengths.

Anticipating what your opponent may try to do during a game, you'll increase your own team's confidence level and minimize the chance for strategic surprises and competitive disasters. After you've done all that you can do to understand an opponent, you can totally focus on your own game plan, one that you can develop to take away your opposition's strengths and take advantage of your opposition's weaknesses.

This will take some time on your part, of course. (Or you can try to convince your assistant coaches to take on the work.) If your league provides game film or video, take advantage of it. You can learn a great deal about a team's tendencies by watching film — the biggest advantage, of course, is that you can watch play after play after play over and over and over again. Exciting, eh? And make sure that you're at the arena or field just about every time any game is in progress. You'll be able to pick up some valuable tips by watching firsthand an opponent play (or an opposing coach coach).

Concentrating on defence

In developing a defensive game plan, the object is to try to come up with the perfect defence that will keep your opposition from scoring more goals than your team. There is no question that all great sports teams win because of their defence; stop your opponent from scoring and all you need is one goal (or touchdown or basket or run) to win. And defensive skills can be taught more easily than offensive skills. You can teach players how to be physical or how to cross-check; you can't teach players how to acquire a shooter's touch around the net. And defences can succeed against any kind of offence: fast-break, slow-down, or in-between.

Create an atmosphere on your team that rewards great defensive play. It's natural for players to think that the fun part of lacrosse is scoring goals. By emphasizing solid defence, you increase the chances of your players considering the fun part of the game to be stopping a player from scoring goals. Play your best defenders on your opponent's best offensive players, regardless of your own player's offensive talents (or lack thereof). Provide incentives for hustling defensive play and hard work, creating quantifiable goals that players can reach, such as number of loose balls recovered. And finally, reward your good defenders with some playing time on the offensive end of the floor; after all, scoring goals is still fun.

Concentrating on offence

The great offensive players seem to be born with a knack for scoring. And then there are some players who practise and practise but never get the "touch" around the net to score. So if you have players who can't score, you better come up with an offensive system that creates open shots, and emphasize that if the shot isn't there, don't shoot. You may also want to build your offence (and your defence) for a low-scoring game.

However, if you have good offensive players, you have a bit more flexibility in creating an offensive game plan. After establishing your opponent's weaknesses, you can add set plays to your game plan that will take advantage of those weaknesses. If your opposing goalie is a great stick-saver, have your shooters focus on the corner of the net that's opposite his stick. And make sure that you have a nice mix of long-ball shooters and inside scorers for each shift.

No matter your team's offensive philosophy, make sure that your offensive players always know who their defensive backup is, that is, which player goes back on defence when a shot is attempted. The pointman is typically the first defender back, followed by the cornerman opposite from where the shot came from.

Finding the Unsung Heroes: Specialty Teams

Probably the best-kept secret to coaching success is an ability to get your players to execute the power-play offence, the man-short defence, and faceoffs. These specialty teams win the close games.

Your primary concern on the power play should be to make the opposition stop you. And you'll have more success when you create a game plan that anticipates what you want to do on the power play, rather than anticipates what your opponent's strategies may be. No matter what defensive formation is thrown at you, you can usually be successful with your power play by either pressuring the ball on goal or by staying back, passing and moving around the zone, and taking what the defence gives you.

The man-short defence is strictly a work-ethic specialty group. If you want your man-short defence to pressure the ball, your defensive players have to be aggressive and smart. They need to be ready to run — out, at an open shooter; back, to help defend the crease; and over, to take away a shooting line. Also, from your advance preparation, find out who your opponent's better power-play players are so that you can overplay them, or at least be aware of them when they have the ball.

Basic Tips for Coaching Lacrosse to Kids

In Chapter 19, you'll find much more information about coaching kids, including how to work with parents, but this section suggests a few things that every minor coach should be able to do.

Minor coaches must be able to teach the game

Teaching the game is the most important thing a coach can do. You can have plenty of knowledge about lacrosse, but your teaching ability will be judged by what your players learn. The most important aspect of teaching is being able to transfer knowledge. You may be the most knowledgeable coach in the world, but if your players cannot translate that knowledge into action, your expertise means nothing. So in addition to sharing what your players need to *know*, make sure that you're giving them the tools they need to know what to *do*.

 Steve Toll of the Toronto Rock gives his philosophy of lacrosse: "First, I believe that young players should learn the game properly and treat the game with respect, and they will always get good results. Secondly, I believe you have to be a team player first; forget personal achievements, you win and lose as a team."

Minor coaches motivate with good teaching principles

Learning improves if you use these basic teaching principles:

✔ **Don't just dictate — explain.** Of course, you need to tell players what you want them to do and achieve. However, players learn best when they're told what to do, how best to do it, why things need to be done a certain way, and what kind of success will come out of it. Be precise, but also be explicit.

✔ **Do as I do, not as I say.** Contrary to the well-known axiom, you *do* want your players to do as you do. So you need to be willing to demonstrate exactly what you're asking your players to do. Use your assistant coaches, other players, or even parents; but whomever you use, make sure that your demonstrations are accompanied by a thorough explanation.

✔ **Practise, practise, practise.** It's time for your players to translate the knowledge they've received from your explanations and demonstrations. Remember to practise enough repetitions so that your players leave the arena or field with confidence in their ability to achieve what you're asking for.

✔ **Watch and analyze — you can walk and chew gum at the same time.** While you're watching your team work on what you've taught them, make notes (mental or otherwise) of your reaction to what you're seeing. You're going to need them when you . . .

✔ **. . . Give feedback.** Make sure to include both positive and negative feedback. You want to reward your players for any success, as well as give them a chance to learn from their mistakes.

Your attitude about mistakes can help create a learning environment of support and security. Because mistakes are an important part of the learning process, don't get upset over them. Instead, present your critical feedback with some more positive comments, making sure that players understand that mistakes are made to be learned from. Also, try not to compare players against players. If you need some comparative examples, use yourself.

The learning process is also influenced by what you do, what types of standards you set, how patient you are, how you react to mistakes, and how you give feedback.

Minor coaches teach confidence more than skill

You need to believe in and see the potential in your players, as well as be able to suffer through your players' growing pains. By doing so, you help your players become more confident, and this motivates them to play better. The skills will come with hard work, preparation, practice, and competition; showing confidence is something that requires your full and constant attention.

Minor coaches need patience — and lots of it

It's okay to set high standards and have high expectations for your team members; but you also need to be prepared for disappointment when they don't meet either of them. In other words, expect a lot, but have patience. Patience is one of the most important characteristics you need, because kids are going to make a lot of mistakes while learning how to play lacrosse. As a minor coach, you have to be a good role model, and the best way to do so is to keep your cool during practices and games.

Minor coaches create commitment

One of the problems of minor sports today is commitment. If you want to coach a good minor team, your players have to be committed to playing their best and playing with respect for the game and for other players.

How do you get commitment? Sometimes the easiest way to create commitment is to hold fast to the most important rule on the team: If you miss practice, you don't play. Make sure that your players expect the consequences of breaking a rule. If a player misses a practice, he may have to sit for the whole game, part of the game, or for a shift. The first time that you give in and don't enforce the consequences, you guarantee yourself more problems, both from the player and other players, as well as from parents.

When a player returns from a missed practice, make sure that you listen fully to the player's explanation, which could be an honest and legitimate excuse, before handing out a punishment. You need to know why a player was late or missed the practice. If it's an excusable mistake, then you can communicate to the rest of the team whether the player is being penalized and why.

Chapter 4

Rules of the Game

• •

• •

As with any team or individual sport, lacrosse is played by a set of rules. The thing about rules is that they help dictate the flow of the game so that all players start on the same level playing field, so to speak. Rules also help the game's fans understand what's happening on that level playing field.

Whether you're curious about the slashing penalty or just need to know how long the playing surface is in a box lacrosse arena, this chapter gives you the basics in lacrosse rules and regulations.

Box of Dreams? Inside the Boards in a Lacrosse Arena

So you've entered an arena to watch a box lacrosse game. As soon as you look at the floor, you notice different markings than you'd find on the ice for hockey or on a basketball court, sports that are also played in an arena. You'll probably also notice that the playing surface is artificial turf, which is called the *carpet*, rather than cement or wood (or ice, for hockey enthusiasts). The reason for using artificial turf is that it's easier on the legs to run on and fall on, plus it looks good. (However, it's not as easy on the legs as an outdoor grass field; see "Examining the field" later in this chapter.)

The box lacrosse playing area must have boards around the sides and the ends of the playing surface with a minimum height of three feet. Because arenas can vary in size (from the 21,000-seat General Motors Place that hosts the Vancouver Ravens, for example, to the intimacy of community arenas such as Rideau Township Arena in Manotick, Ontario), playing surfaces are not always uniform in size. However, most playing surfaces are 200 feet long and 85 feet wide, and the features inside those playing surfaces are the same (see Figure 4-1).

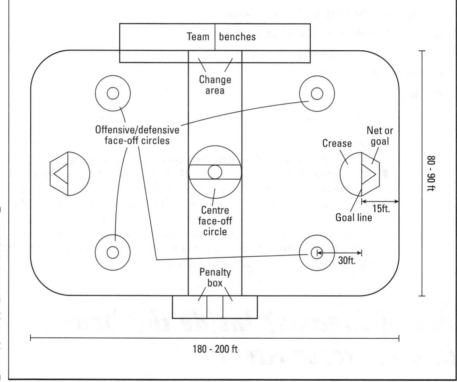

Figure 4-1:
The box lacrosse playing surface can measure 180 to 200 feet long and 80 to 90 feet wide.

- ✔ **Centre faceoff circle:** Despite its location so far from the hub of lacrosse activity — the goal — the big circle at centre floor gets a lot of use. It's used only for faceoffs, including the ones that start the game and each period of play. But the circle also hosts a faceoff after every goal is scored. And believe me, a lacrosse game can feature a lot of goals.

- ✔ **Restraining lines:** The two lines that run across the width of the floor (from the team benches to the penalty boxes) have several functions.

- **Restraining players:** Hence the name (though you won't see any ropes leap off the floor to physically restrain your creaseman). The eight players that are not involved in competing for the faceoff must line up behind the restraining lines until the ball comes out of the faceoff circle, at which time they can pursue a loose ball or defend the ballcarrier.

- **Ten-second threshold:** When a team takes possession in its own zone, it has ten seconds to move the ball over the opposite restraining line, that is, the line closest to the goal that the team attacks. If ten seconds pass before the ball crosses that line, the team forfeits possession.

- **Over-and-back line:** Once the team on offence has crossed over the opposite restraining line, it cannot allow the ball to go back over that line (toward the centre faceoff circle) or it risks losing possession of the ball.

✔ **Change area:** The rectangular boxes that run parallel to the team benches are there for shifting players in and out of the game. A player coming off the floor must have his foot in the box before the player replacing him can come on the floor. If an offensive player comes on the floor too early, the offensive team loses possession of the ball. If a defensive player goes onto the floor too early, the defensive team faces a two-minute penalty.

✔ **Crease:** This semicircular marking around the goal is 9 feet in diameter and serves to protect the goalie. If an opposing offensive player enters the crease, the offence loses possession of the ball. If an opposing offensive player is stepping on the line of the crease or is in the crease and scores, the goal is disallowed. But if the ball goes into the net before he steps into the crease, the goal stands.

✔ **Nets:** Lacrosse nets are a different size than hockey nets. Hockey nets are 6 feet wide and 4 feet high. Lacrosse nets are 4 feet 9 inches wide and 4 feet high.

Field of Dreams: Knowing the Playing Field

The major difference between box lacrosse and field lacrosse is that field lacrosse is played primarily outdoors (though it can be played indoors) on a larger playing surface, with ten players per team, including goalies. It can be played on either grass or artificial turf. Venues for NCAA games are as large as Syracuse University's Carrier Dome (50,000 seats, indoors) and Baltimore's Ravens Stadium (70,000 seats, outdoors), and crowds for the national championship game can be as large as 30,000 people. The larger field space produces a wide-open game with more specialized positions and an added emphasis on team coordination on offence and defence.

The second major difference with the box game is that field lacrosse allows four players to use sticks measuring between 52 and 72 inches. Standard length for sticks in field lacrosse is between 40 and 42 inches, similar to the box game. Those with longer sticks play defence, which makes it harder for opposing offensive players to score but also limits defencemen from getting involved offensively because of the decreased stick-handling that comes from carrying 10 to 20 additional inches.

Two more technical variations in the field game sufficiently alter its style of play. The midline prohibits more than seven players (including a goalie) on one team from being on one-half of the field at any time. This promotes specialization in positions. Also, the field goal is bigger (6 by 6 feet), and the goalies play with much less padding, allowing offensive players the chance to score from farther away.

Examining the field

Field lacrosse traverses a much larger space than the box game, and no walls surround the edges of the field. Outdoor lacrosse is played on grass and artificial turf fields measuring 110 by 60 yards. Fields are sectioned by a midline and two restraining lines 35 yards from the endlines that signify the offensive and defensive zones surrounding each goal. A field's midline serves as the offsides line. When the ball is in one end, seven defensive players (including a goalie) and six offensive players are allowed between the endline and midline. Figure 4-2 shows the field lacrosse layout.

With no walls, out of bounds is called as it is in soccer or basketball on all plays except shots. Throw an errant pass at midfield over the sideline, and possession is awarded to the other team. But fling a shot over the goal, and whichever team has a player closest to where the ball crossed out of bounds gets possession. Once shots are taken that clearly miss the goal, everyone generally sprints to the endline trying to gain or maintain possession.

Goals measure 6 by 6 feet, and the crease is a full-circle 9-yard radius surrounding the goal area. Offensive players are not allowed inside the crease. Goals are waived off and/or possession is given to the defence if an offensive player steps in the crease.

The crease violation is a major difference between field and box lacrosse and a bone of contention among some outdoor fans. The *dive* (trying for a closer shot by entering the crease by air, that is, not *stepping* in the crease area) was taken out of the NCAA game before the 1999 season in an effort to protect goalies from offensive players leaping into the crease. Although he didn't perform the straight-on dive that the NCAA was worried about, Syracuse's Gary Gait made a famous move by jumping from outside the crease behind the goal and dunking a shot around front against Penn in the 1988 national semifinal game. He pulled the move, later coined the "Air Gait," twice in the 11–10 win.

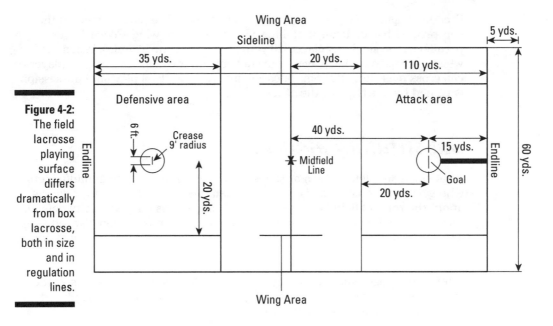

Figure 4-2:
The field lacrosse playing surface differs dramatically from box lacrosse, both in size and in regulation lines.

Keeping the field game moving

Youth, high school, and college field lacrosse games have no shot clock for the offence, but the game does have some rules to help the game keep up its fast-moving pace.

- ✔ **Defensive clear-out:** Defensive players have ten seconds to clear the ball past the defensive area line, or possession is given to the opposing team.

- ✔ **Five-second count:** If any sort of stalling occurs between the defensive area line and midline, officials will give the player with the ball a five-second count during which he must cross midfield or advance within five yards of an opponent.

- ✔ **Ten-second count:** Once over the midline, teams have ten seconds to advance the ball into the attack area. If the offensive team moves the ball out of the attack area once it has entered, a new ten-second count is started.

The summertime professional outdoor lacrosse league, Major League Lacrosse (MLL), has a 45-second shot clock, and many in the field lacrosse community have talked about experimenting with a shot clock in the college game. Without a shot clock, referees can keep teams from stalling by issuing a "keep it in" warning if they are obviously holding the ball from play in the attack area and not advancing toward the goal. In the last two minutes of games, the team with the lead *must* keep the ball in once it enters the attack area.

Faceoffs begin each quarter and follow each goal. Two players meet at the centre X, with each team stationing a player on each wing (20-yard lines parallel to the sidelines placed 20 yards from the centre circle). When the whistle blows, the wing players can converge on the ball, but no other players can cross over the restraining lines and into the middle of play until possession is gained by one team or the other.

Substituting players

Attackmen and defencemen are substituted less frequently than midfielders, who generally come on and off in three-man lines (see Chapter 1 for details about the roles of field lacrosse players). Some teams have specialty defence units, but the first defensive line generally sees the most action. Faceoff specialists and wing players often run directly off the field once possession is gained.

A ten-yard special substitution box straddles the midline and serves as the exclusive entrance and exit for all players to the field — no limit is placed on the number of a team's substitutes.

Unravelling penalties and physical play

Penalties are shorter in field lacrosse than in the box game, generally lasting 30 seconds or a minute, though some penalties last up to 3 minutes. After the team with the player advantage scores, the offending player is released from the penalty box, unless the foul was non-releasable, in which case the penalty is carried out for the duration, regardless of scoring. Only harsher penalties earn non-releasable calls. If the team without the ball commits a technical foul, it has to play without a man for 30 seconds. Technical fouls committed by teams with the ball simply give possession to the opponent.

Lacrosse sticks, or *crosses,* must conform to regulations and one is checked at random after each quarter in field lacrosse. Coaches can specifically request a player's stick be checked. Violation carries a 3-minute non-releasable penalty.

Because most penalties are shorter in field lacrosse, power-play (called man-up) success is lower than in box lacrosse. The best NCAA man-up units generally achieve a 50 percent success rate, while the success rate percentage for the best man-down (penalty-killing) units hovers in the mid-80s. In 2002, the NLL's top power-play percentage was in the mid-70s, while the best penalty-killing units were in the high 50s.

Any player accumulating five penalties is ejected from the game, though this is an extremely rare occurrence, and the player's team does not have to play short-handed after the expulsion. Fighting is almost nonexistent, thanks in part to much higher penalties. Occasional heat-of-the-moment skirmishes break out during games, but actual one-on-one, gloves-off fisticuffs do not happen in field lacrosse. In the NCAA, fighting earns an automatic ejection, 3-minute non-releasable penalty, and suspension from the next game.

In field lacrosse, if a goalie commits a penalty, he must serve the time and is replaced with a backup. This is a significant difference with the box game — facing a cold, often inexperienced backup can be a major advantage for the opposing team.

Another major difference with the box game is that in field lacrosse a player cannot cross-check (using the portion of his stick between his hands to check his opponent). Cross-checking is a personal foul, earning between 1 and 3 minutes of penalty time. In field lacrosse, no check is legal on a player without the ball. Players are allowed to push and use sticks to hold opponents' sticks, as long as they are within five yards of a loose ball.

Understanding the Box Game's Participants and Their Roles

A lacrosse game is a match of skill and wits with three primary groups of participants: the players, their coaches, and the game referees. This section offers a brief rundown of what each group of participants does during a game. For more detailed information about some of these gamers, check out Part III of this book for players and Part IV for coaches.

Introducing tonight's players

Unless a player (or two) is in the penalty box, each box lacrosse team has six players on the floor at any one time, including the goalie, a pointman, two creasemen, and two cornermen.

Because most players these days have either offensive or defensive specialties, you'll see a lot of *line changes,* that is, running to and from the benches as players exchange positions depending on who has possession of the ball. If a team gains control of the ball, some players run the ball up the floor and others run to the bench so that the better offensive players can get on the floor to score. If a team loses possession of the ball, some players run back on defence and others run to the bench to get the better defensive players on the floor to stop the opposition from scoring. A few players can play both ways, offence and defence, and this makes them very valuable to a team.

Leading the team: The coach's role

The coach's primary role during a game is to change the lines and put out special checking assignments against the opposition's best offensive player. When a penalty has been called, the coach calls for either the *power-play offence,* when the opposing team is penalized, or the *man-short defence,* if his team receives the penalty.

Most teams have three coaches: the head coach and two assistant coaches, one of whom works with the offence and one of whom works with the defence. The head coach oversees the whole operation of the game, but the offensive coach changes the offensive players and gives feedback to the offensive players to make them better. The defensive coach does the same thing with the defensive players and makes sure they pick up the correct *checking assignments,* that is, which player to defend. The head coach also makes sure that the bench is organized and makes all final decisions on who should play at what particular time in the game.

Officiating the game: The men in black

In a lacrosse game, two referees are assigned to run the floor, one of whom has been designated chief referee. The referee's job is to make sure that the rules of the game are enforced. Referees try to assure that the game is run smoothly and is played on as close to an even level as possible. If the players try to take advantage of the rules by doing something illegal, the referee will call a penalty on the offender.

In addition to monitoring the play of the game, referees are responsible for ensuring that players are using the proper equipment, including the appropriate game wear, such as helmets and pads, that help prevent injuries, and the proper game equipment, such as the lacrosse stick.

Getting Down to Brass Tacks: The Elements of the Game

As I note in Chapter 1, the length of a lacrosse game varies depending on who the participants are. Pro, major, and junior box lacrosse games go for 60 minutes, while some minor lacrosse games can be as short as 32 minutes. You'll also find variation in the number of periods of play in a lacrosse game, ranging from four quarters to three periods to two halves. Regardless of the length of play, the basic elements of the game are pretty much the same no matter who's playing. This section provides the information you need to understand the nuts and bolts of lacrosse.

He shoots! He scores!

Of course, the primary objective of the game is to score more goals than the other team. And you do this by getting the little white ball past the other team's goalie and into the netting of the goal.

If you're the offensive-minded, run-and-gun, shoot-'em-up kind of sports fan, you'll love the offensive excitement of lacrosse. You won't find many 1–0 or 2–1 final scores in lacrosse. Table 4-1 shows the final scores of championship games (and the champions) at varying skill levels for the five-year period ending in 2002. (Note that for the Mann and Minto Cups, the outcome shown is for the final game of a best four-out-of-seven series.)

Table 4-1	Lacrosse Championship Scores				
Championship	*1998*	*1999*	*2000*	*2001*	*2002*
National Lacrosse League (NLL)	17–12 (Philadelphia)	13–10 (Toronto)	14–13 (Toronto)	9–8 (Philadelphia)	13–12 (Toronto)
NCAA Men's Division I	15–5 (Princeton)	12–10 (Virginia)	13–7 (Syracuse)	10–9 (Princeton)	13–12 (Syracuse)
NCAA Women's Division I	11–5 (Maryland)	16–6 (Maryland)	16–8 (Maryland)	14–13 (Maryland)	12–7 (Princeton)
Mann Cup	7–5 (Brampton)	17–9 (Victoria)	14–9 (Brooklin)	10–9 (Coquitlam)	9–8 (Brampton)
Minto Cup	10–2 (Burnaby)	9–3 (Whitby)	9–5 (Burnaby)	7–4 (St. Catharines)	7–3 (Burnaby)

Why all the scoring?

In 1954, the National Basketball Association instituted a 24-second clock, that is, each team had 24 seconds during an offensive possession to attempt a shot or turn the ball over. In its first year of use, the 24-second clock increased scoring in NBA games by over 17 percent; NBA teams averaged over 13 points per game more than the previous season.

Many levels of lacrosse also play with a shot clock. In the NLL, a 30-second shot clock begins when a team gets possession of the ball. The offensive team must get a shot on net during that time, or it will lose possession of the ball. If the offensive team shoots the ball at the goal and doesn't score, it can recover the rebound or loose ball after which the clock starts all over again with a new 30 seconds. You can get off a lot of shots 30 seconds at a time.

Starting and stopping play and everything in between

To determine possession at the start of each quarter and after every goal, a faceoff occurs, where two players face their sticks at the centre faceoff circle with a referee placing the ball between the heads of the sticks. Play is stopped when a goal is scored, when a penalty is called, and when the ball goes out of bounds. (After a penalty in the NLL, however, the ball is awarded to the non-offending team.)

With these exceptions, just about every other event that starts or stops play of the game involves ball possession. Ball possession is very important in the box lacrosse game. You gain possession from chasing down loose balls, from winning faceoffs, from intercepting bad passes, and from recovering shots at the net.

But you can also *lose* possession of the ball, turning the ball over to your opponent when they may or may not have earned it. You can give up possession by taking more than ten seconds to get the ball into the offensive zone, by setting illegal moving picks, by doing an illegal draw on the faceoff (for example, having a foot inside the small circle), by touching the ball in play with your hand, and by having too many offensive players on the floor.

Refereeing Lacrosse

If you ask the question, "Who would want to be a referee in any sport?" the likely answer would be, "Not too many." Officials are constantly plagued by that question, especially with all the verbal abuse from players, coaches, managers, and of course, fans. Many fans take referees for granted; others believe that referees are there to be abused and are convenient to blame when a game is lost. Well, the truth is, without fans, the game would not be the same; but the game does need officials to interpret its rules fairly and accurately for both teams so that fans can get the most enjoyment out of the sport. And the reason referees do referee is for the sheer enjoyment of the game.

What does it take to be a good referee?

Working as a referee in any sport, you must gain respect from players, coaches, peers, and fans. And you gain this respect by getting a reputation for calling a good game.

Cheers to Beers: The first set of lacrosse rules

The first sign of lacrosse turning into a more organized game came in 1867, when Dr. George Beers, a Montreal dentist, presented a code of rules to a lacrosse convention in Kingston, Ontario. The rules adopted became the basis of the game that developed over the ensuing years, first for field lacrosse and later for box lacrosse:

1. The object of the game is to send the ball, by means of the lacrosse stick, through the enemy's goalposts.

2. The game was opened by the act of "facing-off," in which two centres hold their lacrosse sticks on the ground and the ball is placed between them.

3. The major rule was that the ball could not be touched with the hands except by the goaltender. The goaltender can only block the ball with his hand; he cannot throw it with his hand.

4. The field was to be a minimum of 150 yards.

5. A goal umpire represented each team.

6. Teams were to have 12 men on each side with no substitution except for injury.

7. The goals were 6-feet poles placed 6-feet apart.

8. Fouls included spearing, tripping, holding, slashing with the stick, throwing the stick, stopping the ball with the hands, except the goaltender, and general rough play.

Fouls were penalized either by suspension of the offender until a goal is scored or until the end of the game

9. No one could interfere with a player who is not in possession of the ball.

10. A new stick was introduced at this time with a shaft ending in a sort of crook and a large flat triangular surface of webbing extending as much as two-thirds the length of the stick. Because this new stick was large and flat and there was no pocket; unlike the short narrow bagged stick of the Indians, the game became more of a catching and throwing game rather than a running, dodging game. The new lacrosse stick was held with two hands and it retained the ball in the so-called pocket by a continuous rocking motion.

11. The first side to score three goals won the match.

12. The positions were goal, point, cover point, centre, third attack, second attack, first attack, out home, and in home.

13. The hair-stuffed deerskin ball was replaced with a hard rubber ball.

Because of his efforts in promoting and organizing lacrosse, Dr. George Beers has been known as the "Father of Lacrosse."

You have to enjoy the sport, you have to be physically and mentally fit, and most importantly, you have to know the rules. Proper positioning on the floor — that is, being in the best position to see the most action — is an asset to a referee. Conditioning and practice enables you to be in the right place at the right time. Proper positioning also assures players and coaches that you are up to the tempo of this very fast-paced game.

When you are a team player, you get to know your teammates and what to expect of them. The same is true with refereeing: When you work as a referee, you often have different partners to cooperate with, so you must get to know each other's style.

The hardest and most difficult thing to do as a referee is to let the players play the game while still keeping control of it — referees must know what to call, when to call it, and when to let things go. Patience also plays a big part because referees are constantly challenged by the players who want to find out what they can get away with.

Given that, an official calls what he sees from where he is positioned. A good official keeps up with the pace of the game and quickly covers the play. Since minor lacrosse is generally played during the spring and summer, hot weather can add a lot of friction to the game, and tempers can easily flare when calls are missed.

Are there differences in refereeing systems?

In a word, yes. The Ontario Lacrosse Association (OLA) is refereed by a two-man team. Both referees are equally responsible for the entire playing surface, as well as the conduct of all players, managers, and coaches.

The NLL uses a four-man system. Three officials are on the floor: the crew chief, referee, and technical referee. The technical referee (or tech ref) watches the benches, determines when a team has too many players on the floor, and starts the faceoffs. The crew chief and the referee call the balance of the game as if they were working only a two-man system, with the crew chief having the final say when discrepancies occur or if something is missed. The fourth official operates the shot clock, times the penalty situations, and monitors the game flow.

Managing the games within the game

Throughout any game, referees keep their eyes on what they call the "mini-games," bursts of exciting action that take place over a short period of time, usually benefiting one team only. You may notice some mini-games after a team has been hit with several penalties in a row, or after one team has scored several goals in quick succession, or after a team loses a once-commanding lead. All these events brew frustration among players and coaches, adding an extra challenge to the officials' roles.

NLL referee Paul Ravary's tips for being a good minor lacrosse ref

✔ **Be consistent and be fair.** Refereeing is using fair judgment and allowing fairness in play. Bottom line: That is what players, coaches, and fans all want.

✔ **Enforce according to the danger.** You have to call any deliberate attempt to injure or any hitting from behind with a severe penalty. The risk level seems to be increasing as minor coaches turn to size and intimidation over speed and skill.

✔ **Back up your calls.** On any questionable calls, make sure that you take the time to talk to the upset coach to calm the situation. Just a few words to explain how you saw the play can alleviate a possibly explosive situation.

✔ **Admit your faults.** If you make a mistake or miss a call, just be honest and tell the coach that you made a mistake. Don't think that you are a know-it-all and don't be egotistical because of the power you get from being a referee. Be humble and approachable with the players and coaches.

✔ **Communicate while you arbitrate.** Talk to the players on the floor as the game is going on. Give them a warning if they start to play loose with the rules. If they continue to do so after a warning, give them a penalty. Referees who talk to the players have fewer problems on the floor than those who don't.

Good referees recognize these situations and know how to keep control of the game and to make sure that all calls are legitimate and not overblown. Lose control and fighting will erupt, and this could lead to bench-clearing brawls where out-of-control fans may get involved.

Being a ref in a brawl situation is tough, and when the crowd gets involved, it can be mind-boggling. Not only are you trying to deal with the situation but you also may be asking yourself what went wrong. To further complicate matters, you have a job to do when what you may really want to do is sit back and watch a good fight.

The best any referee can do at this point is to take a step back and make mental notes of what is happening, looking for the dirty stuff that leads to major and match penalties. Once the situation starts to wind down, then the ref's "coaching" begins, with a lot of yelling at players and coaches. The players eventually come to grips and stop fighting, as they too become aware of the game misconduct and possible suspensions looming.

As for unruly fans, leave them to the public law enforcers who are often present; it's their job.

The Fine Print: All the Rules You Need to Know

The sidebar "Cheers to Beers: The first set of lacrosse rules" earlier in this chapter offers an interesting look at how the game was played in its early years. This section looks at how lacrosse is played today, including the rules that dictate the game and the penalties that enforce those rules, from the perspective of how a referee calls the game.

Playing the game

Though the following game situations may seem clear, the referee makes them all official. The referee signals you may see during a game for these situations are shown in Figure 4-3.

- **Faceoff:** The faceoff takes place after a goal, at the beginning of every quarter or period, or when the ball goes out of bounds or over the playing boards. The two centremen — players involved in the faceoff draw — place the frames of their stick flat along the floor with the open face of their stick facing their own goal.

- **Delayed penalty:** When a penalty occurs during play and the non-offending team has possession of the ball, the referee signals a delayed penalty, meaning that a penalty is being called against the defensive team. The offensive team is allowed to continue play until the defensive team gets possession, at which time play is called and the penalty is assessed.

- **Goal scored:** When the ball goes into the net, the referee signals a goal.

- **Shot on net:** When an offensive shot is stopped by the goalie, but the offensive team retains possession of the ball, the 30-second clock is reset on this signal. For the clock to be reset, the shot must hit either the goalie or the pipes on the net; if not, the team loses possession on a shot-clock violation.

- **No goal:** If a team scores, but the goal is disallowed because someone was standing in the crease or for some other violation, the referee signals no-goal.

Losing possession on game violations

These infractions of the rules lead to the offensive team losing possession of the ball. When play is stopped because of these violations, the defensive team receives possession in its own zone. Figure 4-4 shows the referee signals for most of these situations.

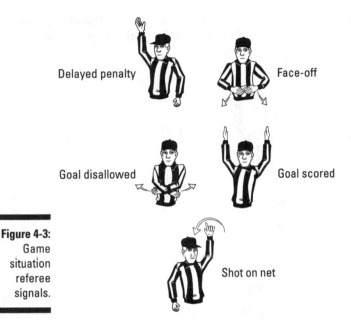

Delayed penalty

Face-off

Goal disallowed

Goal scored

Shot on net

Figure 4-3:
Game
situation
referee
signals.

- ✓ **Five-second count:** After stopping the ball in the crease, the goaltender has five seconds to get the ball out and to a teammate or lose possession of the ball.

- ✓ **Ten-second count:** When a defensive team takes possession of the ball in their own zone, it has ten seconds to push the ball up the floor into their offensive zone.

- ✓ **Back over:** Once an offensive team has the ball in its offensive zone, and the ball goes back over the offensive line into the neutral zone or into the defensive zone, for any reason other than a shot on net, the offending team loses possession of the ball.

- ✓ **Shot-clock violation:** If the offensive team does not attempt a shot in 30 seconds, it loses possession of the ball. (The referee has no signal for this violation; rather, the shot clock buzzes to indicate time has expired.)

- ✓ **Free hand (warding off):** If the ballcarrier pushes off a defending player, usually with his upper arm and forearm, possession is awarded to the non-offending team.

- ✓ **Crease violation:** This violation is called when an offensive player reaches or leans into the crease (except for faking or attempting a shot). Minor and major penalties may also be assessed for illegal play around the net; these are discussed in the section "Paying for penalties and misconducts" that follows.

✔ **Hand ball:** The first rule of lacrosse, if a player other than the goalie touches the ball with his hand outside of the goal crease, possession is awarded to the non-offending team.

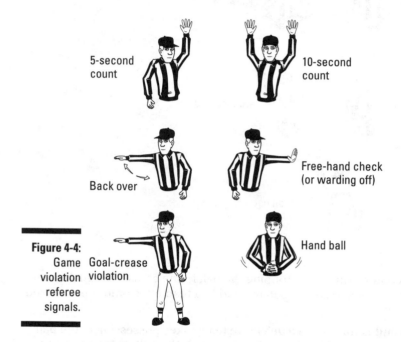

5-second count

10-second count

Back over

Free-hand check (or warding off)

Figure 4-4: Game violation referee signals.

Goal-crease violation

Hand ball

Paying for penalties and misconducts

Lacrosse has timed penalties — two-minute penalties, five-minute penalties, and ten-minute and match penalties — and game and gross misconducts, which are not timed penalties but instead exclude the penalized player from the game, and possibly future games, depending on the severity of the penalty. Combinations of penalties can also be assessed depending on the infractions occurring.

How do you get a penalty? You get a penalty by committing infractions of the rules, and by playing dirty. Slashing, cross-checking from behind, cross-checking around another player's head area, and fighting are a few of the ways you can get a penalty.

Minor penalties (two minutes)

The following are some of the common two-minute penalties, also referred to as minors. Figure 4-5 shows the referee signals for most of these penalties.

- ✔ **Cross-checking:** Cross-checking is legal when the opposing player is in possession of the ball. When the cross-checked player does not have the ball, it is an infraction. Cross-checking is usually delivered to the midsection of the arm or on the back area.

- ✔ **High-sticking:** No stick-check is allowed above the shoulders of an opposing player.

- ✔ **Holding:** When a player grabs hold of another player's body, sweater, and/or stick, thereby keeping him from the play, this penalty is called.

- ✔ **Checking from behind:** This penalty is called when a player cross-checks an opponent from behind. This penalty can be a two-minute, five-minute, or even a match penalty, depending on the severity of the hit. Especially at the minor level, any hit from behind has to be called a penalty rather than a possession call as some minor referees do.

- ✔ **Hooking:** This hockey term may not make too much sense since a lacrosse stick has no angled section with which to hook, but the idea is essentially the same: A player cannot use the stick as a "hook" to slow down an opponent.

Figure 4-5:
Two-minute
penalty
signals.

Cross-Checking High-sticking Holding

Hooking Interference

Slashing Tripping

✔ **Interference:** This penalty applies to several situations. It is used when a player makes contact with an opposing player during a line change, or otherwise interferes with a player or goalie. Other examples include when a player loses his stick and an opponent redirects it so that it cannot be retrieved or when a player gets in the way of another player who does not have the ball but is executing a play.

✔ **Slashing:** No stick swing is allowed against the body of the opponent. This call frustrates the fans because some slashing is part of the game. It is up to the discretion of the official as to how far a player can go before it is called an infraction. Repeated hits and the severity warrant the difference between play and penalty. In the NLL slashing is usually allowed against the limbs of other players.

✔ **Tripping:** Any checking below the waist of an opponent, whether by a stick or by any part of a player's body, is tripping.

Some other two-minute penalties, which may not be quite as common but are similar to penalties in other sports, are described here.

✔ **Unsportsmanlike conduct:** This penalty may be assessed when a player or personnel on the bench conduct themselves, er, in an unsportsmanlike way, such as dallying on the way to the penalty box or questioning a referee's ruling. (Only players designated as captains can question the referee.)

✔ **Too many players on the floor:** This infraction usually occurs when one player is a little too fast to get on the floor during a line change (or one player is a little too slow to get off the floor).

Penalties and goalies

It's not open season on the goalie, as long as he remains in the crease area. When a goalie is outside the crease, an opponent may chase or stick-check him. If the player attempts to check the goalie too hard or tries to take him out of the play, a penalty may be assessed. Goalies are aware of this and sometimes trick opponents into committing stupid penalties. Also, when a goalie has been taken out on a check illegally, it can lead to payback and additional penalties, as most teams stick up for their goalie.

When in the crease, goalies are not to be interfered with at all. Anything from a ball-possession violation to a major penalty may be assessed for messing with the goalie in the crease.

Goalies may be assessed penalties, particularly when they step outside the crease. When a goalie hits or illegally picks on a player outside the crease, he may be called for a major penalty. (All those pads to protect the goalie from flying balls can be painful to the unsuspecting opponent.) Goalie penalties in box lacrosse are served by a teammate who is on the floor at the time of the infraction.

- ✔ **Bench minor:** Similar to an unsportsmanlike conduct call, this penalty is called for inappropriate activity from the bench, usually when the referee can't identify a specific offender, be it player or coach.

Major penalties (five minutes)

All of the common minor penalties can lead to five- or ten-minute penalties, depending on the severity of the infraction and the discretion of the referee. Here are some of the common five-minute penalties. See Figure 4-6 for the referee signals for these penalties.

- ✔ **Boarding:** Players may hold up opponents against the boards to try to slow down their momentum or steal the ball, but checking a player into the boards brings down a major penalty. (If you bring down the player and he doesn't get back up, you may be up for some serious suspension time.)

- ✔ **Butt-ending:** Jabbing an opponent with the butt end of the lacrosse stick (or sometimes even pretending to jab your opponent) will land your butt in the penalty box for five minutes.

- ✔ **Charging:** No credit card will get you out of this penalty; five minutes are given for rushing and running into an opponent.

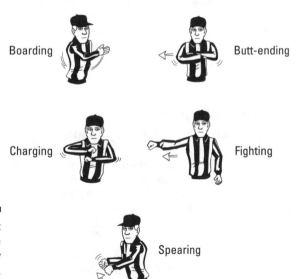

Boarding

Butt-ending

Charging

Fighting

Figure 4-6:
Five-minute
penalty
signals.

Spearing

Rules during penalties

The team that is called for the penalty must serve it, resulting in the offending team playing one player short. The non-offending team goes on a *power play*, which gives them an advantage for the time of the penalty. If the non-offending team scores during a two-minute penalty, the penalized player can leave the penalty box and return to play. For a major or match penalty, the power play can result in two potential goals before the penalty is wiped out. Depending on the league, the penalized player may or may not be released; if not, another player can play for the balance of the penalty time.

When a team is short-handed, it has ten seconds to get the ball over the offensive zone line. Some leagues (though not the NLL) turn off the shot clock when a man-short team has possession of the ball. The team can use this to their advantage to try to run down the penalty. For this strategy to work, however, the short-handed team players must stay inside their own offensive zone. If not, play is stopped, and the ball is given to the power-play unit.

- **Fighting:** Drop your gloves, and you may be finished for the game (and your team will likely spend the next five minutes of the game short-handed). Drop your gloves more than once, and you could risk missing several games or even the rest of the season.

- **Spearing:** Similar to butt-ending, this penalty involves jabbing an opponent with the mouth of your stick.

Beyond major: The most severe penalties

Unfortunately, extreme penalties do occasionally happen in lacrosse. These infractions typically involve getting caught up in a fight between two other players (called *third man in*); severe unsportsmanlike conduct, usually directed toward a referee; and deliberate attempts to injure another player. Get hit with one of these penalties, and you'll be leaving the game earlier than you anticipated. You'll also likely hear from the league about taking a forced break from competition for a few games — that is, you'll be suspended.

These penalties are the ten-minute penalties, game misconducts, and match penalties. For these penalties, you'll be removed from the game and a teammate will take your place in the penalty box. Figure 4-7 shows the misconduct and match penalty signals.

 Misconduct

Figure 4-7:
Misconduct
and match
penalty
signals.

 Match penalty

Part II
Following Lacrosse: The Fan's Point of View

The 5th Wave   By Rich Tennant

"Just how much do you think you can embarrass me? If you think I'm going to the lacrosse game with you wearing those ridiculous socks, you're sadly mistaken!"

In this part . . .

You may just be interested in lacrosse as a fan — that is, you want to find out all you can about the professional game, the collegiate game, the minor game, and the international game. This part gets you started. You can find information here that helps you understand how to watch the game and what to look for amid the frenzied action on the playing surface. You can also read up on the professional leagues (the National Lacrosse League and Major League Lacrosse) and the minor and collegiate action in Canada and the United States.

Chapter 5

How to Watch Lacrosse

*W*hen you see the game of lacrosse for the first time, you may think that you're looking at mayhem. What the heck is going on? Players run around at one end, and then they run up the floor or field and run around at the other end. Some run back and forth to the bench, while others don't run from the playing surface at all. In box lacrosse, players hit everything that moves and then in turn they are hit. And just try following that little ball around — off a pass, off the boards, off the goalie, and off anything else that gets in its way.

As a fan, that last point is the key. Most of lacrosse action follows the ball — following loose balls, following shots on goal, following cross-court or cross-field passes, following fast-break passes, or following where the ball goes on a faceoff. This chapter offers some advice about watching the game of lacrosse from a fan's perspective. Whatever the game — NLL box lacrosse, NCAA field lacrosse, or your community's minor lacrosse league — this chapter will help you follow all the action.

It All Looks a Little Familiar . . .

Box lacrosse especially may seem familiar to you. You're in an arena. If you're at an NLL game, you're probably in a pretty large arena — perhaps even one that you've been in before for a concert or a truck show or maybe a hockey or basketball game. And that may be the rub: Box lacrosse does have some similarities to hockey and basketball.

You'll notice a litany of similarities between ice hockey and box lacrosse — from the rink to the lines and rules to the way the game moves. Partly because they share an out-of-bounds factor, basketball and field lacrosse are quite similar as well. But all these sports are intertwined by a common flow to the game.

Recognizing the game's similarities to hockey

Like hockey, box lacrosse is a very fast game. The two sports are also very physical; go to a pro hockey or a pro box lacrosse event, and you're as likely as not to see a fight break out. And they're both exciting games to watch as well as to play. Here are a few other similarities between hockey and box lacrosse:

- Each team has a goalie and five players on the playing surface.
- Each game is played in an arena 200 feet long and 85 feet wide.
- A faceoff begins play at the start of each game, at the start of each quarter or period, and after a scored goal.
- Each game has two- and five-minute penalties.
- That old hockey joke works for lacrosse too: Went to a fight the other night and a lacrosse game broke out.
- In both hockey and lacrosse, a crease area around the net is a protected area for the goalie.
- Like hockey players, box lacrosse players are legally allowed to hit an opponent with the body or stick.
- Both hockey and lacrosse players wear heavily padded equipment, such as kidney pads, gloves, and helmets (with cages or with fibreglass). In fact, if you play both hockey and lacrosse, you're likely to wear the same equipment for both games.

But the games aren't completely alike. Here are a few important differences between hockey and box lacrosse:

- Hockey is played on ice; lacrosse is played on Astroturf.
- And a corollary to the preceding item: hockey players wear skates; lacrosse players wear running shoes.
- And a corollary to both of the preceding obvious items: hockey players were not born yesterday; lacrosse players were not born yesterday; and neither were their fans.
- Lacrosse has no equivalent offsides or icing violations, so the entire floor is in play.

✔ The dimensions of the goals are different. A hockey goal is 6 x 4 feet; a lacrosse goal is 4¾ x 4 feet.

✔ Lacrosse has a 30-second shot clock during which a team must get off a shot on goal or lose possession of the ball.

Recognizing the game's similarities to basketball

Box lacrosse is similar to hockey because of all the hitting and physical play, but it is even more like basketball because of the passing and ball control. In hockey, a team does not always have complete possession of the puck because of the nature of the game: for example, the puck takes weird and unexpected bounces and ricochets.

However, as in basketball, when a lacrosse team has possession of the ball, it can control the game and possession time; it's pretty hard to get the ball away from a good ballhandler. For this reason, winning a faceoff and collecting loose balls are crucial in the game of lacrosse. Once a team takes possession of the ball, they can control the tempo of the game.

Minor lacrosse coaches coming from the hockey world may have a tendency to play their players like hockey forwards and defencemen — keeping the defencemen back toward centre ice when in their own offensive zone, for example. But lacrosse is more like basketball when it comes to what players do on each end of the floor. When a team has possession of the ball, everybody has an active role on the offence; when a team does not have the ball, everybody plays defence.

Other similarities between box lacrosse and basketball are:

✔ Each sport has a shot clock to regulate offensive play and help speed up the action. For example, the NLL's shot clock is 30 seconds; the NBA (National Basketball Association) has a 24-second shot clock.

✔ Although you won't see any teams scoring 100 points in a game, lacrosse is a bit more like basketball in that it has many more legitimate scoring opportunities than hockey does.

✔ The basketball equivalent of a faceoff is the tipoff (or jump ball), which takes place at the start of each game, at the start of an overtime period, and in the pros, on the occurrence of a held ball (when players from opposing teams have possession of the ball at the same time). Thankfully, for a game where teams can score over 100 points each, tipoffs aren't required after the scoring of every goal.

Recognizing what keeps all three games flowing

In talking about the similarities between lacrosse and hockey and basketball, however, the rules and other logistical elements as noted in the preceding two sections are not the most telling. The style of play really shows how very similar these games are — to both box and field lacrosse.

Fast breaks are spliced into the action, but most of the games are dictated by half-court offences and defences. In these sets, the offence works the ball around in an effort to get the defence out of position and thereby create a scoring opportunity. The three options of a basketball player with the ball are pass, shoot, or try to fake out the defender — same as in lacrosse. The cuts and movement of off-ball play are crucial in creating space and opening opportunities. Two-man plays such as the pick-and-roll work in lacrosse as well as they do in basketball and hockey. Vision, that knack of seeing peripherally and being able to play with your head up, is very important to follow teammates and know where they will be. When a forward posts up in basketball, he uses the same body positioning and similar power moves to create space with the defender as an attacking player would in lacrosse. Zone and man-to-man defensive play appear in lacrosse as they do in basketball. Individual and team defence are virtually identical in basketball and lacrosse. The footwork, lateral movement, and bent knee translate from one sport to the other. The communication, sliding/shifting, double-teams, and cover schemes characterize team defence in both games.

The scoring runs and tempo of basketball and lacrosse are also familiar. Knowing how to push the ball, how to play a numbers advantage or disadvantage, and when to slow things down are as important in lacrosse as in hockey or basketball. Like hockey, lacrosse uses different lines and shifts so that matching up personnel is crucial.

Hockey and basketball players make great lacrosse players because they have advanced overall understandings of lacrosse. Outside the stick skills, virtually everything else will be familiar to a hockey or basketball player new to lacrosse.

Knowing What to Watch For

You've made it to the game in time to buy a program or pick up a lineup so that you know who the players are. If you're already a fan, you probably know the home-team players. If you're new to the game, you'll want to read up on both teams. You should be able to find out who the outstanding players are on both teams — the ones to watch during the game. Teams usually match up their best defensive player with the opponent's best offensive player, so you're sure to see at least one classic struggle.

Another great way to get information about either team is to ask the fans sitting around you. Most fans love to share information and advice on who to watch, what to watch for, and what other exciting things to anticipate during the game, such as a player who may be approaching a scoring record or a team fighting for a playoff spot.

 Don't worry about trying to figure out the rules of the game: I've been coaching lacrosse for decades, and I'm still trying to figure some of them out. For example, box lacrosse players are allowed to slash another player's stick, but they can also be penalized for slashing. If you really want to learn more about the rules of the game, check out Chapter 4 of this book. At the game, it may be helpful to remember some of the referee's signals (also discussed in Chapter 4) so that you have some idea of what has happened to cause a play stoppage.

The balance of this section offers some suggestions about what game action to watch for. You'll probably concentrate on what your favourite team is doing during the game, so these tips are written from that perspective. Of course, if your team is playing against a team known for its defensive prowess, for example, you may want to pay closer attention to that team's defence when your team has the ball.

Watching the offence

When your team has the ball, they're obviously looking for ways to score. As a fan, you want to try to figure out their style of play or what type of play they're running that will give them the best chance to score. Here are some things to look for:

✔ **Getting open:** Following the ball doesn't always take you to the most action. Often, the most exciting thing to watch is how the offensive team gets its better players open or away from the best defenders. Look for offensive players off the ball who set picks for their teammates. A pick occurs when an offensive player positions himself in front of a defensive player defending one of his offensive teammates so that his teammate can have an opening to receive a pass or take a shot. The player setting the pick has to be stationary (a moving pick is illegal). When it's done correctly, picking off a defender can be the most exciting event in an offensive set; fans (and players) love it when a defender is picked right off his feet.

✔ **Executing plays:** Most teams have a tendency to run similar plays all the time. They rely on a particular play because of the type of players they have on offence. For example, you may see offensive players habitually taking on a defender one-on-one. Or you may see a lot of pick-and-roll plays. Motion offences are those where players cut and pass all the time. Or a team's offence may simply run through the player who has the hot hand during a particular game.

✔ **Controlling the tempo:** Is your team dictating the pace of play? If you're familiar with the style of play that your team prefers, you may be able to tell whether they're controlling the tempo of the game. For example, if your team is loaded with smaller players, they probably have to play a fast-paced running game to be successful. If their opponents are a bigger team that always run the shot clock down to two or three seconds before they shoot, then two distinct styles of play are colliding. In this case, if both teams are scoring a lot of goals, then your team is probably controlling the tempo. However, if it's a low-scoring game, then your team is likely losing the tempo battle, and probably the game.

Besides watching for a fast or slow tempo, you may spot another kind of tempo in a game: a scoring run, where a team scores a bunch of goals in a row over a short period of time, also known as having momentum. But momentum shifts swiftly in a lacrosse game. If your team quickly finds itself down by four or five goals, don't worry: A scoring run could be right around the corner to get those four or five goals back. These scoring runs tend to come from playing good aggressive defence that forces a lot of turnovers.

✔ **Pressing on the power play:** When the opposition takes a penalty, it gives the offence a one- (or two-) player advantage. How does your team take advantage of the situation? Some teams have a series of set plays that they save for the power play; other teams prefer to stay back and pass around the zone until the defence allows an opportunity for a cutter or an open shot. The power play also is the time when some of the best offensive players have a chance to really show off their skills, taking on a defender one-on-one because eventually his opponent will run out of help and a teammate will be open.

Watching the defence

Are the teams playing man-to-man or zone defence? How are they defending the great offensive players of the other team? Does the defence pressure the ballcarrier or just sit back and let the offence take shots from long distance? These are a few things to look for on the defensive side of the ball. However, defence is also where you see most of the activity that results in turnovers or loose balls.

✔ **Forcing turnovers:** Turnovers occur when possession of the ball changes teams. Turnovers can be the result of careless offensive play (a bad pass, dropping or missing a pass, or an offensive penalty) or aggressive defensive play (a stolen pass, stripping the ball from the ballcarrier, or causing an offensive penalty). But the action doesn't stop once the ball has been turned over. Good teams look to score off turnovers, creating those scoring-run opportunities discussed in the preceding section. Aggressive play that forces turnovers can turn a game around, making the opposition pay the price for dropping the ball.

✔ **Forcing missed shots:** A missed shot can technically be considered a turnover, but a missed shot can also be thought of as part of the natural flow of the game. No matter how you look at them though, missed shots are often the result of good solid defensive play. From the offence, look for examples of long-distance shots through a phalanx of other players; awkward, off-balance shots from poor angles toward the goal; or arcing, slow-moving shots from players who've been hit as they shoot. These poor shots are all the result of a good aggressive defence forcing low-percentage shots.

✔ **Going after loose balls:** Loose balls should not be taken for granted. Whoever controls the loose balls, controls the game. Watch what happens after most of the loose balls are picked up. If players are constantly running down to the other end of the playing surface after a loose ball, then chances are you're watching a good defence control the game. Also, you're likely to see one or two players who just seem to have a nose for the ball and are always in the middle of a pile, fighting for that loose ball.

Watching the goalie

The goalie is the backbone of the team. Watching a great goalie perform is a bit like watching a great artist at work: The best goalies not only rely on fundamental skills but also on their shot-saving creativity in goal. Here are some things to look for:

✔ **Playing the angles:** Goalies that play the angles move around in goal more than you may expect. They're looking to cut off any angle that an offensive player may have at a shot. You'll often see angle goalies reaching back to feel where they are in relation to the net (they try to keep themselves centred between the posts). And because they've usually cut off a shooter's angle when they make a save, you'll see a lot of body saves from angle goalies.

✔ **Relying on reflexes:** Reflex-oriented goalies will make more stick, leg, or glove saves than body saves. That's because they're depending on their reflexes for seeing the ball as it approaches the net. Reflex goalies will still try to play the angles, but they also tend to take more risks than angle goalies, thinking that their quick reflexes can save them from poor positioning.

✔ **Releasing the ball:** After every stop, goalies have an opportunity to start the offence with a well-timed and well-thrown pass. Scoring runs, for example, can be extended with a quick and accurate pass from a goalie to a fast-breaking offensive player.

Watching the game action

Remember that any activity on the floor or field is relevant to the outcome of a lacrosse game, even if the clock isn't ticking.

- ✔ **Winning the faceoff:** Watch the faceoff strategy between the two teams (see Figure 5-1). Some teams may place three players back on defence to defend against losing the faceoff; other teams may place just two players on the defensive end, playing to win the faceoff and get an offensive start. How they line up around the circle usually gives you a pretty good idea about whether a team is trying to score off the faceoff or just trying to get possession of the ball (or not let the other team get possession of it). You'll also notice that teams have specific players who play the draw in almost every faceoff.

Figure 5-1:
Lining up for
the faceoff.

✔ **Noting substitution patterns:** Most coaches do have a specific substitution strategy for their players, but often that strategy is thrown out with the bath water because of line changes made by the opposing team. Teams try to match up their best defenders against the opposition's best offensive players. So you're bound to see a cat-and-mouse game between the two coaches as each tries to run players on and off the floor to get a match-up that's in their favour. You can also keep track of which players play on both the offensive and defensive ends or which coaches operate an offence–defence strategy.

✔ **Monitoring injuries:** Because of the physical nature of the game, it's not unusual that a player is not able to finish a game. When a player limps off the playing surface (or is carried off), make note of it and consider how his absence may influence the ending of the game.

✔ **Spying on the fans:** Lacrosse, especially NLL lacrosse, has some big-time die-hard fans. They dress to the nines with their home-team sweaters, hats, buttons, and colours. They get into the game, and anybody who hurts their team will hear about it, especially the referee; fans love to harass a referee about any little thing that may hurt the home team, no matter how accurate the complaint is. You should get involved in the game — cheer for the home team and wear the home-team sweater — but be an enthusiastic spectator without acting like an idiot. There's nothing as exciting as sitting among hometown fans to cheer on the home team, but maintain respect for the opposition — and for the referee.

Closing out the game

In the last five minutes of a close game, hang onto your seat. Every possession could turn out to be the difference of the game. At this point in the game, you should be able to figure out who the real stars on each team are. With the game on the line, the best players — offensive and defensive — step up to challenge the opposition and find out who blinks first.

Look for the offensive player who handles the ball on every possession. He's likely to be the one who wants the ball in that situation, the one who plays with composure and doesn't panic. And he's likely to score the game-winning goal. But he needs help. He probably has a teammate who will sacrifice a little pain to set him up for that game-winning goal, stepping in front of the opposition's best defender to set a crushing pick.

At the end of a close game, you're almost guaranteed to see a one-on-one match-up between the best players on each team. Look for the little things that may give one player an edge over the other on that particular night, such as who looks more tired and who looks more alert at this stage of the game. And then just sit back and enjoy; these one-on-one battles are what the game is all about — a healthy confrontation between a top scorer and a top defender to determine who is the best.

COACH TIP

Calling it a night in the NLL

Stick around after an NLL game is over because you'll see two interesting things. First, the players from both teams line up and shake hands. Now, these warriors have just beaten up on each other for 60 minutes, but like true athletes, they shake hands to thank their opponents for the game. Second, the league also has a postgame tradition where the players run around the arena and wave to the fans to thank them for their support.

If you are willing to hang around long after the game, you may be able to get an autograph from your favourite player. In fact, your favourite player may be your teacher or your neighbourhood policeman or fireman. Most players in the NLL work at another career.

Following Lacrosse on Television

Watching lacrosse on TV is a good way to keep up with your team's rivals, whether they're playing in Calgary or in Colorado. But a televised game can't match the entertainment value and intensity of watching a game in person. Plus, the ball moves so quickly that television cameras are often playing catch-up just to keep pace (though television crews are getting better as more games are broadcast). If you can't get to the arena and the big game is coming up, however, catch it on the big screen in your den.

As this book goes to press, televised lacrosse is fairly widely available, especially in lacrosse-crazy areas of North America. And as with any sport, increased television coverage is monumentally crucial to the growth of lacrosse.

✔ **National Lacrosse League:** The NLL has national coverage in Canada through Rogers Sportsnet, with both national and regional broadcasts that focus naturally on the league's four Canadian franchises. Five markets in the northeast U.S. also offer broadcasts of their local teams.

✔ **Major League Lacrosse:** This outdoor professional lacrosse league broadcasts its games virtually nationwide through FOX Sports Net regional programming. Nearly all games are delayed — that is, not broadcast live.

✔ **Major and junior A levels:** Local enthusiasm for the hometown team is regularly supported by regional cable-access channels across Canada. That enthusiasm increases, of course, if the hometown team's appearance in the Minto Cup or Mann Cup series is televised.

- **NCAA field lacrosse:** In addition to local broadcasts of NCAA lacrosse in a variety of markets, ESPN owns the rights to broadcast the lacrosse version of the Final Four — the Division I national semifinals and final — each May. ESPN's broadcast of the final game also includes highlight coverage of the Division II and III final games.

  Regular-season NCAA men's and women's games are broadcast live in select markets, with a game televised every spring week on the ABC affiliate in Baltimore.

Chapter 6

Keeping Up with the Pros: Following the National Lacrosse League

*P*rofessional lacrosse leagues have come and gone in the decades during which the game has taken root in North America. From the Canadian Professional Indoor Lacrosse League to the National Lacrosse Association, the success of these leagues against that of the minor lacrosse organizations or NCAA field lacrosse has been markedly measured.

The National Lacrosse League (NLL), however, seems to be taking hold of the attention of lacrosse fans in a way that may indicate it's around to stay. This chapter discusses, from a fan's point of view, what to look for when watching the teams and games of the NLL.

What You Should Know about the NLL

While those who don't follow professional sports of any kind may suggest that you don't need to know *anything* about the NLL, this section (and this book, for that matter) suggests otherwise. Any fan of any professional sports league needs to know at least the bare necessities about what teams are in the league, how long the season lasts, what the teams play for, and what the playoff structure is like. This section offers a quick peek at the bare necessities of the NLL.

How many teams are in the league?

For the 2002–03 season, the NLL fields 12 teams, divided into three equal divisions:

- **Northern:** Calgary Roughnecks, Ottawa Rebel, Toronto Rock, and Vancouver Ravens
- **Eastern:** Colorado Mammoth, New Jersey Storm, New York Saints, and Philadelphia Wings
- **Central:** Albany Attack, Buffalo Bandits, Columbus Landsharks, and Rochester Knighthawks

Placing the Colorado Mammoth in the Eastern division is a bit like keeping the Dallas Cowboys in the National Football League's NFC East division, but not quite. The Cowboys stayed in the east following the league's 2002 realignment in order to maintain strong division rivalries with its division-mates: the Washington Redskins, the New York Giants, and the Philadelphia Eagles. The Mammoth moved west to Denver after two years as the Power in Washington, D.C. The franchise is an original member of the NLL, joining the league during its first season in 1987 as the Baltimore Thunder, going on that year to win the league's first championship.

How long does the season last?

During a season that runs from late December through late April, each team plays 16 regular-season games: 8 games at home and 8 games away. The schedule is unbalanced, but each team at least plays both home and away games with every other team in its division. Most games are played on Fridays, Saturdays, and Sundays, though the league scheduled five games for Thursdays during the 2002–03 season.

While the major league baseball player (and Kevin Costner) may claim that they play "for the love of the game," this cliché is a way of life for players in the NLL, who are effectively moonlighters in a profession that they love. Because the maximum player salary in the league is US$18,750, players have to report to their regular (if not necessarily first-love) jobs during the week. By the way, the *minimum* player salary in major league baseball is US$200,000; the average salary was a little over US$2.3 million in 2002.

What is the playoff structure?

By the end of the regular season, 6 of the 12 teams earn their way into the NLL playoffs.

> ✔ The first-place team in each division gets in. The two first-place teams with the best records earn a playoff bye — that is, they don't have to play the first game of the playoffs and can use the extra time to rest tired players and plan for their first playoff opponent.
>
> ✔ The remaining three playoff spots go to the teams with the three best records that did not win their division.

Playoff games are seeded so that teams that finished the regular season with the better records are rewarded with a playoff game against a team with a worse record. In the first round of the playoffs, the team with the worst record (seeded sixth) plays the divisional winner who didn't earn a bye; the fourth- and fifth-seeded teams play each other in the other first-round game.

In round two, the winners in the first round face the two divisional winners who earned the bye, with the lowest-seeded remaining team playing the top-seeded team. The winning teams in the second round vie for the Champions Cup, the league's championship trophy, in a winner-take-all single-game championship.

Because division winners automatically get in, the possibility exists that a team with a better regular season record may be seeded lower than a division winner. For the 2001–02 season, the Rochester Knighthawks finished with a record of 13–3, not good enough to win the NLL's Central division, captured by the Albany Attack with a 14–2 record. The Knighthawks entered the playoffs as the fourth seed, behind the third-seeded Washington Power, who won the NLL's Eastern division with a 9–7 record. (In fact, the possibility exists that a division winner may enter the playoffs with the worst record of the six teams and still be seeded third. It hasn't happened yet, but this same Washington Power team entered the 2002 playoffs only one game ahead of the sixth-seeded Philadelphia Wings and their 8–8 record.)

Where do the players come from?

The NLL draws players from all over North America, whether the sources are NCAA field lacrosse or Canadian junior and senior associations. In fact, of the 107 players selected in the league's 2002 entry draft, 60 players came out of Canadian associations, such as the Ontario Lacrosse Association and the British Columbia Lacrosse Association, and 47 came from NCAA schools in the United States. (See Chapter 7 for more information about these lacrosse training grounds.)

The team rosters are still primarily filled by Canadian players. During the 2001–02 season, Canadian players filled nearly 75 percent of NLL roster slots, with 143 (almost half) from Ontario alone.

These statistics represent the prevalence of box lacrosse as the preferred style of play in Canada. Look through any team's roster, and you're certain to find players who came out of junior and senior lacrosse hotbeds such as Peterborough, Ontario; Coquitlam, British Columbia; Brampton, Ontario; and Victoria, British Columbia.

Nevertheless, the number of NCAA players in the league is moving upward. Though the number of players drafted in the 2002 draft who actually play in the league is pretty small, the number who come out of the U.S. is substantial. And the 2002 NLL all-star teams featured ten players who came out of U.S. collegiate lacrosse.

Some of the league's top players had no box-lacrosse experience when they entered the league, coming out of NCAA field-lacrosse traditions. These top American players (and the U.S. universities where they played) include Jake Bergey (Salisbury State University), Roy Colsey (Syracuse University), Tim Soudan (University of Massachusetts), Mike Regan (Butler University), Mike Law (Denver University), Brian Reese (University of Maryland), Hugh Donovan (Bucknell University), Jamie Hanford (Loyola College), Paul Cantabene (Loyola College), and Tom Ryan (Bowdoin College).

When attending an NLL game, check out each team's roster for players from your hometown (or nearby). Especially if you come from Ontario or British Columbia, or from the northeastern United States, you're likely to find someone on a team to watch.

Each team can dress 15 players and 2 goalies for each game. They carry 23 players on their roster with 3 practice players.

What to Look For from the Top NLL Teams

Each team creates its own personality, establishing a reputation among players and fans about the style of game it plays. Of course, that style of play depends on the strength of its players. Some teams are stronger defensively because their better players are more defensive-oriented. Others are strong at breaking out of their own end and rely heavily on scoring from fast-break transition goals. Then there are the offensive teams that have such great offensive talent that they just want to score, score, and score. Keep in mind, though, that a team's style of play is likely to change, sometimes seemingly overnight. Nevertheless, here is my list of the top five teams in the NLL, in order of strength, through the 2002–03 season.

- ✔ **Toronto Rock:** The NLL came to Toronto in 1998, and subsequently, the Rock won the NLL championship three out of its four years of existence. They have had great goaltending from Bob Watson; a great defence anchored by players such as Pat Coyle, Glenn Clark, and Dan Ladouceur; a great transition game with Jim Veltman and Steve Toll; and a great offence that has been led by Colin Doyle, Kim Squire, and Blaine Manning. Toronto has always been a team that can score from anywhere, out of their fast break or from their offence. The team is very unselfish in their offensive play, which is shown by their spread-out scoring on the team.

- ✔ **Albany Attack:** Albany's first season in the league came in 1999. Building an offence similar in style to Toronto, the Attack made it to the NLL championship game in its third year. Albany lacks stellar offensive scoring skills from its defence. They play defence similar to Toronto and are blessed with great defenders in Cam Woods and Jim Moss. Their offence is awesome to watch led by Josh Sanderson, Gary Rosyski, Dan Teat, Mike Regan, and Nick Trudeau. Their goaltender, Rob Blasdell, had his best year ever in 2002.

- ✔ **Rochester Knighthawks:** In 1995, the Knighthawks entered the league with a bang, advancing to the championship game before losing to the Philadelphia Wings. Rochester won the league championship in 1997. When you talk about Rochester, you have to talk about their offence, which includes some of the best offensive players in the NLL. John Grant Jr., Shawn Williams, Derek Malawsky, and Cory Bomberry lead this potent offence. The defence is anchored by Mike Hasen, Regy Thorpe, and Casey Zaph. Pat O'Toole is their experienced goaltender.

- ✔ **Colorado Mammoth:** This franchise is an original member of the NLL, joining the league as the Baltimore Thunder and winning the inaugural championship. The organization played in Pittsburgh and Washington before landing in Denver in 2002, the first U.S. team to be based west of the Mississippi River. If you mention Colorado, you have to mention Gary Gait. Gary, and his twin brother Paul, played together for years for this franchise, making their team instant winners. Paul retired at the end of the 2002 season; Gary remains with the franchise, supported in the scoring department by Ted Dowling and Del Halladay. Most of the defence is made up of solid American players who are tough and big. Their goaltender is Erik Miller, one of the few American goalies to play the NLL.

- ✔ **Philadelphia Wings:** Philadelphia typically fields the most all-stars of any team in the league, which helps explain their six league championships since joining the NLL in 1987 as an original member. Jake Bergey and Tom Marechek are one of the best offensive combinations in the league. But the real key to Philadelphia is Dallas Eliuk, their all-star goaltender. He wins more games and championships for them than anybody in the league. Their defence is not bad, but they have a tough time scoring on their breakouts.

What to Look For in the League's Second-Tier (for Now) Teams

The times they are a changin' — even in the National Lacrosse League. So the teams you see today at the top may not be the teams at the top in five years. Some of the teams in this list reflect that inevitable change. But for now, this group rests in the bottom tier of the league's elite, listed in alphabetical order.

- ✔ **Buffalo Bandits:** This franchise started play in 1992 and has won three league championships, the last one in 1996. This once-proud franchise was led by players such as Darris Dilgour, now the team's head coach; Jim Veltman, now with Toronto; and Derek Kennan. However, Buffalo has had difficulty making the playoffs in the past few years. Buffalo's best player is John Tavares, who has been a perennial all-star.

- ✔ **Calgary Roughnecks:** The Roughnecks joined the NLL as an expansion franchise in 2001. Calgary is led by Kaleb Toth, Jason Wulder, and Tracey Kelusky, who came to the Roughnecks after his previous team, the Montreal Express, shut down after the 2002 season.

- ✔ **Columbus Landsharks:** This franchise's first year in the league came in 2000. Columbus has built its team around youth and speed, with players such as Pat Maddalena, Dan Dawson, Kasey Beirnes, and Gewas Schindler.

- ✔ **New Jersey Storm:** Another 2001 expansion franchise, the Storm may be most infamously known as the team owned by former NBA star Jayson Williams. Players such as Cam Bomberry, Scott Stewart, and Roy Colsey, formerly of Buffalo lead the Storm.

- ✔ **New York Saints:** With Colorado and Philadelphia, the Saints are the third of three original franchises still with the league. (The fourth, the Washington Wave, folded operations after the 1989 season.) The Saints only championship came in the league's second year in 1988. A team that seems to always be in flux, the Saints nevertheless have featured such all-star players as Mark Millon, Matt Panetta, Pat McCabe, Roy Colsey, and goalie Sal LoCascio. Current franchise cornerstone players include Gavin Prout and Gee Nash.

- ✔ **Ottawa Rebel:** This franchise entered the league in 1998 as an expansion team playing in Syracuse (the Syracuse Smash). Moving to Ottawa for the 2000 season, the Rebel has not met with much on-field success in its history in the league, despite the efforts of solid players such as Kevin Howard, Matt Giles, and Chris Konopliff. Brad Watters, owner of the Toronto Rock, also owns this franchise.

TECHNICAL STUFF

Growing pains

The professional sports world is littered with failed franchises and leagues, from the American Basketball Association of the late 1960s and 1970s (remember the red, white, and blue basketballs?) to the United States Football League of the mid-1980s (at least no red, white, and blue footballs) to the North American Soccer League (which operated from 1967 through 1984 and gave North American soccer fans an opportunity to see the remarkable Pelé in action).

The National Lacrosse League has had its share of disappointments as well, but signs of steady growth exist, including five expansion teams joining the league in the last three years. But perhaps the best sign of growth is that the following six franchises are the only teams forced to pull the plug in the league's 16 years of existence:

- Washington Wave: 1987–1989

- Detroit Turbos: 1989–1994

- New England/Boston Blazers: 1989–1998

- Pittsburgh Bulls: 1990–1993

- Charlotte Cobras: 1996–1996

- Montreal Express: 2001–2002

- **Vancouver Ravens:** Another of the four 2001 expansion franchises, the Ravens have drawn much of their talent from players out of the British Columbia Lacrosse Association. Vancouver surprised veteran NLL observers by making the playoffs in their first year of play, led by players such as Chris Gill, Peter Morgan, Ryan O'Connor, and goalie Dwight Maetche. The addition of Dan Stroup from Toronto and first-year player Cam Sedgwick makes them an even stronger team.

Building on History: Professional Lacrosse through the Decades

In 1931, a group of hockey promoters came up with the idea to create a professional box lacrosse league. They wanted their hockey arenas to be in use during the summer, and they wanted to keep their players in shape for hockey during the winter. The team Canadian Professional Indoor Lacrosse League formed with four teams — Montreal Canadians, Montreal Maroons, Toronto Maple Leafs, and Cornwall Colts — using players from their hockey teams.

Although the league enjoyed a successful first season, it closed down in 1932, but not before introducing the lacrosse world to a new game. Though several modifications to the field game were made, the indoor lacrosse game was basically the field game played in an enclosed space. The number of players

FIELD TIP

Fielding the pros

The field lacrosse game has entered the world of professional sports with the birth of Major League Lacrosse (MLL), which began play in 2001, after a barnstorming tour to try out markets in 2000. Six teams make up the competitive landscape in this league: Baltimore Bayhawks, Boston Cannons, Bridgeport (Conn.) Barrage, New Jersey Pride, Long Island Lizards, and Rochester Rattlers.

The league has two divisions: the National (Baltimore, New Jersey, and Rochester) and the American (Long Island, Boston, and Bridgeport). The winners of each division and the two teams with the next best records make the playoffs. Baltimore and Long Island met for the championship in both of the first two seasons, with the Lizards winning the title in 2001 and the Bayhawks taking it in 2002.

The league begins play in late May and continues through the end of August, playing mostly weekend games in minor-league baseball stadiums. Crowds hover around 5,000 per game. Salaries are higher (roughly US$8,000 to $30,000) than in the NLL and the season is shorter (12 games per team). The players come mostly from NCAA Division I programs, though Canadians such as John Grant, Jr. (Rochester), Tom Marechek (Baltimore), and Gary Gait (Baltimore) played major roles in the first couple seasons of play. A host of players play in both professional leagues, but MLL is dominated by Americans. Among the league's top players are Casey and Ryan Powell (Rochester), Mark Millon (Baltimore), Jesse Hubbard (New Jersey), Greg Cattrano (Baltimore), and Christian Cook (New Jersey).

One major rule change that differentiates MLL from the NCAA is a 45-second shot clock. The league instituted this (and only allows three long sticks as opposed to the standard four) in an effort to speed up play and make it more appealing to people new to the sport. Also introducing an orange ball, the league has put its games in homes throughout the U.S. thanks to a TV deal with Fox Sports Net. Another addition is a two-point arc that is located 15 yards from the goal; goals scored from behind this line count for two points (similar to basketball's three-point line).

was reduced from 12 to 7 (and then down to 6 in the 1950s). From the wide-open field game, lacrosse was transformed to a hard-checking game when cross-checking was introduced, and games were played in a restricted boarded area. This new lacrosse came to be known as box lacrosse, or *boxla*.

In 1968, the National Lacrosse Association began play in eight cities in Canada and the United States. The teams were the Montreal Canadians, Toronto Maple Leafs, Detroit Olympics, Peterborough Lakers, Vancouver Carlings, Victoria Shamrocks, New Westminster Salmonbellies, and Portland (Oregon) Adanacs. This league introduced the 30-second clock to speed up the game, but the league only lasted until 1969.

An earlier incarnation of the National Lacrosse League made a go of it in 1974 and 1975. Again, teams were based in both the U.S. and Canada, but the league wasn't successful. Over the two years of play, the league fielded teams in Baltimore, Boston, Long Island, Montreal, Philadelphia, Quebec, Rochester, Syracuse, and Toronto.

Then came the NLL, which started play in 1987 as the Eagle Pro Box Lacrosse League, with four teams playing a six-game schedule. In 1988, the league upped the schedule to eight games, and in 1989, the league became the Major Indoor Lacrosse League (MILL), with six teams playing an eight-game schedule. Just before the 1998 season, the MILL abandoned its single-entity ownership strategy — that is, teams were operated by the league itself — in favour of franchise ownership by individuals, and renamed the reorganized league the National Lacrosse League.

Chapter 7

The Future of the Game: Minor and University Lacrosse

*W*hile the National Lacrosse League receives most of the attention today from lacrosse fans and media, the league is not the only place where lacrosse is competitively played. Lacrosse remains Canada's national summer sport, and an estimated 25,000 Canadians play in the country's major and junior box lacrosse leagues. Field lacrosse reigns in the United States, with more than 250,000 players located primarily in the northeastern states and along the eastern seaboard, with the NCAA men's and women's collegiate play pulling in most of the attention.

This chapter introduces you to the levels of box and field lacrosse that compete all over North America. You'll probably find out about a team in your area for which you can start rooting.

Understanding Lacrosse's Competitive Balance

Distinguishing between amateur and professional lacrosse is no longer as cut-and-dried as it was before the success of the National Lacrosse League. Today, so many professional players of the NLL continue to compete in the so-called amateur organizations that they really shouldn't be considered amateur organizations anymore.

That said, this chapter introduces the various levels of *non-professional* or *minor lacrosse* competition that exist in Canada and the United States. In Canada, these minor levels range from, well, minor to major in box lacrosse. (Canada fields men's and women's field organizations, but box lacrosse provides the greatest opportunity for minor play.) In the United States, field lacrosse dominates, with men's and women's teams at NCAA Division I, II, and III levels, as well as at the high school level, with competitive and club teams.

Introducing Minor Box Lacrosse in Canada

Canadian box lacrosse at the minor level features three age levels, each with additional divisions, according to age or according to the quality of players:

- **Minor lacrosse:** A variety of leagues for players between the ages of 7 and 20.
- **Junior A and B leagues:** For players ages 17 through 21; the A league features the better players.
- **Major A and B leagues (also called Senior):** For players over 21 years of age; also has the more highly skilled players at the A level.

With levels such as *Tyke* (ages 7 and 8), *PeeWee* (ages 11 and 12), and *Midget* (ages 15 and 16), the minor lacrosse level offers the greatest opportunity for young players to play the game. You can find minor leagues around the country, called *house leagues,* usually affiliated with a community's arena. Teams typically are formed at the youngest ages, with the more successful teams staying together through the duration of their players' minor careers. And the best of these teams — *rep teams* — represent the community in national tournaments. At age 17, the best players from these house leagues reach the next level in a player draft conducted by teams in the Junior A and Junior B leagues.

The Junior and Senior leagues operate somewhat like professional or university competitive leagues. The leagues are made up of teams from communities primarily in Ontario, British Columbia, and Alberta who draw on the best players in their particular house leagues. The teams then compete during the regular season for the right to participate in playoffs that can lead to a national championship series.

Because teams — franchises, almost — are responsible for fielding players, coaches, equipment managers, and so on, as well as for the fees required to maintain membership in a league, the number of teams participating may vary from year to year. In 2003, for example, three teams were added to the Junior B league of the Ontario Lacrosse Association, increasing the number of franchises from 22 in 2002 to 25 in 2003.

Playing for the Minto Cup: Junior A lacrosse

The oldest competitive championship trophy in lacrosse is the reward for each year's national champion at the Junior A level. The Minto Cup (see Figure 7-1) was first awarded in 1901, originally to the Senior champions of Canada. It became the Junior A championship cup in 1937. The most valuable player in each Minto Cup championship receives the Jim McConaghy Memorial Award.

Figure 7-1:
The Minto
Cup.

(Photo: Canadian Lacrosse Association)

The champions of Junior A leagues from the Ontario Lacrosse Association (OLA) and the British Columbia Lacrosse Association (BCLA) compete for the Minto Cup. The championship is a best-of-seven series (first team to win four games) that in 2002 concluded a playoff competition among 12 teams (8 in Ontario, 4 in British Columbia). The Burnaby, British Columbia, Lakers won the 2002 Minto Cup, defeating the St. Catharines, Ontario, Athletics.

The Junior A playoff participants are determined by a regular season schedule. Between April and July, teams in the BCLA (there were seven teams in 2002) play a 24-game schedule. The OLA (11 in 2002) starts the season a little later (May), and plays a 20-game schedule through July.

Other Canadian national trophies

Canadian lacrosse players have more than the Mann and Minto Cups to aim for. The following trophies are also highly coveted by players, coaches, and fans at other competitive levels:

✔ **The President's Cup:** For the national box lacrosse champions at the Senior B level, this trophy was first awarded in 1964. Past champions have included the usual array of teams from Ontario and British Columbia, as well as three teams from Alberta — including the Edmonton Outlaws in 2002 — and a team from Tuscarora, New York, in 1994.

✔ **The Founders Trophy:** Since 1972, this trophy has been awarded to the national box lacrosse champions at the Junior B level. Nearly all past champions have come from the Province of Ontario.

✔ **P.D. Ross Cup and Victory Trophy:** Two divisions of senior men's field lacrosse teams vie for these prizes, both first awarded in 1984.

✔ **First Nations Trophy:** Junior men's field organizations compete for this championship, first awarded in 1985.

Since 1953 — the year that the Canadian Lacrosse Association (CLA) modified box lacrosse rules to reduce the number of players per side from seven to six (including the goaltender) — the following teams have collected the most Minto Cups:

✔ Ontario teams have dominated the series, winning 35 cups:

- Peterborough has won 10 Minto Cups.
- Oshawa has won 7 Minto Cups.
- St. Catharines and Whitby have won 5 Minto Cups each.
- Brampton has won 4 Minto Cups.

✔ British Columbia teams have won 15 cups, most of them won by the following teams:

- Burnaby has won 6 Minto Cups.
- New Westminster has won 3 Minto Cups.
- Vancouver and Victoria have won 2 Minto Cups each.

Playing for the Mann Cup: Major lacrosse

The Mann Cup was first awarded to the major champions in 1910. The most valuable player in each Mann Cup championship receives the Mike Kelly Memorial Award. The champions of major leagues from the Ontario Lacrosse

How 'bout them Salmonbellies?

Why has New Westminster won so many Mann Cups? Maybe the answer lies in the source — of the Mann Cup, that is.

The New Westminster Salmonbellies was formed in 1889, making it one of the oldest sports franchises in North America — older than such storied franchises as the New York Yankees of Major League Baseball, the Green Bay Packers, of the National Football League, and the Montreal Canadiens of the National Hockey League.

As the oldest lacrosse franchise at the time, the New Westminster club served as trustee of the Mann Cup in the cup's early years, which may have been made more expedient by the fact that the Salmonbellies won 10 of the first 18 Mann Cup competitions. The club turned over control to the Canadian Lacrosse Association (CLA) in 1925.

New Westminster was also the last home of the Minto Cup before the CLA took control of it. However, its heritage hasn't had the same effect on the Salmonbellies Junior A history, with only three Minto Cups to its credit since 1937.

Association (OLA) and the Western Lacrosse Association (WLA) compete for the Mann Cup. The championship is a best-of-seven series (first team to win four games) that in 2002 concluded a playoff competition among 8 teams (4 each in Ontario and British Columbia). The Brampton, Ontario, Excelsiors won the 2002 Mann Cup, defeating the Victoria, British Columbia, Shamrocks.

The major playoff participants are determined by a 20-game regular season schedule. Both the WLA (there were seven teams in 2002) and the OLA play a May-through-July schedule.

Since 1953, the following teams have collected the most Mann Cups:

- British Columbia teams have a slight edge in this series, winning 26 cups, most of them won by the following teams:
  - New Westminster has won 12 Mann Cups.
  - Vancouver has won 6 Mann Cups.
  - Victoria has won 6 Mann Cups.
- Ontario teams have won 24 cups, most of them won by the following teams:
  - Peterborough has won 7 Mann Cups.
  - Brooklin has won 7 Mann Cups.
  - Brampton has won 5 Mann Cups.
  - Six Nations has won 3 Mann Cups.

Keeping Pace with the Field: U.S. Field Lacrosse

Though the traditional strength of U.S. field lacrosse has been in the northeastern states and along the eastern seaboard, field lacrosse has now found its way across to the West Coast. This section introduces the levels of varsity play you may find in your area.

Heading to college

Nearly 240 schools at the Division I, II, III, and junior college levels sponsored varsity men's lacrosse teams in 2002 (see Figure 7-2). The Division I level, with 54 men's teams in 2003, features the best talent and attracts the most attention from fans and media, thanks primarily to scholarships and much bigger budgets. Though Division I schools such as Michigan State, University of New Hampshire, and Boston College have recently dropped men's lacrosse, SUNY Albany, SUNY Binghamton, and Wagner (N.Y.) College have helped keep the number of teams at a steady level.

Figure 7-2: The NCAA men's field lacrosse game is most popular in the northeastern United States.

(Photo: Joe Apaestegui/Inside Lacrosse)

The most growth in collegiate lacrosse can be found on the women's side, which has seen a 46-percent increase in varsity programs since 1997 (see Figure 7-3). At the start of the 2003 season, more than 250 women's varsity programs were active, including 78 at the Division I level. Close to 50 new Division III teams have been added since 1997.

Most of the NCAA schools that sponsor varsity lacrosse are in the northeastern U.S., though varsity men's Division I programs are at the Air Force Academy and the University of Denver, both in Colorado, and a men's Division III team plays for Whittier College near Los Angeles. Schools such as Vanderbilt (Tennessee), Northwestern (Illinois), Stanford (California), and the University of Oregon (starting in 2005) sponsor varsity women's Division I programs.

Figure 7-3:
The NCAA women's game is the fastest growing segment of collegiate lacrosse.

(Photo: Joe Apaestegui/Inside Lacrosse)

College lacrosse starts its official season in late February and culminates with the Division I men's championship game in late May (on Memorial Day). Teams play an average of 13 regular-season games each spring, mostly on Saturday afternoons. Crowds can range from a few hundred to nearly 10,000 for top games in Syracuse University's Carrier Dome or at Hofstra University's James M. Shuart Stadium.

The culmination of every college lacrosse season is the Final Four, played on Memorial Day weekend and traditionally broadcast live on ESPN2 and ESPN. The Division I semifinals take place on Saturday, the Division II and III championships on Sunday, and the Division I final plays on Monday. In the Division I tournament bracket, 16 teams compete for the title; 4 teams make the Division II playoffs, and 16 teams vie for the Division III championship. The University of Maryland's Byrd Stadium and Rutgers University's Rutgers Stadium previously alternated turns hosting the Division I final, a massive event that can draw crowds of more than 30,000 people. Baltimore's state-of-the-art Ravens Stadium took over in 2003, offering a video-replay screen and 40,000 available seats.

Following the star programs and players

Much to the dismay of some college lacrosse fans, two teams dominated the 1990s — Princeton University and Syracuse University. Heading into the 2003 season, these two schools had combined for 12 of the 15 championships since 1988, not counting Syracuse's 1990 championship, which was vacated by the NCAA due to an eligibility infraction. Not counting the 1990 title, Syracuse and Princeton each had six championships during that stretch, meeting in the final game three straight seasons from 2000 to 2002. Other perennial Division I powers include Johns Hopkins University, the University of Virginia, the University of Maryland, and the University of North Carolina.

Most of the NCAA's stars come from traditional field-lacrosse backgrounds. Syracuse stars Ryan, Casey, and Mike Powell grew up in upstate New York. Johns Hopkins legend Dave Pietramala came from Long Island. Princeton's Jesse Hubbard played his prep lacrosse around Washington, D.C. Virginia's Michael Watson was weaned on the sport in Baltimore.

And plenty of Canadians have also made a large impact on the NCAA and that influence seems to be increasing as more players in Ontario and British Columbia are looking for scholarships at U.S. colleges. Legends such as Gary and Paul Gait (British Columbia to Syracuse), Tom Marechek (B.C. to Syracuse), Mike French (Ontario to Cornell University), Gavin Prout (Ontario to Loyola College), John Grant, Jr. (Ontario to University of Delaware), and Tracey Kelusky (Ontario to University of Hartford) dominated college lacrosse during their tenures. Heading into the 2003 season, two Canadians returned after leading their teams in scoring as freshmen in 2002: Cornell's Sean Greenhalgh, from St. Catharines, Ontario, and Denver's Matt Brown, from Burnaby, British Columbia. Division II power Limestone College (South Carolina) has long been a popular draw for Canadian talent.

Beyond the NCAA

Recent years have also seen an explosion on the club scene, as roughly 400 colleges (making up about 8,000 players) are home to some sort of non-varsity lacrosse team. The most popular and organized league is the U.S. Lacrosse

Intercollegiate Associates (USLIA), which has more than 150 men's teams and 35 women's teams. Both men's and women's play culminates with a championship tournament in St. Louis in May. Most of the schools in the USLIA are big universities outside the northeastern U.S. (such as Utah's Brigham Young University, Colorado State, Arizona State, and Georgia Tech University) that do not sponsor varsity programs.

High school days

At the varsity and club high school level, you can find close to 1,000 girls teams and just over 1,000 boys teams in nearly every state. Counting only varsity programs, 81,000 boys and girls played high school lacrosse in 2002 — up from 74,000 in 2001. That number jumps to nearly 100,000 when you count club programs — programs that aren't sanctioned by regional scholastic athletic organizations.

Not all states sanction the sport officially, especially those outside the northeast, but more and more are coming along (Georgia and California recently made the move). As the game spreads, more players from non-traditional areas are popping up on NCAA varsity lacrosse rosters at all levels. One of Syracuse's leading scorers during its 2002 NCAA championship season was Spencer Wright, a midfielder from San Diego, California.

Taking on the World: The World Lacrosse Championship

The pride of wearing your home country's sweater in competitive lacrosse started in 1967, the year of Canada's centennial celebration. Canada invited the U.S., England, and Australia to compete in an international field lacrosse tournament, the beginning of the World Lacrosse Championship, now held every four years and sponsored by the International Lacrosse Federation. Of the eight championships that have been held, the U.S. field lacrosse team has won seven of them. The only time the U.S. lost was in 1978, when Canada defeated the U.S. squad.

Since the first tournament, the games have been held in Melbourne, Australia; Stockport, England; Baltimore, Maryland; Perth, Australia; and Manchester, England. The 2006 World Lacrosse Championship will take place in July in London, Ontario.

Nations compete in a weighted round-robin tournament during which higher-ranked teams play an easier schedule based on their record in the previous World Lacrosse Championship. The nations scheduled to play in 2006 are Argentina, Australia, Canada, the Czech Republic, England, Finland, Germany, Hong Kong, Ireland, the Iroquois Nation, Japan, The Netherlands, New Zealand, Scotland, South Korea, Sweden, Tonga, the United States, and Wales.

Lacrosse has been a competitive sport in the Summer Olympic Games only four times: in 1904 as a medal sport (Canada won the gold) and in 1928, 1932, and 1948 as a demonstration sport.

Part III

Playing Lacrosse: What You Need to Know to Succeed

The 5th Wave   By Rich Tennant

"Hey! I said 'pick-and-roll', not 'kick-and-roll'!
Everybody off the assistant coach!"

In this part . . .

Discover how to be a player with the information in these chapters. For the offensive player, this part includes tips and tricks to improve your passing, catching, and shooting skills. For defenders, you'll find out about proper positioning, delivering legal checks, and defending the most popular offensive plays, among other topics. And I've thrown in a separate chapter just for goaltenders.

This part also discusses the value and fundamentals of playing team offence and defence, and includes some tips on physical and mental conditioning.

Chapter 8

Getting the Ball into the Goal: Developing Offensive Skills

In This Chapter

▶ Creating magic with the stick: Ball-handling skills

▶ Cradling the ball

▶ Catching and passing

▶ Moving — with and without the ball

*T*he name of the game is scoring. Well, actually, the name of the game is lacrosse, but the fundamental determinant of the game — well, you get the idea.

The team with the most goals at the end of the game is declared the winner. You can't get much simpler than that. How your team gets to that stage, however, requires you and your teammates to possess certain offensive skills that lead to the highest possible number of scoring opportunities. This chapter shows you ways to develop the skills to help your team achieve the best possible outcome.

Grasping Basic Ball-Handling Skills

Ball handling is "magic with the stick." Only a few players are great ball-handlers, the kind you watch with awe from the stands. A backhand shot into the top corner of the net or an over-the-shoulder long bounce shot, a great stick fake on the goalie or on a defender, a great pass threaded through a crowd of players into the receiver's stick — you wonder how they saw any opening and how they could get that shot or pass off. All these moves, and more, make up ball handling. The ball seems to be glued to the stick and it has "eyes" on every pass and every shot.

How do you become a great ballhandler? That's easy. You practise and practise on your own time. You shoot at the wall, you play one-on-one with an imaginary defender, and you do crazy tricks with the ball in your stick. You practically sleep with the stick and ball. It is with you all the time wherever you go. You do this until the ball and stick feel like they are an extension of your body and until you can do almost anything you want with the ball.

Handling (holding) the stick

The key to handling the stick — whether you are cradling, catching, passing, or shooting — is the grip. You hold the stick with your fingers, snugly but loosely, so that your wrists can turn and rotate freely. You definitely don't want to grab the stick tight with your fingers wrapped around the shaft and the palms of your hands touching the shaft.

Where you place your thumbs is an individual preference — wherever they feel comfortable. Some players like to let them just gently wrap around the shaft; others like to place them along the shaft.

Where you place your top-arm hand also depends on where it feels comfortable. Your top-arm hand can be placed slightly below the midpoint of the handle or slightly above the midpoint of the handle. Your bottom hand is usually placed at the butt end of the stick. Some players like to make a bump with tape at the end of the handle so that their hand does not slip off the end of the handle, and for better support of the stick.

Your *top-arm hand* is the hand that's attached to the arm that's closer to the, er, top of the stick. If you're a left-handed player — that is, if most of your passes and shots come with the stick on your left side of your body — then your top-arm hand is your left hand. Right-handed players, of course, use the right hand as the top-arm hand.

Your grip on the stick doesn't change much during a game. In other words, a player keeps the same grip whether passing or catching. For a beginner who may have trouble catching the ball, you should try to grip the stick higher up on the shaft, even at the throat of the stick, to make it easier to catch. Holding the stick this way is almost like holding a baseball glove, and you have more of a chance of catching the ball. When passing, you can always slide your top hand down the shaft to the midpoint area.

When shooting, players typically slide their top-arm hand down closer to the bottom hand so that they can get more of a whip in their shot, which helps them get more power into their shot.

Cradling the ball

Cradling is the art of keeping the ball in the stick without looking at it. With practice, you'll know when the ball is in your stick by feeling its weight, not by looking at it. By cradling, you can look at the net, see your teammates cutting, and concentrate on beating your defender, all without worrying about whether you have the ball in your pocket. Players practise three basic styles of cradling, depending on the game situation:

✔ **Small cradle:** You use the small cradle (see Figure 8-1) when standing stationary, looking to pass to a teammate, or getting ready to shoot. You hold the stick in a horizontal position while rocking only the stick's head back-and-forth slightly by the wrist of the top-arm hand, getting ready to pass or shoot. The small cradle locks the ball into the middle of the pocket, setting it up for a quick shot, dodge, or pass.

Figure 8-1:
The small
cradle.

✔ **Medium cradle:** You use the medium cradle (see Figure 8-2) when running up the floor with the ball in a passing or shooting position. Here, you hold the stick at a 45-degree angle to the floor and the cradle is a little more vigorous, swinging the stick and head forward and backward by the top-arm hand to keep the ball in the stick while looking to either pass or shoot.

✔ **Large cradle:** You use the large cradle (see Figure 8-3) when taking a cross-check. You hold the stick in a vertical position with large movement of the stick swinging in and out from your body using the top-arm hand. Holding the stick in this position, your body protects the stick while you can still cradle to feel the ball in your stick.

Figure 8-2:
The medium
cradle.

Figure 8-3:
The large
cradle.

Because you have more room to run in the field lacrosse game, players must be more versatile using both hands with the cradle than in the box game. Conversely, most box players have better stick skills and protection because they can't simply run away from defenders. They are constantly under pressure from someone. Because field players have more space to work with, they can sometimes employ a one-handed cradle, using the free arm to protect the arm and keeping the stick vertical. Be careful, though, as warding can be called if you use your free arm in any way to hold, push, or control the defender.

Beyond Handling: Catching the Ball

In my experience, most minor players have more difficulty catching the ball than passing it. It's amazing how the ball can fall right into a minor player's stick and he still drops it. Beginners have a tendency to tighten up on their grip as the ball approaches their stick rather than relaxing their grip and relaxing their top-hand arm. By tightening up, the stick acts like a tennis racquet and the ball ricochets off it. So, this section starts with the basics of catching before moving on to passing.

Catching the ball may seem like such a simple skill that parents think their kids can do it every time. Keep in mind, however, the difficulty of catching the ball that I discuss in this section. You can always help your child develop catching skills by practising with her in the backyard, at the local park, or even in your basement. Of course, if she's trying to catch the ball while standing in front of a stack of her favourite CDs, she may catch on more quickly.

Positioning your body for the catch

Get the player to face his receiver and hold his stick up over his shoulder and in front of his body for a target. The player holds the stick with his fingers — in other words, he doesn't grab the stick hard — and places his thumbs along the shaft. The top hand is slightly below midpoint of the handle while the bottom hand is placed at the butt of stick (see Figure 8-4). For beginners, keep your eye on the ball all the way into the pocket of the stick.

Giving — and then you shall receive the catch

To explain the importance of "giving" on the catch, consider whether you could catch a tennis ball with a tennis racquet. If you hold the tennis racquet out straight and without movement as the ball hits it, the ball will bounce off the racquet. But if you try to absorb the tennis ball onto the racquet by moving it back as the ball goes toward it — "giving" — the ball drops onto the racquet without bouncing off.

Figure 8-4:
Establishing
position for
the catch.

Catching in lacrosse is the same motion. Start with the stick beside your head and as the ball approaches the stick, drop the stick back to gradually absorb the ball into the pocket of the stick. By the time you actually catch the ball, the stick is behind your body (see Figure 8-5). And now you're in a position to pass the ball back to your partner. You can achieve this motion with the stick by relaxing the top arm backwards.

More players in the NLL are cocking, or winding up, their sticks less. Instead, they hold the stick beside the head to catch and shoot all in one motion. This adjustment helps them get off a shot quickly, giving the goalie less chance to stop the shot.

What's the Catch? Building Your Passing Skills

I can't stress enough the importance of improving your ability to pass. To play lacrosse successfully and confidently, you have to know how to handle the ball and pass. And as with catching the ball, one of the most important places to begin is with the stance you take up to pass the ball.

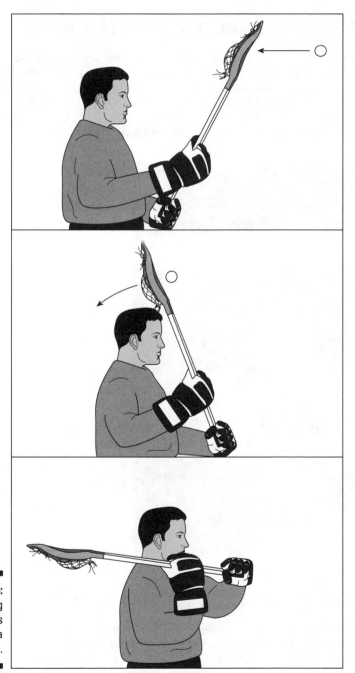

Figure 8-5:
Catching
requires
giving a
little.

Positioning your body for the pass

A sideways stance is your most optimum position for passing the ball because it also helps you protect the stick in a game (see Figure 8-6). Before you pass, you first need to position yourself sideways from the player who will receive the pass. This position is more realistic in a game situation because if you have the ball in your stick you are probably being checked or bothered by a defender. Turning your body sideways protects the ball from the defender.

Figure 8-6:
Establishing
your
position for
the pass.

Gripping the stick for the pass

The grip of the stick is the same as ball handling and catching: top hand at the midpoint of the shaft while the bottom hand is at the end of the handle. Some players like to move their hands closer for passing and farther apart for catching, but I recommend that you not move your hands when either passing or catching. When you have the ball, hold the stick vertically at a 45-degree angle with your top hand beside your head.

Moving the stick forward with the pass

To start your passing motion, cock your stick by moving the top hand straight back, the butt of the stick pointing at your target. As you prepare to release the ball, step with your front foot to get power into your pass. On the forward motion of the stick, transfer your weight from the back foot to the front foot, that is, the foot opposite your stick. Be careful not to step with the foot on the same side as your stick because you'll not only lose power but also look awkward.

As you bring the stick forward, you'll snap both your wrists and bring the stick's head straight ahead, not across your body, with the top arm fully extended and the butt of your stick touching your elbow (see Figure 8-7).

Figure 8-7:
The passing motion.

Touching your elbow is a reference point for you to make sure that you have thrown a perfect overhand pass. In reality, the butt of your stick does not usually end up touching your elbow, missing it by a few inches to the inside. What you want to avoid altogether is the butt ending up in the stomach area, which creates a side arm passing motion that is not as accurate as the overhand passing motion.

Remembering the keys to good passing

Here are some other important passing points to keep in mind:

- ✔ **Pass and catch with two hands.**

- ✔ **Throw hard, crisp passes that are short and parallel to the floor.** It is amazing how the great passers have a touch to their passes that makes them catchable.

  The great players are able to read their receiver — to determine whether he is a beginner, intermediate, or experienced player — and then pass accordingly. An experienced player will likely have no trouble catching a hard pass. A pass to a beginner, on the other hand, needs to be thrown with less intensity so that it's easier to catch.

- ✔ **Stress accuracy over power.** Pass quickly but don't sacrifice accuracy.

- ✔ **Use the head of the receiver's stick as your target.**

- ✔ **Every pass thrown is the responsibility of the passer.** You must make eye contact with your receiver to let him know that you are looking for him. When you do so, you become the eyes of your receiver. If your receiver is covered or turning his head for the pass, keep your eye on your teammate's defender to see if he is going to hit him.

- ✔ **Don't catch the ball and then think.** To make good game decisions, you must concentrate all the time, and that includes thinking ahead about what you're going to do with the ball after you catch it. Keep your head in the game all the time.

If you drop passes regularly, you could be thinking too far ahead of yourself, that is, thinking of shooting the ball before you catch it. You drop the ball not because of poor technique, but because of poor concentration. Concentrate on catching the ball first, before you think of shooting or making a play.

Working on Catching and Passing Drills

The drills in this section are designed to help you improve your catching and passing skills. You can work on these drills by yourself, with a partner, or with your teammates at the arena before or after practice. Or you can play a little pass and catch around the neighbourhood with a group of friends.

What to focus on during passing and catching drills

While you're working on the catching and passing drills in this section, here are a few things to keep in mind:

- ✔ Make sure you are fixing or correcting your stick's head all the time: check where the pocket should be, how deep the pocket should be, and how many shooting strings there should be. (See Chapter 2 for more about shooting strings.)

- ✔ Look at your partner's stick head.

- ✔ Think about catching the ball as if it were an egg.

- ✔ After catching the ball, drop your stick farther back so that you pass the ball from behind your body, with your stick level to the floor.

- ✔ Throw hard, level passes, staying away from rainbow passes. Rainbow passes are high-arcing (blooping) passes that take forever to reach their destination. By the time the receiver catches the ball, he is being hit by the defender and he can't make a good play.

- ✔ Snap your wrists forward on the release of the ball.

- ✔ Freeze your stick on the follow-through — that is, hold your stick for a second at your target so that you get more accuracy on your pass.

- ✔ Take pride in hitting the receiver's stick.

Individual passing drills

Here are a couple of passing drills that you can practise on your own. These drills emphasize the progression of passing and catching that is grip first, catching second, and passing third.

- ✔ **1-on-0 form passing:** Pretend to pass without a ball. It's a good idea to get a friend to watch you, someone who can tell whether you're doing all the basics right. Good passers should be able to analyze themselves or other players and correct their mistakes.

✔ **1-on-0 stationary passing:** This is how all the great players develop their passing skills, constantly shooting and passing against the arena boards, a wall, or a target high on the Plexiglas.

Partner passing drills

The following drills are ones that you can practise with a teammate or a parent or a coach. These drills are how great passers are made. Do a few of them every day to develop into a good passing player.

✔ **2-on-0 stationary passing drills:** These drills will definitely help with your passing form. In these drills, just two players pass back and forth; it may help to have a third player around to help correct any flaws.

- **Practise catching with one partner throwing the ball with his hand, not with his stick, to the other partner.** You can start with tennis balls so that you avoid the tendency to "cheat" by using the weight of the lacrosse ball to help you catch.

  This simple drill is so important because if players start to throw the ball back and forth with their sticks, the balls will be on the floor or anywhere except near the receiver's body. By throwing the ball with the hand, at least you throw accurately and your partner will have a chance to practise catching.

- **Pass and catch with only one hand, usually the top hand.** This is a good drill for catching.

- **Pass and catch from a passing distance you would normally throw from in a game, about 15 feet.**

- **Move closer together and pass from a short distance, about 5 feet apart.** Continue making hard and level passes, even at this distance.

- **Move to opposite sideboards to practise passing from a far distance.** Again continue making hard and level passes from this longer distance. A player may have a slight arc on the pass because of the distance, but not enough to slow the ball down.

- **Practise fake passes.** From a normal distance, partners fake a pass one way and then pass the other way to their partner.

- **From a normal distance, partners do "hot potato" passing.** This is passing without any real catch; the ball goes in the stick and is thrown back, all in one motion.

- **Practise winding up for a long shot and then passing.** Partners take a wind-up position, stick level to floor, as if they are going to shoot. Then fake a shot by twisting the top wrist in before passing.

- **Practise fake shots.** Partners fake a shot by bringing the stick across the front of the body and then back as if shooting, but instead pass to the partner. Or a partner can fake a shot by turning his stick in with his wrists, freezing the defender, and then step across as if shooting, but instead passing to his partner.

- **Throw only behind-the-back passes.**

✔ **2-on-0 stationary timed passing:** Partners count the number of passes they can catch in 30 seconds.

Variation: If practising with a number of teammates, find out who can be the first pair to catch 20 passes.

✔ **2-on-0 stationary passing with two balls:** One partner throws a ball in the air while the other partner throws bounce passes.

✔ **2-on-1 "monkey in the middle":** This defensive-pressure drill helps players avoid panicking with the ball when being pressured. The two passers are about 15 feet apart with a defensive player in the middle of them. The defensive player attacks the ballcarrier and tries to intercept his pass. The ballcarrier passes around the defender's stick to his partner. The ballcarrier cannot pass until the defensive player is close to him.

Variation: The passer fakes a pass and steps around the defender and passes. The defender then goes after the other partner and plays his stick.

✔ **2-on-0 full-floor passing on the run:** In this drill to work on with a number of teammates, players form two lines, right-shots and left-shots, beside the net. Partners run down the floor to the other end passing back-and-forth. Start in a narrow width, about crease-width apart, and then go wide, close to the boards, and finally a normal distance apart.

Passing and shooting on the run is one of the most important elements of lacrosse. Especially in field lacrosse, being able to seamlessly pass, catch, and shoot on the run is much more important than any behind-the-back shots, bounce passes, or stick fakes. Behind-the-back passes and bounce passes are not nearly as common in the field game. Players usually have enough room so that behind-the-back passes are not necessary, and with many games played on grass, the bounce pass isn't as reliable a form of moving the ball.

Team passing drills

Here are some passing drills that you can work on as a team, either at practice or before a game. Your coach may have some other team drills that you can work on as well.

- ✔ **Knock-out drill:** Line up six players, three sets of partners opposite each other. Start the drill with two balls. The players pass the balls back-and-forth in random order. If a player throws a bad pass or drops a good pass he gets a point. When a player has three points, he is out of the drill. The drill continues until there are two players left passing two balls back-and-forth and one winner. The only rule is that you cannot pass to a player who already has a ball.

- ✔ **Pepper drill:** Line up four passers with one ball opposite one receiver who has a ball. The passers pass to the receiver quickly, and as soon as the receiver passes a ball, the next passer passes to him. Make him pass quickly so that as soon as a ball is released, another one is coming at him.

- ✔ **Zigzag drill:** This drill (see Figure 8-8) improves ball handling because of its high repetition of passing. Line the whole team up with everybody opposite a partner. Place a bucket of balls at both ends of the line. From one end, the players pass all the balls down to the other end of the line in a zigzag formation.

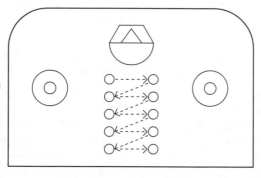

Figure 8-8:
Diagramming
the zigzag
drill.

- ✔ **Zigzag full-floor:** Form five stations, each consisting of one player; all other players have a ball at one end of the floor. A player passes the ball to the first station and follows his pass. Then the player who received the first pass passes to the next station and follows his pass. The players do this all the way down the floor. The last player at the far end of the floor on receiving the ball runs back up to where the other players are lined up.

- ✔ **Shuttle passing drill:** In this drill for six players, three players are on one side of the floor (in a single line) and three are opposite on the other side of the floor (also in a single line). Players pass across the floor and then follow their pass and go to the end of that line; then when that player receives a pass he passes back across the floor and follows his pass and goes to the end of that line (see Figure 8-9). This drill is great for improving passing while on the run using quick, hard, and level passes.

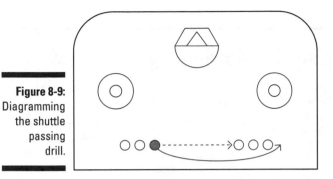

Figure 8-9:
Diagramming
the shuttle
passing
drill.

You can set up two groups of players or have three lines compete against each other. The groups compete to see who can pass the longest without dropping the ball, or who can make 20 completed passes first, or who can make the most passes in 30 seconds. You can vary the width between the two lines in the group, for example, sending the lines almost to the boards, putting the lines at a game-distance apart (about three-quarters of the width of the floor), or putting the lines close to each other to improve close passing.

Variation: Form four groups in a corner formation. Players make passes to the line positioned diagonally from them and follow their pass. Take care not to run directly into other players (though you will) and try to go around them.

Beating the Defender: Moving with the Ball

The great players of the game are great because they can easily beat a defender and score. It's important for players to be able to pass or collect loose balls, but the biggest offensive asset that a player can have is to be able to beat his opponent one-on-one.

Protecting the ball in the stick

You are going to handle the ball sometime during a game, so you better know how to protect it from a defender. The key here is the ability to cradle, pass, and shoot the ball without looking at it. You must know that the ball is in the stick by cradling and by feel, because this gives you freedom to concentrate on protecting the ball from a defender by looking at him rather than trying to look at the ball and at the defender at the same time. (For more about cradling and carrying the ball, see "Grasping Basic Ball-Handling Skills" earlier in this chapter.)

COACH TIP

Coaching the zigzag drill

Coaches: The zigzag drill is a good opportunity to work with the players on your team to help them with their passing and catching flaws. Because your players are spread out and all together at the same time and because they are all involved in the drill, you can work with them both individually and as a team. Following are a few things that you can work on:

✔ You can easily go around to each player, teaching and correcting (and praising) his passing while everyone else remains active.

✔ Consider adding some negative motivation to the drill. For every dropped ball, a player must do one push-up after the drill is finished.

✔ Motivate your team by using statistics. Ask the team to try to catch 17 passes out of 20

thrown. If they do not reach that number, the whole team does push-ups.

✔ Get your team to work on short-term success by challenging them to find out how many times they can pass a ball down and back up the line without dropping it.

✔ Work on team ball movement by getting your team to find out how long it takes to pass the ball down the line. Use a stopwatch to time the drill. You can use this time as a standard for comparing the time of future drills, always trying to improve the time.

✔ Add some competition to the mix: Have the lines compete to see who can pass the ball the longest without dropping it.

Some defenders like to attack the ballcarrier and try to steal the ball from him. If you have the ability to cradle, you can watch your defender and you can spin and turn to protect the ball from the defender as he tries to slash and dislodge the ball from your stick. This basic cradling move is important even before you start to go one-on-one because you have no reason to beat anybody if you don't have the ball in your stick.

Taking a cross-check

Another step in the basics of beating a defender is learning how to take a check. The natural tendency when you get hit is to tighten up with your body, but this move can cause you to become rigid with the stick, and when hit, the ball will be jarred loose out of your stick. Instead, do the opposite when you receive a cross-check: Relax and lean into the direction of the force of the hit.

When you see or feel a hit coming, take a wide stance to absorb the hit and cradle the stick, making sure the ball faces away from the force of the direction of the hit so that the ball doesn't pop out of the stick (see Figure 8-10). As you approach your defender with the ball, hold the stick low and horizontally across the front of your body. Just before you get hit, bring your stick up in a vertical

Figure 8-10:
Getting in
position to
receive a
cross-check.

position and turn your body sideways to take the hit on the arm, protecting the ball in the stick. Keep your head up to look at the net; you may want to shoot or watch your checker over your shoulder to see what he is going to do next.

You can slide your top hand up to the throat of the stick to cradle the ball on a hit, or you can keep your top hand at the midpoint mark of the handle to be in a position to pass or shoot. However, unless you are an experienced player, you should not try to pass when being cross-checked.

One-on-one offensive moves with the ball

This section suggests a few possible moves that you can make against a defender to shake yourself free for an open shot or to make a clean pass to a teammate. These moves are used by the best offensive players in the NLL to help them beat the best defenders.

The inside slide

The *inside-slide* or *bull* move is the most common one-on-one move used by NLL players to cut across the top of the zone. All you do is lean into your defender and try to muscle your way past him across the top of the offence, a natural move (see Figure 8-11). Usually this move starts on the side of the floor so that when you eventually get by your defender you are in the middle of the floor in a good position to shoot. You have to turn your body sideways to take the cross-check on your non-stick shoulder, remembering to take a wide stance for balance and support and to lean with your body and dip your shoulder into the cross-check. Swing or cradle your stick vertically to know where the ball is. When you have the ball in your stick, it should never stop moving.

Figure 8-11: Making an inside-slide move.

Relax on the hit; don't resist a cross-check because this is counterproductive. Rather, you should relax your body to become dead weight and equalize pressure, which makes it harder to push you out of the way. And protect your stick after you go by the defender because the defender will go after your stick from behind you to dislodge the ball. In fact, some defenders even let you go by them on purpose — the *matador defence* — and then try to stick-check you from behind.

Nick Trudeau of the Albany Attack on one-on-one offensive moves: "I try to read the defender but have no pre-planned move, as I may try something I would never do in another situation. My best move is a stutter step to the middle. I make a hard cut with my strong side out, or I go opposite to the boards and make it look like I'm going outside before cutting back inside. I find that my body is big enough to get back to the middle. When taking a hit, I still try to get a shot off. My first thought is to keep shooting even to the point where I'll take a shot around someone."

Keys to beating a defender

The qualities of a good one-on-one player are the following:

✔ The ability to hang on to the ball when being cross-checked

✔ The ability to move both ways: inside to the middle of the floor and outside toward the boards

✔ First-step quickness to change direction

✔ Balance to stay standing

✔ Upper-body strength to receive a hit and overpower your defender

✔ Intelligence to out-think the opponent

✔ Deception to make the defender expect an action and then see something else

✔ And especially instinct — great players have a knack for beating defenders without thinking about how they do so

A great saying in lacrosse is to be quick, but don't hurry. When beating a defender, you should have control of your body. Keep your offensive moves simple; the less movement, the better. Stay relaxed and loose with your knees bent. Slow down and do things with a purpose, using patience before you accelerate. When you hurry, you tend to appear unsettled, frantic, flustered, and confused.

Remember, however, that if you don't attack the defender, he will attack you. So neutralize your defender by making him react to an offensive move.

The outside slide

This move is being used more and more often. The ballcarrier just leans into his check and cuts outside toward the boards to slide back in toward the net. You need this move to counter the inside-slide move when defenders overplay you to force you to the boards. At one time, this move was used only periodically, but now it is executed as much as the inside-slide move.

When you approach the defender, turn your body outward facing the boards while at the same time swinging your stick outside to protect it. Taking the cross-check on the stickside, or inside shoulder, lean your body weight on the defender as you move down the side of the floor, trying to weasel your way back in to get on the inside of the defender.

The trick with the outside-slide move is to use your inside elbow and forearm to push the defender behind you and get your body completely in front of him. Once you beat him, the defender could be behind you, so keep your stick out in front of your body so that he cannot stick-check you from behind.

A word of caution: Be ready for any type of stick-check, over-the-head check, wraparound check, or straight slash that tries to dislodge the ball.

Offensive moves on the field

Offensive moves in field lacrosse are called *dodges*. The field game has five primary dodges:

🡒 **Face dodge:** This involves an offensive player running at a defender, pulling the stick across the face to the opposite side of the body, and then continuing around the defender using the body to shield the stick.

🡒 **Split dodge:** This involves more of a fake, running right at the defender, stutter-stepping, and switching the stick from one hand to the other. This move is very similar to the crossover dribble in basketball.

🡒 **Roll dodge:** This is a spin move to slip around a defender using the body to shield your stick. Run at a defender with your stick in your right hand, plant with your left foot, and spin away from and around the defender. Do the opposite if starting left-handed.

🡒 **Bull dodge:** This move is common in the box game and really can only be used effectively by an offensive player with size and power. It is simply leaning in to a defender while cradling the stick away on the opposite side and using your size and strength to create enough room to pass or shoot.

🡒 **Question mark dodge:** This is the most complicated of the moves. The offensive player starts behind the goal. You can go left or right, curling around and in toward the goal, before sharply spinning back away from the cage and shooting, creating a question mark path. This move is not used to beat a defender as much as it is to create enough space to get off a shot.

The inside and outside spins

To execute the *inside-spin* move, you fake the outside-slide move (make it look real), lean on your defender cutting to the outside while receiving a cross-check, then quickly roll back inside and cut across the top for the shot.

To execute the *outside-spin* move, you fake the inside-slide move (again, make it look real), lean on your defender cutting to the inside while receiving a cross-check, and then quickly roll back and cut outside for the shot.

Chris Driscoll of the New York Saints comments on spin moves: "My favourite move is to beat my defender with speed. I like to make a spin move coming across the top of the floor. My counter move is to cut outside, making sure that I keep my stick protected and beat my defender with speed."

Just the fakes, ma'am

A body fake is a deception where you make your defender think you are going to do one thing and then you do something else. The body fake is a move more of quickness than of strength. Your quickness helps make the fake move look like the real thing, rather than looking like a fake. You make a body fake usually on the run to get your defender off-balance by reacting to your fake.

Making a game of drills

Running drills doesn't have to be all work and no play. Here are a couple of suggestions for turning your practice sessions into a competition:

✔ **Tag game:** Use five balls with six players in a confined area marked off by cones. The player without the ball is "it," and he must go after the ballcarriers and try to steal a ball from one of them. If he is successful, the player that he stole the ball from is now it.

✔ **British bulldog game:** There are two teams, one along the sideboards with balls, the other in the middle of the floor. On the call "British bulldog," players with the balls run across the floor to the other side trying not to get checked off or lose the ball. If a player is checked and loses the ball, he now becomes part of the defensive team to check the ballcarriers. Last man with a ball is the winner.

You can make one or two body fakes: the outside-fake move, where you fake a cut to the outside and then cut back inside; and the inside-fake move, where you fake a cut to the inside and then cut back outside.

The other type of fake is the fake shot, which is an offensive move that has more to do with the stick than the body. A good fake shot freezes the defender for a split second to give you enough time to go around him. You can wind up to fake a shot and then pull your stick in front of your body and go around the outside of the defender.

Cutting: Moving without the Ball

Moving without the ball helps you, when you're not carrying the ball, to beat a defender and get in the clear for a pass. The most basic play and effective move without the ball is the *go play,* where you just cut past your defender from the off-ball side. It can be a move of first-step quickness and deception, you can knock your defender's stick down and go, or you can cross-check your defender and then push off and go.

Some stronger players use an inside-slide move without the ball when receiving a cross-check, physically sliding past their defender. Another common move is the outside fake, where you fake a cut to the outside, then cut back inside.

Practising Individual Offensive Drills

Though it is a team game, you can play lacrosse by yourself to get better. The great players have always stressed how important it is to their games to go to a wall or sneak into an arena to practise on their own. The main point is that they always have a stick in their hands. Instead of putting it away between practices, they constantly cradle or shoot. They play against imaginary defenders, practise stick faking or body faking, or shoot at a net or a wall. All this practice is never work to them, but fun, helping their drive to be the best.

You can practise many of the drills in this section on your own. But most importantly, take a tip from the game's great players and work with your stick whenever you have the chance, not just in practice or during a game.

Individual cradling drills

These drills help with both cradling and ball handling:

- **1-on-0 stationary cradling:** Just stand still and practise cradling the ball in your stick. This is one of the best drills that you can do at any time, anywhere, on your own.

   Variation: Try jogging while cradling.

- **1-on-0 fake shot:** From all positions (overhand, sidearm, and underhand), just keep the ball in your stick and circle your body without dropping it. Or keep the ball in your stick and wave the stick out in front of your body.

Offensive ball-handling drills with a partner

Try your hand at these 2-on-0 catching and passing drills with a partner:

- Pass two balls simultaneously. You can try both players passing through the air, or one partner passing through the air, the other throwing a bounce pass.
- Throw underhanded passes only.
- Throw sidearm passes only.
- Throw behind-the-back passes only.

✔ Pass and catch the ball with only one hand on your stick, first your left hand, then your right hand.

✔ Swing your stick to your opposite hand and then flip the ball underhand or overhand to your partner.

Protecting-the-ball-in-the-stick drills

Working with your teammates or a couple of friends, these drills help you with ways to keep defenders from poking the ball out of your stick:

✔ **1-on-1 circle drill:** The defender tries to check the ballcarrier's stick using the over-the-head check, wraparound slash, or stick-check. The ballcarrier looks over his shoulder to protect the stick while constantly cradling. The ballcarrier can only move in a confined area. Start and stop on whistle or whoever can hang onto the ball the longest is the winner.

✔ **1-on-2 circle drill:** The ballcarrier can move a little bit more as he now has two defenders trying to get the ball off of him.

Taking-a-cross-check drills

As a lacrosse player, you have to be ready to take a hit, even when you're practising. Working on these drills will help you get your body ready to absorb a real hit during a real game:

✔ **1-on-1 bump drill:** The defensive player pushes the ballcarrier with his hands, and then he bumps the ballcarrier with his body. The key here is that the ballcarrier has to relax his body on any hit rather than tightening up.

✔ **1-on-1 charging defender drill:** The ballcarrier is stationary while the defender runs at or charges the ballcarrier to hit him with his body and dislodge the ball. Stress that the ballcarrier must relax on the hit.

✔ **1-on-1 equalize pressure:** Ballcarrier leans on the defender and moves across the top of the floor trying to slide off the check for a shot. If he runs out of territory, he rolls or spins back and still leans on the defender, but tries to cut around the defender on the outside. Or the ballcarrier leans on the defender and moves outside trying to slide off the check and back inside for a shot. If he runs out of territory, he rolls or spins back and still leans on the defender, but tries to cut around the defender cutting across the top.

✔ **1-on-1 man-in-the-middle drill:** The defender plays behind the offensive man who receives a pass from the pointman at the top of the offence. The defender can only push on the offensive player while the offensive player leans into him relaxed to catch the ball, turn, and shoot.

Beating-a-defender drills

These drills are best practised with teammates or friends. You need to have the experience of seeing a defender lose his balance or get fooled in some way so that you can anticipate when to blow past him.

✔ **1-on-1 offensive-move progression:** A progression to practise offensive moves, first when neither player has a stick, then when only the offensive player has a stick, and finally when both players have sticks.

- Partner practises one offensive move to beat his partner; defender plays token defence by just leaning on the ballcarrier with his stick.

- Partner practises one offensive move to beat his partner; defender pushes and shoves with his stick.

- Partner practises one offensive move to beat his partner; defender uses solid cross-checks.

✔ **Gauntlet drill:** Ballcarriers zigzag, or go in-and-out, around a straight line of stationary players. This drill helps players work on balance, quickness, protecting the stick, and relaxing when taking a hit.

The stationary players cannot move, but they can cross-check the ballcarriers as they go through the line to force them to protect the ball in their stick. They can try to stick-check the ballcarriers to try to get the ball from them, either while the ballcarrier faces them or after the ballcarrier has past them.

✔ **1-on-1 offence from a stationary start with a cross-floor pass:** Start with two lines with balls, left-shots and right-shots. The first offensive player in each line is covered by a defender. The first offensive player in one line doesn't have a ball, but he receives a cross-floor pass then goes one-on-one against the defender just like a real game. The offensive player who just passed receives a pass from the next player in line and goes one-on-one. You rotate from the offensive line to a defender.

✔ **1-on-1 live half-floor drill:** Start these one-on-one drills with the ball-carrier having a ball, with the defender having the ball and passing it to the offensive player, from a loose-ball situation, or from a pick situation. Here are some variations:

- Ballcarrier tries to beat defender by turning sideways to receive the cross-check.

- Ballcarrier tries to beat defender by turning his back to the defender and rolling back-and-forth.

- Ballcarrier tries to beat defender by working him (rolling back-and-forth, faking one way or the other) for as long as he can. With patience and continual movement, an offensive player can beat any defender.

- Ballcarrier tries to beat defender when the defender tries to take the ball from him. Defender can slash, over-the-head check, or wraparound slash.

- Ballcarrier tries to beat defender facing him in just five seconds.

Tell the offensive player to keep his stick cocked as much as possible, to always look to shoot, and not to shoot from the wrong side of the floor but to go back to his proper side to shoot (that is, left-shot or right-shot side).

✓ **1-on-1 off the bench:** A right-shot player rolls the ball to the goalie and breaks for a return pass around centre floor. When he catches the ball, a left-shot defender comes off the bench to play defence. They go one-on-one.

✓ **1-on-1 game:** Make up two teams — right-shots and left-shots. The defender has the ball and passes to the offensive player in front of him. The offensive right-shot gets one point if he beats his defender and another point for a score. You can play to 15 points.

Here are some variations for the 1-on-1 game.

- Ballcarrier on the run attacks the defender.

- Ballcarrier, from a stationary position attacks the defender.

- The stationary offensive player receives cross-floor pass, and then goes one-on-one.

- The offensive player cuts to the ball on the run for a pass and shot.

- The offensive player receives a down pass in the corner area or pops out and goes one-on-one.

Taking shots after beating a defender

The section "One-on-one offensive moves with the ball" earlier in this chapter offers suggestions for some of the most basic offensive moves that you can make to try to get in position for an open shot. You can use the following drills to work both on those moves and on the shots that follow the moves. Shoot against an outdoor target or at the net before or after practice.

- ✔ Inside-slide move, across the top of the zone, or an outside-slide move and shoot. If you're working with a friend or teammate, ask him to hit you while running or shooting.

- ✔ Inside- or outside-spin move and shoot. Practise shooting while running.

- ✔ Outside body fake and shoot. Fake outside, cut inside, and shoot.

- ✔ Inside body fake and shoot. Fake inside, cut outside, and shoot.

- ✔ Fake shot, cut to outside, back to inside, and shoot.

- ✔ Fake shot, cut to middle of floor, and shoot.

- ✔ Fake shot while sidestepping down the side, and then cut across the top for a shot.

- ✔ Fake shot while sidestepping down the side, and then spin outside and in for a shot.

- ✔ Bait move while being cross-checked. Expose your stick over your shoulder, and when the defender goes after it, pull it back in and shoot.

Chapter 9

Putting the Ball in the Goal: Shooting Fundamentals

Shooting is the most important skill a lacrosse player needs. Passing is second. You can do everything — get loose balls, play good defence, throw great passes — but if you can't score, all the rest is for naught. Great shooters are looking to shoot all the time!

And great shooters have the knack of not only shooting the ball straight and hard but also "thinking" their way around a goalie. Shooting is just like passing a ball against a wall, but a little bit harder. In lacrosse, everybody should be allowed to shoot and therefore score. Why? Because scoring is the fun part of lacrosse, and no other feeling in the world is better than hitting the twine behind a goalie.

In this chapter, I offer the fundamentals of shooting to score, as well as the skills you should work on and some drills to help you to build those skills.

Becoming a Great Shooter

Being a great shooter is not the same as being a great goal scorer. A great goal scorer can score from anywhere — outside (say, 15 feet out) or inside (around the crease area, close to the net).

A great shooter, on the other hand, scores on long shots. Some lacrosse players seem to be able to score at will; others can't "put the ball in the ocean" or "hit the side of a barn," to borrow a couple of sayings that show how bad some players can be at it. If you work on your shooting form, you will definitely improve your shooting percentage (that is, the number of goals made divided by the number of shots you take), making you a better shooter — but you still may not become a great goal scorer.

Some players just don't have the touch or feel for shooting. Their technique, their body size (usually too bulky), their stick, the way they hold their stick, their confidence, their selection of shots, or their timing (shooting at the wrong time) — one or more of these traits could be what keeps a player from becoming a good shooter.

Acquiring a shooter's stick

Now don't forget the tool of the trade for the shooter: the lacrosse stick. The great shooters can take the head of a stick apart and re-string it the way they like it. The pocket is crucial to becoming a great shooter. You will never meet a good shooter who has a pocket that is at the throat of the stick (that is, where the head joins the handle of the stick); a stick with a deep pocket (about the depth of a ball) that can't be used to pass and shoot quickly and accurately; a pocket so shallow, almost flat, that the ball has a hard time staying in the pocket; or a pocket with no shooting strings.

To have a shooter's pocket, the mesh must have two to three *shooting strings* (the strings that run horizontally below the head of the stick that players can adjust); the ball should rest at the tip of the pocket on the last shooting string. The depth of the pocket is about a ball's depth, and the ball should come out of the pocket nice and smooth. Some shooters like the feel of the ball hitting the end of the plastic frame of the head just slightly so that they know the ball has left the stick.

Can great shooting be taught?

Do great shooters have a touch, a natural thing, something they are born with? To a degree, some players are born with *soft hands,* that is they can catch, throw, and shoot effortlessly and accurately. But most players have to put in the practice time to make themselves better shooters.

After you have mastered the proper mechanics of shooting, you have to practise every day to take your shooting skill to the next level. Confidence comes from taking 100 to 200 shots a day until you feel confident about where the ball is going and can hit that spot on the wall almost every time.

Depending on the type of shooter you are, you may find different types of pockets to be more effective. The deeper the pocket, the more whip and power it has. Outside shooters generally employ deeper pockets to put more behind their shots. Shallower pockets are better for quickly getting the ball away. Inside players don't need as much power. They benefit more from a shallower pocket that zips the ball right off the stick.

Putting an 8-inch ball into a 4-foot net

To shoot a little white ball behind a goalie into a 4-foot net (actually, 4 by 4¾ feet) takes more than just the ability to hit an open spot. Why? Because goalies tend to move. If goalies just stood there and gave you the shot, lacrosse wouldn't be much of a game. So the first trick to shooting is to learn to read the goalie.

Some goalies, called *reflex goalies,* show you an open spot and then take it away. Others come out on an angle to take away openings; they're ready to move sideways by anticipating where you are going to shoot by reading your eyes, reading the position of your stick, or by just plain guessing where they think the shot is going. For more about the types of saves that goalies make see Chapter 11.

The great shooters feel that they can shoot faster than a goalie can move, so if they see an open spot they just shoot it. Goalies can be scored on because they have more to contend with than just a stationary shooter. Goalies have to move according to where the ball is, have to watch for cutters through the middle of the floor, and have to be aware of opponents around the net.

Developing soft hands is really developing proper form

To become a player with *the touch,* that is, someone who can shoot hard with the ball always going where it should, really has to do with recognizing your shooting form. Great form means never looking as if you're forcing your shot.

Soft hands come from having proper form: using your wrists, holding the stick with your fingers loose, extending your wrists back when cocking your stick, and then extending your wrists fully on the follow-through.

Resolving shooting problems

If you can make the shot in practice, however, why can't you make it in a game, especially when it's a shot you've mastered in practice? A number of things can contribute to your misfires:

- You may have stopped believing in yourself. By practising your shooting until you know you can hit whatever you're aiming at, your confidence will again soar.

- You may be *telegraphing* your shot, that is, looking directly at where you are going to shoot. Limiting your wind-up — just catching and shooting — keeps the goalie on his toes.

- You may be taking bad shots, for example, from a bad angle or from the wrong side of floor, or you're being pressured or cross-checked when you shoot.

- You may be rushing or hurrying your shot. Be patient: If you don't have a good shot, don't shoot.

- You may be *bombing* your shot, that is, just winding up and shooting at no particular spot. NLL players take a short wind-up, if they wind up at all, shooting almost as soon as the ball hits the pocket.

- You may lack concentration by not focusing on the open spot. Great shooters can focus on one thing — the open spot left by the goalie — and block out everything else.

If your fundamentals are fine, but you're still having trouble shooting, you may be in a scoring slump. Sometimes players play uptight, so remember to laugh and relax. Or, you may be trying too hard, so remember not to force your shot. Finally, just go back to the basics and practise, practise, practise.

Target-shooting

Great shooters are made, not born. They develop into shooters from shooting practice either at a wall or at a net. Shooting at a net gives the player that extra feeling of exhilaration when the ball hits the twine. The shooting board, however, is a shooter's laboratory. It is a board made of plywood or plastic that covers the whole net with the four corners cut out for top corner shots or low corner shots. Or you can cut out a curve on the side of the board for hip shots. (Figure 9-1 shows where hip shots and corner shots are with a goalie in net.)

High Corner Shots

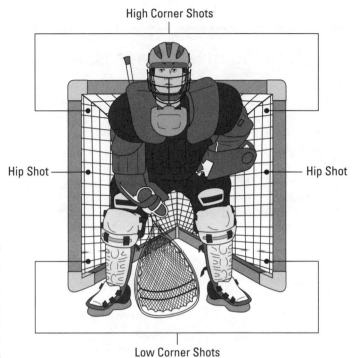

Hip Shot

Hip Shot

Figure 9-1:
A goalie in
the crease
with target
areas to
aim for.

Low Corner Shots

The size of the holes depends on your skill level. If you are a beginner, make the holes big so that you can score easily and get the good feeling of the ball going into the net. If you are experienced, make the holes big enough to score, yet small enough to make the shot challenging.

Remember to be relaxed when shooting, not forcing your shot. You'll want to practise shooting at game speed, shooting from the distance you would shoot from in a game, and shooting from spots you would shoot from in a game.

Shooting from a Long Distance

The variety of long shots that you can work on include the overhand long shot, the sidearm shot, the underhand shot, and the back-hand shot (see Figure 9-2). It doesn't matter what type of shot you use. The options for long shots include the straight long shot for either top corner of the net, the long bounce shot for either top corner or mid-corner, and the long low shot for either bottom corner. You also have in your repertoire the fake long shot, which takes a quick stick fake — bringing your stick across your body while stepping to the outside and then back in for the shot.

Shooting in field lacrosse

Shooting on the run is crucial in lacrosse, but it's more common in field lacrosse. Field lacrosse players are more likely to need to shoot on the run than from a stationary position, so developing that skill needs to be mastered before learning different shots and fakes.

Great shooters can score from anywhere. Having a great outside shot is one thing, but being able to pick corners at high speeds in front of the crease is just as impressive and effective.

Because players have more space to score in field lacrosse (with less-padded goalies and larger nets), shooting percentages are generally much higher. Top shooters in the NCAA usually average around 50 percent scoring accuracy. And by studying the skills and tendencies of a goalie, you can improve that percentage. Some goalies more prone to getting beat on bounce shots, others on high or low shots. Knowing a goalie and tracking what shots he commonly saves and what shots give him trouble can make it much easier to score.

Another difference in field lacrosse shooting strategy is that the player closest to the ball when it goes out of bounds gains possession for his team. So if an attackman sails a shot over the goal and out of bounds, if a teammate is back there when he shoots, his team retains possession. After shots miss the cage, most goalies dash out and behind the goal in a race against opposing players to the endline to try to obtain (or retain) possession.

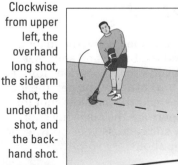

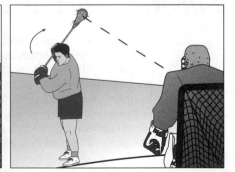

Figure 9-2: Clockwise from upper left, the overhand long shot, the sidearm shot, the underhand shot, and the backhand shot.

Because of the way the goalies are "bulking up" (over-padding), it's getting harder and harder to score in those top corners. But you still have to take those long shots, of which 70 percent should be bounce shots.

These are a few of the main points you should consider when working on your long shot:

- ✔ **Look at the whole net on your shot and pick the open spot.** Avoid looking directly at the spot you are shooting at because some goalies watch your eyes. To counter this, some players look at one corner and shoot to the other corner.

- ✔ **Learn to shoot with rhythm rather than flat-footed.** Players, whether they know it or not, *hop-step* (hop with back leg, and step with front foot) into their shot to synchronize all their body parts with the stick. Besides the hop-step, players at the end of their shot should take a forward step to create a wide stance for the all-important transfer of body weight from the back foot to the front foot. This again helps to get more power into your shot.

- ✔ **Make sure that you *cock the stick* by dropping your stick straight back to wind up for your shot.** This gives you the much-needed power to shoot long.

- ✔ **The actual release of the ball from the stick is important in getting velocity in your shot.** Shoot the ball when it is in the stick and still behind your head (see Figure 9-3). This gives you more power than releasing the ball when it is beside your head or in front of your body.

Figure 9-3:
Winding up
to shoot.

You want to shoot hard but you don't want to sacrifice accuracy for hardness. I have seen players with the hardest shot in the world who never hit the net.

Nick Trudeau of the Albany Attack on shooting: "I try not to think too much; if I think too much, I may miss the net. I try to use my wrist a little bit and will shoot around people and use them as a screen. I try to take a quick shot with not too much of a wind-up. I don't cock my stick; in other words, I put my stick level to the ground and just shoot from wherever I catch it."

✔ **Get used to snapping both your wrists at the end of your shot to give you that extra velocity.**

✔ **Do not shoot just for the sake of shooting.** If you can't see the open spot, don't shoot. In lacrosse, you'll very seldom find screen shots or deflected shots where the ball ends up in the net. So make sure that you see an opening to shoot at.

✔ **Shoot relaxed to get power.** Do not grab the stick as hard as you can to get hardness in your shot. Learn to hold the stick with just your fingers, which gives you more flexibility.

Shooting to obtain a high percentage

Every player would love to have a 25 percent shooting percentage. This means he would score one goal out of four shots. Some keys to getting a shooting percentage that high are offered in this section.

✔ **For a quick release, be ready to shoot before you receive the ball.** It takes time to catch the ball and then get into a shooting position. Try to catch and shoot from the same spot in your pocket. On the release of the ball from the pocket, you want the ball to run out smoothly from the pocket, but at the end of the shot you like to feel the ball "tick" the top of the plastic to know it has gone. Great shooters know that they can shoot faster than a goalie can move.

✔ **Shoot from your proper side of the floor.** When you shoot, make sure that you are at the proper angle, inside the side faceoff circles in the prime scoring area (see Figure 9-4).

✔ **Shoot in your range.** If you are in your range and feel able to make your shot, it will be more relaxed. If you are not in your range, if you're too far out from the goal to feel comfortable about the shot, you will probably force your shot trying to make up for the distance. Great shooters feel that the hardest shots are the ones they swing easy with. They do not try to swing or force the shot too much.

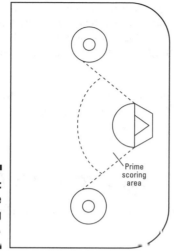

Figure 9-4:
The prime
scoring
area.

✔ **Before you shoot, make sure your stick is not being interfered with.** That means no stick or body is in front of your shot. If you have beaten your check, you should be one step ahead of him and be wide open before you shoot. If you received a cross-floor pass and are about to shoot, you can use your defender, who is likely coming out at you as a screen, but there should be a gap so that he doesn't interfere with your shot. You do not shoot around opponents (screen shots) unless they are playing back from you and cannot interfere with your stick.

✔ **You should be able to hit the open spot you are shooting at.** Wow, that sounds really simple, but it is amazing how many players cannot hit that little hole. You must have patience when shooting. Just before you shoot, take a split second to look at where you are going to shoot. Some players rush their shots, that is, take *automatics,* shots without thinking, and end up hitting the goalie in the chest area.

✔ **"Think" your way around the goalie.** Positioning and strategy are also critical to developing good shooting accuracy. Sometimes you don't need to just shoot the ball straight and hard. Instead, make it look as if you are going to shoot to the far corner by holding your stick in the sidearm position, and then bring it over your shoulder in an overhand shot, shooting for the near side.

If you are shooting straight on with the goalie, step into the middle of the floor slightly to move the goalie sideways and get him away from his near goalpost. This move gives you two options to shoot at: the far corner or the near corner.

When coming across the top of the floor, you should look for the far top corner or mid-post, but if you can't see anything, shoot a bounce shot or a straight shot to the near-side corner. Similarly, if you see no openings in the top corners, bounce! If you see no openings on the far side of the net, shoot to the near side!

If you don't have a good shot or don't see an opening to shoot at, don't shoot. You need shooting discipline. A lot of players end up just shooting at the goalie, whether they have something to shoot at or not.

Knowing the two best areas to shoot long

I have seen teams shoot from anywhere on the floor; it happens. These teams feel that if they shoot more than their opposition, they will win the ball game. How wrong they are.

Striving to get a high shooting percentage gives teams a higher chance of winning. To help your team achieve that percentage, here are the two best areas on the floor from which to shoot long shots:

- ✔ Exactly in the middle of the floor, where a player has many options to pick from on the goalie. Here a player still has good options from the far corner (high or low) and the near side (high or low).
- ✔ Off-centre on your proper shooting side.

Chris Driscoll of the New York Saints on shooting: "I usually pick an open spot on the net, but sometimes I just shoot at no spot. I like to shoot when the goalie is not expecting it. I like to shoot quickly and on the run. My favourite spot is the far top corner, but I will go somewhere else if I have to."

Shooting the overhand shot

In making the overhand shot, your stance is important because in a real game you will be turned sideways most of the time to protect your stick from your check. You hold the stick with your fingers loosely with the top hand just below the halfway point on the shaft. Hold your stick high and behind your head, vertically at a slight 45 degree angle, or if you are really winding up to shoot, you move your stick backward, level to the floor in a cocked position. The shot originates from behind your head and you release the ball when it is behind your head, but still follow-through after it is gone. Pull the stick forward by extending your top-hand arm forward and snapping the wrists. On the follow-through, make sure you fully extend your top-hand arm and that the head of your stick points at the target. The stick motion is directly over the shooting shoulder or to the side of that shoulder for the overhand shot. To get power, synchronization, and rhythm in your shot, step or hop-step into it. Step with your front foot to give you a wide stance, which gives power in your shot.

Shooting Closer to the Goal

It is important for crease players to step out in front of the net to execute close-in shots and not stand on the side of the crease. Timid players tend to stand beside the crease rather than taking the step out in front of the net to take a better shot because of the possibility of getting hit from behind.

When taking a straight close-in shot, no fake, just look at one corner and shoot at the other corner of the net. If taking a close-in shot to the far side of the net, you have three types of shots you can take:

- ✔ Start from an overhand shooting position to an overhand shot.
- ✔ Start from an overhand shooting position to a sidearm shot.
- ✔ Start from a sidearm shooting position to a sidearm shot.

This last type is done at least 80 percent of the time. When taking a close-in shot to the near side of the net, you can start from an overhand shooting position to an overhand shot or from a sidearm shooting position to an overhand shot.

What to do on a breakaway

If you get a breakaway in a game, make sure that you run down the floor off-centre, not down the middle or straight at the goalie. This gives you the option of cutting across the crease to move the goalie so that you can shoot to the short (or near) side or the far side of the net.

Breakaways can occur two to three times a game and usually originate from the defensive end when a defensive player anticipates an opponent's shot and heads for his offensive zone early, although you sometimes can pass to an open player coming off the bench.

Developing a great fake

Stick faking is important to discuss here because most faking in lacrosse happens around the net, though you will see it occur from far out with the ball or when in trouble with the ball. Faking is used in lacrosse more than any other sport in the world. You should develop different fakes for different situations:

- ✔ **Fake with your body:** Jab your foot one way and go the other way.

- ✔ **Fake a long shot with your stick:** This fake freezes your defender and allows you to then go around him.

- ✔ **Fake a close-in shot against a goalie:** This fake allows you to get the goalie's reaction or to freeze the goalie, and you can then shoot to the open spot.

- ✔ **Fake a pass:** You freeze your defender to get yourself out of trouble when being pressured by a defender and don't know what to do. A good fake pass against a defender checking you either freezes him or gets him to react by looking to intercept the pass, giving you time to go around him or at least giving you time to make a play.

Becoming a good close-in shooter

Patience is an extremely important asset around the net. But the longer you hang onto the ball around the net, the higher the chance of getting hit. So if you want to be a good player in close, you better not be afraid to get hit, because you will.

If cutting or running across in front of the net, the general rule is to put the ball back where you came from, that is, in the short side of the net. However, with the larger nets in the National Lacrosse League, you're likely to see players going to the far side of the net 80 percent of the time.

When you fake a shot at a goalie and he doesn't move, shoot at the corner you just faked at. You can fake right at a big goalie's body, knowing he will not move, but you will freeze him so that you can then pick and shoot. The other option you have against a big goalie is not to fake at all, just pick and shoot; the bigger goalies tend to rely more on angles.

Practising Shooting Drills

You can work on long-ball shooting drills on your own with some kind of fashioned target that matches the dimensions of the net, or with a friend or teammate acting as the goalie. These drills, however, focus on what you can do in practice or with a group of teammates.

Focusing on long-ball shooting drills

As you're working on your long-ball shots, here are a few fundamentals to keep in mind:

- React back toward the centre of the zone after you shoot, which puts you in position to be a defensive safety to stop any breakaways.
- On your wind-up to shoot, your stick should be level to the floor.
- Release the ball when it is behind your head.
- Cock or twist your wrists before you release the ball to make sure it's in the shooting pocket.
- Visualize a perfect shot.
- When incorporating cutting into your drills, cut hard to the ball or pass the ball hard to the cutter. And before you cut, fake a cut the opposite way in which you want to cut, and cut with your stick up and ready to shoot.

Remember to mix up the spots on goal at which you'll be shooting. You may want a teammate or a coach to shout out where to aim. Alternate between shots at each corner, mix bounce shots in with shots aimed to the top or bottom of the net, and don't forget to practise your fakes.

Work with several teammates to practise the following long-ball shooting drills. Remember to alternate right-shot and left-shot shooters in the drills.

- **Single-line breakaway drill:** Every player has a ball and lines up at centre. Players run down the middle of the floor and take a straight long shot from near the top of the zone. Change shot locations each time down the floor; for example, shoot at the far corner and then at the near corner.
- **Semi-circle long-ball shooting drill:** Form three lines in a semi-circle near the top of the zone, each with two shooters and a pointman; players in each line stand in single file. Each line shoots continuously, first around the horn and then alternating from side-to-side. After a player shoots, he should fade off to the side.

✔ **Two-line cornerman shooting drills:** With each player cradling a ball, start the two lines from the top sides of the floor and then from the top middle (see Figure 9-5). The lines can alternate sides shooting, first all right-shots and then all left-shots.

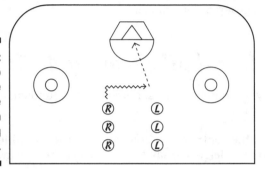

Figure 9-5:
The setup for the two-line cornerman shooting drill.

- Lines start from the top side of the floor and cut across the top, alternating among planting their feet and shooting an overhand shot; shooting on the run; and faking a shot, pulling the stick across their body, and shooting.

- Lines start from the top side of the floor, facing an imaginary defender, and just wind up and shoot.

- Lines start from one side of the floor and cut across the top, alternating among planting their feet and shooting an overhand shot; shooting on the run; and planting, faking a wind-up, pulling the stick across the body, and shooting.

- Lines start from the top corner area of the zone and then cut across the top shooting on the run.

Working on close-in shooting drills

When practicing your close-in shots, don't forget these tips:

✔ Follow your rebound, either off the goalie or off the boards.

✔ Make sure that you step around in front of net before you shoot.

✔ Place your top hand higher on your stick when faking. You can fake with your wrists only (no arm action), or you can fake with your wrists and arms together.

Don't forget the goalie

While working on shooting drills with your team, remember to tell your goalie what's expected of him during the drill. You want your goalie to make improvements as well as your shooters.

Have your goalie practise making saves from different positions; rotating his body positioning will help both the shooter and the goalie. The goalie will become comfortable defending the net from different positioning perspectives; the shooter will be able to practise against a goalie in a variety of different positions.

✔ Goalie can sit back in his net and not move.

✔ Goalie can sit back in crease and react to the shots.

✔ Goalie can take one step out and not move.

✔ Goalie can take one step out and react to the shots.

✔ Goalie can take a butterfly position (low to the ground with his legs spread out to the sides) and stay that way while players shoot.

✔ Goalie can play as if in a live game situation.

Finally, don't forget to warm up the goalie.

✔ On faking, turn your wrists in and fake hard. Think to yourself, "I'm going to shoot," so you make your fake look real. But remember to check back so that you don't end up shooting instead.

✔ Against bigger goalies, don't fake; just pick and shoot.

Remember to mix up the spots on goal at which you'll be shooting. You may want a teammate or a coach to shout out where to aim. Alternate types of fakes before shooting to alternating corners; for example, fake high and then shoot low or fake low and then shoot high.

Work with several teammates to practise the following close-in shooting drills. Remember to alternate right-shot and left-shot shooters in the drills.

✔ **Single-line breakaway drill:** Every player has a ball and they line up at centre floor. Players run down the middle of the zone, one right after the other, and take straight close-in shots in rapid succession. Run the line of players again, this time giving players the option to fake or just shoot.

✔ **2-on-0 creaseman shooting drill:** Players form two lines, right-shots and left-shots, on each side of the crease. All the players cradle a ball. On the run, the players alternate from side-to-side, shoot around a cone, which is placed in the middle of the crease. So that you don't have players running into each other, keep the left-shots inside and the right-shots outside.

✔ **2-on-0 cornerman makes diagonal pass to creaseman shooting drill:** One line, the passing line, is in the side cornerman position, passing diagonally to players in the other line, a stationary player in the crease area who takes a quick shot. The passer should work on looking at the net while passing to the creaseman.

Shooting games

Here are a couple of games that you can work into your shooting practice routine:

✔ **Shooting game "21":** Make up two teams, usually left-shots against the right-shots. A game goes to 21 points. Players can take any type of shot. You get one point for a close-in shot, two points for a long shot, and three points for a long bounce shot. For variation, try close-in shooting only.

✔ **Breakaway shooting game "15":** Ballcarrier runs full length of floor. Coach calls out which shot to take: a straight close-in fake and shot, a long shot on the run, or a long shot from a stationary position in the cornerman's area. Game is to 15.

Chapter 10

Keeping the Ball out of the Goal: Developing Defensive Skills

In This Chapter

▶ Defending the ballcarrier

▶ Defending other offensive players

▶ Drilling defensively

The fast pace of a lacrosse game is generally dictated by the offence. That speedy offensive pace requires quickness and stamina from lacrosse players on the defensive side of the floor too.

This chapter gives you the strategies and tactics you need to make yourself a better individual defender on the lacrosse floor and field. For information about building team defensive skills, see Chapter 12.

Stopping the Ball: Taking On the Ballcarrier

Keeping up with the ballcarrier requires the solid combination of a number of resources, both physical and mental. This section reviews some of the skills that are needed to play good individual defence:

✔ Practising solid cross-checking.

✔ Being vocal on the floor.

✔ Using your feet to move and maintain balance.

✔ Anticipating what is going to happen.

✔ Knowing your opponent.

✔ Playing with your heart.

Cross-checking

A cross-check involves a defensive player applying pressure to the ballcarrier with his stick. The defender holds the stick with two hands and applies it to the upper body area of the ballcarrier (see Figure 10-1). This defensive strategy works to slow down the ballcarrier's momentum toward the goal, perhaps forcing him to try an off-balance shot or pass off to a teammate.

Figure 10-1:
Cross-
checking the
ballcarrier.

A huge difference between box and field lacrosse is that cross-checking is illegal in the field game. Field defencemen play with both hands on their stick, but they cannot use the space between their hands to check an opposing player. One hand on the stick may be extended toward the offensive player to keep him at bay so that either the head of the stick or the butt end (covered by a fist) is used for this *poke-check*. Both hands can be involved in the same check if they are used together, generally at the bottom of the shaft, to push off the opponent. Contact between each stick head is common, as the defensive player tries to check the ball out of the opponent's possession. Defencemen can also use their elbows and shoulders to hold off offensive players.

The poke-check has worked its way into the box lacrosse game and has become one of the main weapons that players use to pressure and stop the ballcarrier.

Taking the stance

The defensive stance is called *being in a position of readiness.* To be in this fighting stance, you must play with your knees bent to make sure that you stay low, and with your feet placed a shoulder-width apart for balance (see Figure 10-2). Taking this low body position allows you to make quicker and stronger moves against the ballcarrier.

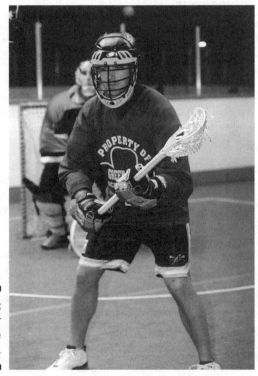

Figure 10-2:
The proper defensive stance.

Also, make sure that you keep your head up by keeping your eyes directed to the top of the ballcarrier's chest area or the top of the numbers on his jersey. You should avoid looking directly at the ball as you'll probably end up trying to go after the ball, stick-checking, and being beaten off the ball. Also, if you drop your eyes to look at the waist area, you'll end up dropping your head, again giving the ballcarrier the chance to beat you.

In box lacrosse, you want to force the ballcarrier toward the boards by overplaying him half-a-man. In other words, don't stand directly in front of him but rather slightly off to the side of him toward the centre of the floor. This defensive stance essentially gives you a one-player defensive advantage, except that the extra player is really the sideboards. Make sure that your hips are parallel to the sideboards and your head is in alignment with the head of your opponent's stick.

Holding the stick in a cross-check position

When holding the stick to cross-check, your hands should be about body-width apart and your arms cocked. The open face of your stick should point backward to allow for easier pickups of loose balls by just turning your handle. Cross-checking should only be used to stop a ballcarrier and therefore you should keep both hands on the stick.

Positioning your feet for the cross-check

The best positioning for your feet is whatever leaves you the most prepared to move to defend your player. You should focus on keeping your feet active and being ready to move them quickly and explosively.

Good defence requires the defensive player to make two to three good cross-checks on a play, rather than one big hit. He must move his feet constantly to keep up with the ballcarrier so that he can make multiple cross-checks.

Waiting to cross-check

Patience is the key in not getting beat by the ballcarrier. One of the most important things to do to play good defence is to wait for the ballcarrier to come to you instead of reaching or lunging at him. While waiting, make sure that you keep your feet active and ready to move. So get low, relax the muscles, and wait.

You may have to move out on the ballcarrier to maintain pressure, but you still have to wait for him to come to you. Now this may sound like a contradiction. But really when you go after the ballcarrier, you should shuffle the last two steps so that you maintain control, keeping a safe distance away so that he can't make his way around you, but effectively moving toward him to prevent a quick shot. Against a good long-ball shooter, you cannot afford the luxury of thinking that a player cannot score from a certain scoring distance and then let him shoot. Defenders cannot stay back and let shooters shoot because they will score.

Establishing contact on the cross-check

On contact, try to remain stationary so that you have a solid base with your feet. On the cross-check, try to keep the ballcarrier in the middle of the stick, between both hands. Follow these steps to deliver an effective cross-check:

1. **When you hit, extend your arms upward and outward.**

   Never overextend on your cross-check as you'll become vulnerable and off-balance.

2. **As you hit up and under, make contact on your opponent's arm between his elbow and shoulder and stay down.**

   If you stand up on the hit, you'll lose your power and quickness.

3. **During the hit, make sure that your feet are under your body for balance.**

4. **Cross-check and get off the ballcarrier!**

   Make your hits short and hard, and then recoil, filling the gap you created with the hit by shuffling out with small steps. Just keep continually cross-checking. If you lean on the ballcarrier's body with your stick when cross-checking, he will roll and slide past you.

When cross-checking, don't hit too high up on the ballcarrier's arm because the stick may slide up his arm pad and onto the neck, resulting in a high-sticking penalty against you.

Here are a few more cross-checking tips to keep in mind before (or after) delivering that defensive blow:

- ✔ **Never finish your check after the ballcarrier passes the ball.** Finishing your check puts you out of the play because of your over-commitment to a player who no longer has the ball. Also, the former ballcarrier can now get out of your cross-check and more easily cut to the net for a return pass.

  When the ballcarrier you're defending passes the ball to a teammate, instead of finishing your cross-check, drop to the level on the floor where the ball is to provide defensive help on the ball.

- ✔ **Defend the body, not the stick.** You should not play a great player's stick on a wind-up for a shot, that is, challenge what you think may be an upcoming shot. The ballcarrier could fake his shot and go around you, looking for an easier shot or for a teammate cutting to the net. Play your opponent's body, not the stick.

Slashing or cross-checking?

In major lacrosse now, you'll see both *wrap-arounds,* that is, the defender working around the ballcarrier to get at the ball, and *slashing* or *poking* to dislodge the ball, pressure the ballcarrier, or stop the ballcarrier. The *poke-check,* also known as the *can opener,* is a move to dislodge the ball. The defender tries to poke his stick between the ballcarrier's stick and body to pry the ball loose.

Slashing also has a place in lacrosse. When coaching slashing, be sure to encourage players to give a two-handed slash on the ballcarrier just to let him know what kind of game he is going to be in. But even while using the stick to slash, the players have to stay down.

Of course, in field lacrosse this kind of slashing is illegal. Checking players with a stick is just that: a check.

✔ **Don't forget the fake cross-check.** To counter a player who is much bigger than you, try to overplay his stick side or make him think that you're going to cross-check. Instead, at the moment of contact, step back to try to get him off-balance — for example, he may try to negate your cross-check by aggressively hitting back — and then, while he is fighting for his balance, slash at his stick.

Communicating to teammates

For some reason, most players have a hard time communicating on the floor. Being vocal on the floor is a must because of all the action and movement that happens in a game. This is especially true when you're on defence; good defensive communication in a game should include the following messages:

✔ **Picks and screens:** Warn your teammates when they're about to be picked off or become the victim of a set screen. (Picks and screens help free up an offensive player so that he can get a more open look at the net or can cut to an open spot on the floor for a pass.)

✔ **Cuts:** Let your teammates know when an offensive player is cutting toward another spot on the floor to receive a pass, usually a position that allows an easier shot on goal.

✔ **Who's guarding whom:** When defending an offensive player, let your teammates know who you're playing against, especially when a pick or screen causes you and another defender to switch checks. By not communicating, you may create a situation where two defenders are inadvertently guarding the same offensive player, leaving someone somewhere wide open for an easy shot.

✔ **Helping:** Of course, some game situations dictate when it's okay to have two defenders guarding the same offensive player (called *double-teaming*). If you leave your check to double-team the ballcarrier or another offensive player, let the teammate you're helping know so that he can apply more defensive pressure and play more aggressively than usual.

Playing with your feet

One of the keys to defending well is to keep your body in balance, and your feet play the biggest role in keeping your body in balance, whether you're a size 10EEE or a size 13A.

You play defence with your feet to maintain good position; as the offensive player moves, you slide your feet while staying in your position of readiness with your knees bent, back straight, looking directly at your opponent's chest, not at his stick or the ball. A few particular steps can help you defend in certain situations:

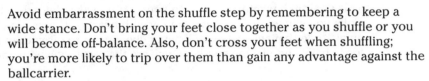

✔ **Retreat step:** You take a *retreat step,* that is, a step back, when the ballcarrier makes a move to the net. The retreat step allows you to be ready to cross- or poke-check by having weight on your front foot so that you can push off from this front foot to stay with the ballcarrier. If the ballcarrier decides to attack the net quickly, you are in a position to retreat quickly.

✔ **Shuffle step:** As you move with the ballcarrier, often down the sidelines as he tries to beat you, you take short *shuffle steps,* or lateral sidesteps, shuffling sideways to stay with him.

Avoid embarrassment on the shuffle step by remembering to keep a wide stance. Don't bring your feet close together as you shuffle or you will become off-balance. Also, don't cross your feet when shuffling; you're more likely to trip over them than gain any advantage against the ballcarrier.

✔ **Attack step:** Often on defence, you have to go out after the ballcarrier on a cross-floor pass and you do this with the *attack step,* where you run out and, shuffling the last two steps, stay low, and approach him at an angle to force him to the boards. By focusing on those last two shuffle steps and staying low, you avoid the mistake of overcommitting against the ballcarrier's stick or setting yourself up for the body fake.

Playing with your head

I'm not suggesting you make a header shot on goal like in soccer, although lacrosse balls have been known to ricochet off helmets. Rather, playing effective individual defence requires a lot of on-the-spot thinking.

On defence, you have to play with your head a bit more differently than you do when you are on offence. On offence, you can do a lot of things without thinking; on defence, you're always thinking and trying to anticipate what is going to happen before it happens. And knowing your opponent's strengths, favourite moves, and tendencies helps you in this anticipation. Is he quick? Does he like to shoot from the outside? Does he like to work inside?

Offensive players are creatures of habit, always trying to make the same move; as a defender, you have to know what your opponent is trying to do so that you can take away his primary move.

Establishing effective defensive positioning

Defensive positioning simply means being in the right place at the right time. In fact, many coaches feel that establishing good defensive positioning is half the battle of playing solid defence.

Taking the correct floor position against the ballcarrier helps you a great deal in stopping the ballcarrier. In most game situations, the most effective defensive positioning against the ballcarrier is to force him to the sideboards. To do so, overplay the ballcarrier *half-a-man,* which means that you turn your shoulders to the sideboards either a quarter turn or parallel to the boards.

Playing with heart

This final tip has more to do with your attitude as a defender than with any skills you can learn. You have to play with heart — that is, you should have an attitude that suggests you'll never give up. More often than not, getting to loose balls and playing solid defence are the result of who wants it the most.

Lacrosse is an aggressive game; to defend well you need to be aggressive not only in your play but also in your attitude. Defenders who have a reputation for being cocky and mouthy, for pushing opponents in the face with a glove, for example, are thought of as pests; they bother people defensively, irritate their opponents, and generally tick people off. They're also usually thought of as good defenders.

Defending the field of play

The size of the field in outdoor lacrosse is larger than in the box game, and so too is the length of the sticks used to defend. Teams generally use three long-stick (72 inches) defencemen at once, though a fourth can be deployed as a midfielder. The longer reach of the defencemen, and the fact that offensive players have more room to run, makes playing defence in field lacrosse different than in box lacrosse.

Space is important. A defensive player needs to use his stick to hold off and keep the midfielder or attackman at a distance. If you get too close, it's easy for the offensive player to make a quick move and zoom away. Defencemen need time to recover and that requires a space buffer with the offensive player.

Another important element of defence in field lacrosse is to keep your head on a swivel — figuratively, of course. You should always keep your eyes moving between your man and the man with the ball.

Stopping the Player: Defending Offensive Players without the Ball

Defensive floor positioning is the primary weapon a defender has against offensive players who don't have the ball. Your goal as a defender is to maintain a position that limits the possibility of your check receiving a pass or cutting to get closer to the net. How you achieve that goal depends on which side of the floor the ball is on.

Off-ball side defending

When defending an offensive player on the off-ball side of the defence, you should form a flat triangle. In this triangle, you're at the apex of the triangle, and the ballcarrier and your check form the base of the triangle. It is called a *flat triangle* because you should play off your check slightly and towards the ballcarrier in case you need to be in a position to help; you're therefore flattening the triangle a bit (see Figure 10-3). If your defence takes the shape of a deeper triangle, you're more likely to be protecting the net than keeping yourself available to help against the ballcarrier. In this situation, the opponent could cut very easily for a pass and shot.

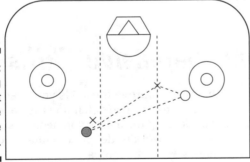

Figure 10-3: Diagramming the flat triangle defensive positioning.

On the off-ball side, always keep your opponent in front of you. If you play your check even, that is, parallel to the goal, he could fake up and cut behind you for a quick pass and shot. If your opponent goes behind you (a *backdoor cut*), always assume that a pass is coming and turn and play his stick hard.

Off-ball defenders should play an open stance, facing down the floor using their peripheral vision to see both their man and the ball.

In the NLL, with its highly skilled offensive players, off-ball defenders play closer to their opponents, using more of a closed stance, belly-to-belly.

Ballside defending

The defenders defending non-ballcarriers on the ballside of the floor should play in a closed stance, belly-to-belly to their check, looking over their shoulder at the ballcarrier in case their teammate needs help.

A good rule is that if the ballcarrier passes the ball, drop to the level of the ball immediately and then adjust your position according to your check. You're now in a position to collapse, help, and rotate, especially from the top of the defence.

Moving before the ball

The final rule for positioning when defending against offensive players without the ball is that the defence moves before the offence moves on any movement of the ball. And here are a few more tips for this type of individual defence:

- Never let a player lean on your stick without the ball; he can equalize pressure, giving himself the chance to catch the ball and score before you can adjust using your stick.

- Never let a player lean against you while cutting through the middle; he can neutralize your ability to use your body to stop a pass.

- Play your man to deny him the ball, that is, stay between him and the ball, not between him and the net.

Drills to Build Your Defensive Skills

The drills in this chapter can help you improve the skills you need to be a strong defensive player. You'll be able to practise defending the ballcarrier and other offensive players, as well as develop the agility you need to successfully defend the ball. From footwork to stickwork to defensive stance, you can work on these drills either alone or with teammates.

Developing defensive agility

These drills are designed to help you improve your footwork. The majority of defensive drills deal with lateral action, footwork, communication, and quickness, all actions that are part of every successful defensive player's repertoire. Remember to keep your drills short, quick, and hard.

✔ **Footwork:** More often than not, running on defence involves moving backward or sideways, rather than forward. A couple of ways to work on improving your footwork are running backward (say, the length of the floor and back a couple of times) in a drill I call *carioca*. While facing the sideboards, run sideways the length of the floor and back twice, taking lateral steps and keeping your body low.

✔ **Defensive steps:** To develop some of the defensive steps you need for defensive situations, this drill focuses on repeating each step in order. Start with an advance step, move into the retreat step, and swing sideways with the shuffle. When working on this drill, make sure to keep your body low as you would in a game situation. For a refresher about when to use these steps, see "Playing with your feet" earlier in this chapter.

✔ **Reaction:** This *wave drill* prepares you for game situations in which you need to react to a quickly passed ball or a cutting player. Working with a teammate or with your whole team, you react to the direction your partner or coach waves to, simulating the movement of the ball, for example. You can alternate the steps you take with the reaction, using a shuffle step during one set or a slide step during another. Again, make sure that your knees are bent and you're in the proper stance (see Figure 10-4).

Figure 10-4:
The wave drill improves defensive reaction to the ball.

✔ **Covering the defender:** In this shadow drill, work with a teammate to practise following the movements of an offensive player. To do this, you just need to mirror the other's movements for ten seconds, alternating so that your partner can also work on his defensive skills. Make sure to work on this drill both with contact and without contact.

✔ **Slide steps:** This defensive slide drill asks you to do the slide step back and forth ten times within a ten-foot area, timing yourself so that you have something to gauge your progress. Alternatively, you can practise this slide drill in 30-second time periods, counting how many times you can slide back and forth in the area before the 30-second period ends.

✔ **Lateral movement:** This defensive square drill works on lateral motion, agility, and quickness. Place four cones (or other objects) to mark a square; the distance between the cones should match the distance you would normally move in a game. Move laterally around the cones both clockwise and counterclockwise. Try going around the square four times, or time it for 20 seconds.

✔ **Stopping and starting:** Using the same square set-up, this drill lets you practise for those game situations when you have to stop or start suddenly. Start in the middle of the square, run to a corner, backpedal back to middle, and go to another corner. Do this with all four corners. You can also sprint to the corner and sprint back to the middle or slide to the corner and slide back to the middle.

Drills for defending the ballcarrier

The following drills help you work on some of the skills discussed earlier in this chapter for defending the ballcarrier:

✔ **1-on-1 defensive progression:** This drill is best with the whole team broken into partners, one offensive and one defensive. The offensive players play token offence so that the defensive players can work on defending different situations.

1. While cross-checking, the defender leans on the ballcarrier and experiences what happens when the offensive player steps backs or rolls.

2. While stationary, the ballcarrier leans into the defender and rolls to try to beat the defender.

3. The ballcarrier just stands and lets the defender cross-check him, feeling what it is like to hit and fill the gap created by the hit.

4. The ballcarrier fakes one way with the defender reacting to catch up to the fake, and then the ballcarrier fakes the other way. This becomes a reaction drill for the defender.

5. The ballcarrier fakes a cut inside and then cuts outside and down. The defender hits and slides down to prevent ballcarrier from beating him on the outside.

6. The ballcarrier fakes an outside cut and cuts inside the floor. The defender hits and slides across the top of the floor to prevent the ballcarrier from getting an inside position to go to the net.

7. The ballcarrier runs down the outside of the floor, and then stops and rolls back into middle for a shot. Defender works on his footwork to stop him from coming back.

8. The ballcarrier fakes a shot, and cuts outside and back in. The defender should stay low, keeping his stick up to interfere with the shot, but not stick-check.

✔ **1-on-1 closing-out drill:** This drill is related to the attack step discussed earlier in this chapter under "Playing with your feet." Run this drill with a teammate or with the whole team. Partners are spaced 15 feet apart, and one partner passes to other and *closes out* hard on him, that is, he follows the pass to his partner and takes his defensive stance. (Remember to shuffle the last two steps as with the attack step.) Then he moves back to his original position, and the other partner with the ball passes and closes out on him.

✔ **1-on-1 steal-the-ball drill:** Two players go one-on-one against each other. The ballcarrier is trying to score, and the defender can only slash and wrap-around to get the ball from the ballcarrier.

✔ **2-on-1 fight-through-pick drill:** This drill uses three players: a defender, a ballcarrier, and another offensive player. The defender plays the ballcarrier while the second offensive player tries to set a pick on the defender. The drill is designed so that the defender can either step back or step up to work around the pick and get back to defending the ballcarrier. For one variation, use three offensive players with two trying to set picks for the ballcarrier, from either side or with double picks, and the defender has to fight through both.

Drills for defending other offensive players

The following drills help you work on some of the skills discussed earlier in this chapter for defending other offensive players:

✔ **2-on-1 denying man on ballside or off-ball side:** This drill uses three players: two offensive players and one defender. The defender covers one offensive player while the other tries to pass to his offensive teammate. Defender takes a closed stance, belly-to-belly, to deny one pass away. Deny the pass from the same side of the floor or from the opposite side of the floor.

✔ **1-on-1 multiple defensive teaching drill:** This progression drill works best with two coaches controlling the ball, and it stresses stance, positioning, and communication. When communicating, players should call out "cutter," "help right," or "pick right." The defender starts on the side, defending an offensive player without the ball; the coaches set up on opposite sides of the floor, one with the ball.

1. Positioned on the ballside, the defender denies the entry pass using a closed stance, close to the offensive player as he goes in and out to get in the clear for a pass from a coach or another teammate. Coach then throws a cross-floor pass to the other coach.

2. Switching to the off-ball side, the defender denies the cross-floor pass using an open stance, following the offensive player as he moves up and down the sidelines trying to get into the clear for a pass.

3. The offensive player tries to cut in front of the defender to the ball while the defender yells "cutter" and takes away the cut.

4. The offensive player circles the net and then fakes a cut in front of the defender before cutting backdoor, that is behind the defender; the defender yells "cutter," turns his back to the ball, and plays the cutter's stick hard with a slash.

5. After the cut, the offensive player circles the net and comes back to the cornerman's spot, all the time the defender playing between him and the ball.

6. On the off-ball side, the defender calls "help right" and helps on penetration by the coach or other teammate with the ball and makes a quick recovery back to his check.

7. On the recovery following the help, the defender closes out on the pass back to his check by the coach.

8. Bring another offensive player into the drill, starting him in the crease before moving to set an *up pick,* where the offensive player picks the defender from behind, between the net and the defender.

9. The defender steps back and plays the picker as he rolls or slides down to the net for a pass.

10. The ballcarrier cuts outside down the sidelines while the picker runs back to the top for a return pass from the ballcarrier, who is now in the crease area.

11. The defender defends the *cross pick-and-roll* on the ball by stepping back and playing the picker rolling to the net while the ballcarrier makes a cut across the top to pass down to the picker.

12. The picker after his cut to the net goes to the crease position to receive a down pass and the defender defends a *down pick-and-roll* by stepping back on the pick and switching to the picker.

13. Another defensive player calls out "pick right" and the ballcarrier comes out of the pick and then runs the ball back down into the corner area while the defender follows his check to the top.

14. The defender is now in the top area and his check is going to set a screen for the ballcarrier in the corner area. The defender fights off the screen to get position between his check and the ball. When the ballcarrier comes off the screen, the defender comes out from the side or goes around the screen and comes out on the net side to switch and check him.

15. The defender is now on the ballcarrier who backpedals to the top to finally go one-on-one.

Chapter 11

Goaltending

· ·

In This Chapter

▶ Assessing who has the right stuff

▶ Picking up the goaltending basics

▶ Making saves

▶ Starting the offence

· ·

*T*he most important task of a lacrosse goalie is to stop the ball from getting into the net. How to do that — by moving in front of the shot, which is the *reflex* part of goaltending, or by moving out on the crease so that the ball hits him, which is the *angling* part of goaltending — is what this chapter is all about.

Unfortunately, many parents and coaches leave goaltenders on their own to learn how to play the position through trial and error. Practice sessions in which the goaltender is simply someone to shoot at rather than a vital team member who needs coaching also don't help.

Fortunately, this chapter does not share that attitude. In fact, here you have the privilege of reading tips and tricks from three of the top goaltenders in the National Lacrosse League. They are sure to answer your questions about goaltending.

Recognizing Who Can Play in Goal

No doubt about it, goaltender is *the* glamour position in hockey or soccer. Unless you have the charisma (and goal-scoring ability) of a Mario Lemieux or a Wayne Gretzky, you're not likely to get too many endorsement opportunities from the left wing. (And forget about it completely if you're a defenceman.)

One of the primary reasons why goalies get all the ink is that they have many opportunities to put up some impressive numbers, such as stops, shutouts, and wins. Curtis Joseph wouldn't get too many Vector commercials if his game headlines regularly read something like "Joseph Still Hot: Habs Score 14."

Allowing 14 goals is an everyday occurrence for a lacrosse goalie. So to be a successful lacrosse goalie, you need to recognize that you're going to get scored on.

Scoring leads to improvement

Bob Watson, goaltender for the Toronto Rock of the NLL, believes that a key quality for a goaltender is to remain confident and focused because in lacrosse there are no shutouts. You will be scored upon, so don't get too high and don't get too low. When scored upon, analyze how your opponent scored, learn from it so that you can minimize the chances of it happening again, and then forget about it.

For example, a few goals scored against you by a particular opponent can sure motivate you to get to know a little bit more about that player's shooting tendencies. When a player scores a handful of goals against you in a particular game, analyze where he liked to shoot from, what types of shots he preferred, whether he shot in the open floor or from behind a screen. This kind of analysis will improve your chances against the same player the next time you meet him.

After this analysis, forget about it. Don't forget about your analysis or how you've improved your game because of it; forget about the fact that he beat you for a handful of goals.

Staying focused

The other primary quality that a good lacrosse goalie should have is an ability to stay focused during a game. Admit it, your mind has a tendency to wander no matter what you may be doing. It's a job in itself to keep yourself mentally in the game at all times, whether your game is lacrosse or beach volleyball. (Insert your own bikini-related joke here.)

Being a lacrosse goalie doesn't reward a wandering mind. You have to keep your eye on the ball no matter how many offensive players run in front of you, how many picks and screens take place off to your side, or how many cheerleaders are on the sidelines waiting to dash onto the floor at the next break in play. (Insert your own pompom-related joke here.)

Who wants it bad enough

As a coach, picking a goalie can sometimes be very easy; you may have one young player who wants to do nothing but play goal. Or you may have a standout player who is made for the position. He just loves to stand in the net and let the ball hit him where it will. He is fearless of the ball, he is quick with his body at getting in front of shots, and he can handle the goalie stick well enough to pass the ball.

But what if there isn't anybody who wants to play goal? Then your best bet as a coach is to rotate each player on your team, say, by his number, to play in the net. But regardless of whom you get to play in goal, improvement comes from hard work and practice, not from game-situation trial and error.

Bob Watson, with whom the Toronto Rock has won three NLL championships in four years and who has been selected to the NLL all-star team four times, says about becoming a better goaltender: "To improve my ball handling when I was younger, I spent a lot of time with my stick passing with my friends or finding a wall and passing against it. To improve my stopping ability, I would get my dad or somebody to take a video of my performance and then I would diagnose my stance and angles. And finally I watched a lot of different-style goalies and learned from them."

The Basics of Goaltending

The following list offers a complete starting point for a review of the basics of goaltending, all of which will be discussed in greater detail in this section.

- ✔ Stay in your ready stance for the shot.
- ✔ Start all movement from the centre of the net on the goal line.
- ✔ Follow the ball, using your eyes and your body.
- ✔ Move out at least one step to challenge the shooter.
- ✔ Keep your stick on the floor even when moving.
- ✔ Wait out any fake.

Where it all starts: The ready stance

As a goalie, you have to take a stance, the *ready stance*. You have to be balanced and relaxed so that you are ready to react quickly forward, backward, and sideways. Take a crouching position with your knees bent, back straight, and shoulders and chest square to the ball, that is, with your body on the goal line facing the ball. Your feet should be shoulder-width apart; your body weight should be on the balls of your feet. Hold the stick between and in front of your feet, maintaining a firm grip on your stick to have control over the stick so that it doesn't turn in your hand (see Figure 11-1).

Figure 11-1:
Assuming the position — the ready stance — in goal.

The goalposts can become part of your stance as well, providing a reference point for where to place your body in goal. Start all movement from a centring position where you stand on the goal line and grab both goalposts.

Stay centred

This tip is pretty basic; position yourself on the goal line in the centre of the net, that is, between the goalposts. In fact, Bob Watson of the Toronto Rock makes it a practice to grab a goalpost with each hand. This position gives him the best flexibility to move his body with the ball.

Follow the ball

Because your primary task as goalie is to allow as few balls as possible into the net, you need to make every effort to know where the ball is at all times, even when it's behind you (see Figure 11-2). This involves more than just that age-old expression, keeping your eye on the ball. You need to follow the ball with your body as well.

You do, of course, need to keep your eye on the ball — well, both of them, actually — following it around the playing area. And you not only want to follow the ball on a shot on goal but also as it's passed around from player to

Figure 11-2:
Watching the action behind the net.

player. And, of course, says all-star goaltender Dallas Eliuk of the Philadelphia Wings, "To stop a shooter you have to focus on the ball and only the ball."

Following the ball with your body involves moving your body when the ball moves, keeping it square to the ball in the shooter's stick. When the ball swings to your right side, swing your body to the right, keeping it parallel between the ball and the net.

You should begin the following progression drill, designed to help you improve your lateral motion in the crease, without a stick so that you use your body to stop shots:

- Players form a semicircle and shoot for the far top corner of the net. Shooters should start firing shots at 50 percent strength and work up to 75 percent.

- From the same semicircle, players alternate shots to any target at the net. Players should fire shots from alternate ends of the semicircle.

- Re-run the same drills, but this time, you get to use your stick in the crease.

Challenge the shooter

Move out one or two steps from the goal line to challenge the shooter. You're not likely to be a successful goalie if you're looking at the position as one of comfort, waiting around for the occasional shot. Playing in goal requires you to challenge the shooter so that he is more likely to rush a shot and send it off-line or decide not to shoot at all.

Moving out depends on how far away the shooter is, who is shooting, and how big the goalie is. You have to test your positioning to find out the perfect spot that reduces your opponent's shooting area. Generally, though, three steps out, or at the top of the crease, is a bit much, unless the shooter is way out and definitely shooting. If you're that far out in the crease and the shooter fakes a shot, he can easily attack and put the ball over your shoulder.

The biggest problem for goaltenders is getting caught moving out when the shot is taken. When you move out, you cannot move laterally. And if the shooter picks his shot, he will score. When you do step out, remember that recovery is just as important as coming out. As the ball moves from side to side, shuffle your feet by taking small sidesteps and keep your stick on the floor. If the ball is passed down low in the zone, retreat by stepping back and to the post. If the ball is passed up high, step out to challenge.

Challenging long shots

As you can tell, challenging the shooter is an especially good strategy against long shots. Bob Watson of the Toronto Rock says about stopping long-ball shooters cutting across in front of the net: "I step out, stay square to the shooter's stick, and just follow him across in front of the net with small side-steps in my ready stance. My concern on stepping out is my recovery in case the shooter tries to get in closer to the net."

Gee Nash of the New York Saints also uses this strategy on stopping long shots: "On long shots, I try and step out about two feet from the goal line so that I can cut down the shooter's angle as well as protect against a quick pass to the crease. At two feet out, I can still recover in time if the shot is faked."

As you work on your goaltending skills, try to keep in mind how many steps it will take you to get back into your net or get to the post.

Drills for stopping long-ball shots

You can run these drills for three distinct save styles: the goalie steps to the ball, the goalie stays back in his net for reflexive saves, or the goalie takes a step out for the angle saves.

✔ Players take controlled shots so that the goalie can work on his technique and positioning.

✔ Players take rapid-fire shots so that the goalie can work on his reflexes and quickness.

✔ Coach calls out, at random, the types of shots for players to take:

- Long, top-corner shots

- Long, bottom-corner shots

- Long shots directed at mid-waist area of body

- Long bounce shots for top corner

- Long bounce shots for mid-waist area of body

- Close-in shots, no fake

- Close-in shots with one strong fake

Challenging the breakaway

The step-out can be a good strategy for goalies in defending against the breakaway, that is, when an offensive player breaks away from the rest of the players on the floor and anticipates a one-on-one opportunity against the goalie.

Gee Nash of the New York Saints says: "On a breakaway, I usually step back to the goal line and get set up in my net. From there, I take about a step out, but no more than one step because any more than one step and a shooter can put the ball over the goalie. I try not to stay flat-footed and I am on the balls on my feet so that I can react to a fake and make a save."

Bob Watson comments on stopping breakaways: "I start at the goal line and centre set. I take one step out to challenge the shooter. As the ballcarrier attacks, I move backward. I know patience is the key, so I let him make the first move, but I hold my ground. I feel the toughest save to make, especially on a breakaway, is the over-the-shoulder shot.

Keep your stick low

Stick saves are critical to a goaltender's success, so how you position the stick is also critical, especially against long, low shots. Earlier in this chapter, I discuss how the stick position is part of the goaltender's ready stance — low, between and in front of your feet. And the stick should stay low as you move your body to follow the ball.

Gee Nash of the New York Saints urges young goalies to follow his experience and concentrate on stick saves when practising: "And on the low shots, I take round after round and try and catch the lower shots in my stick."

Tending the field goal

Larger goals and less body padding in field lacrosse translate into a different technique for goalies. With so much more space to cover in goal (6 by 6 feet), sticks become the most important tool to make saves. As a result, goalies wear less padding (chest protectors and throat guards are the only extra equipment not worn by the rest of the players on the field). They also use their sticks differently — field goalies stand with the head of the stick upright, as opposed to the box style of keeping the head on the floor.

Despite the larger size of the goals, field lacrosse generally has less scoring. Scores average around 20 goals combined per game, while impressive save percentages for NCAA goalies average in the mid-60s. Shutouts are rare, but not impossible. Impressive one-game save totals in field lacrosse stand at around 25, as opposed to the 50-some marks posted in box lacrosse. One-on-none breakaways are almost unheard of, but goalies frequently find themselves on their own with shooters who beat their defenders and get open in front of the goal. They also have to deal with players buzzing around behind the net, with 15 yards between the goal and the endline. This space serves as the area through which much of a team's offence flows, and goalies have to actually turn completely around so that they face the goal to watch the ball. When the ball swings to the front, it is generally best for a field goalie to take a couple extra steps out to slice a shooter's angle.

In addition to bigger goals, field goalies have to negotiate a larger area when clearing the ball — once possession is gained, a team has ten seconds to advance past the restraining line (35 yards from the endline) and out of its defensive end. Attackmen do not sprint away once possession is lost. They stick around to help scramble a goalie's effort to clear the ball out of the defensive end. This means that goalies need to be athletic enough to run around and coordinated enough to handle the ball in the open field.

The following drills are designed to help you work on your stick saves:

- **Drills for long low shots:** A semicircle of shooters shoots long low shots. Focus on moving the stick to the ball with your body backing up the stick.

- **Drills for mid-waist area shots:** Use your stick only to stop shots. Form a semicircle and shoot mid-waist area shots.

- **Drill for bounce shots:** Use your stick only to stop shots. Form a semicircle and shoot bounce shots to any target in the net.

Don't bite on the fake

As a goaltender, you're sure to see your share of stick fakes. In fact, you're likely to see stick fakes of stick fakes, before yet another stick fake that leads to a shot. The idea, of course, is that the shooter wants you to move in one direction to block a shot that he fakes so that he can score on a shot the other way. Not only does a successful stick fake lead to a goal for the other team but it can also make even the best goalies look a little silly.

Basically, the only tip that is helpful to protect against the fake is to practise patience. If you can wait out a shooter's stick fakes, you're more likely to be able to react effectively against the shooter's actual shot. Actual practice may not help against stick fakes as much as knowing your opponents' tendencies. Knowing which shooters are more likely to try a stick fake, and which shooters are more likely to just shoot away, will help you be the most effective against stick fakes.

Bob Watson of the Toronto Rock says about playing the stick fake: "When a goalie sees a stick fake, you must stay square to the shooter's stick and rely on your angles. You must have patience and not overreact; let the shooter make the first move. Do not react to the first fake but wait out the shooter. Many shooters have problems when a goalie does not do what they think he is going to do, that is, react to the fake. Knowing the type of shooters you are playing against will also help you anticipate their moves."

Making the Reflex Save

The reflexive part of goaltending relies on your athletic ability to get your body in front of shots. No matter how much you're able to cut down on the angle that a shooter may have on goal, you still have to move laterally or step sideways to make saves, whether it's with your body, your stick, your leg, or even your arm.

- ✔ **Using your body to make saves:** Most saves in lacrosse are made with the upper body. The rule of thumb is to try and stop all high shots in the centre of your chest, and if you can't get your chest in front of a shot, then use your shoulders to take away top corner shots. You should try to maintain a straight line between the ball and the net.

Beginning goalies have a tendency to turn their body on a shot so that the ball hits their side or their back. A coach should build confidence by using tennis balls in shooting drills so that goalies know that they can't get hurt and are well protected.

- ✔ **Using your stick to make saves:** Use the goalie stick to stop long low shots, that is, all shots below the waist on both sides of the body. The stick starts between the legs, but on a low shot, it is moved to the side to catch the ball.
- ✔ **Using your legs for making saves:** The legs are a backup to stick saves. Sometimes you just can't get to the ball with your stick, so you use your leg to kick the ball away.

Making the Angle Save

The angle part of goaltending involves getting good body positioning, being in the right place at the right time, stepping out, and cutting down with the body some of the open areas of the net to shoot at. As a goalie, you want to be out and set in a ready stance before the shot is taken. You have to know how to play angles to stop shots and thereby be a good goalie.

All-star goaltender Dallas Eliuk of the Philadelphia Wings says about angling: "On a good defensive team, a goalie can take an extra half- to full-step out to cut down on the amount of net to shoot at. But on a weaker defensive team, it's best for the goalie to stay close to his goal line so that he doesn't have to scramble to follow a cross-floor pass or a quick pass to the crease for a quick-stick shot. Also by staying on his goal line, it gives the goalie a longer look at the ball from a long shot and more time to react."

Here are a few drills to help you develop your angle-save skills:

- ✔ Form a triangle with a rope attached to you and to both posts. You must learn to stay in the centre of the posts — that is, stay in the middle of the net.

- ✔ Find an ideal spot against shooter. Shooter takes a position within good scoring range and shoots at the goalie. If he scores, he tells the goalie to move slightly over as he is giving too much to shoot at.

- ✔ Five players spread out on the floor just to pass ball the around quickly and shoot quickly and randomly.

The Goalie on Offence

The goaltender plays a key role in a team's offence, primarily by starting the offence following a stopped shot. A crisp accurate — sometimes breakaway — pass can set the offence off on a good start. The goalie has only five seconds once receiving the ball in the crease before he has to get rid of it.

Gee Nash of the New York Saints second-team all-star goalie talks about his ability as a goaltender: "My strength as a goaltender would be my ability to get the fast break started with a quick release from my goal crease to a player up the floor in order to get into the offensive end."

Goaltending tips from the pros

Dallas Eliuk of the Philadelphia Wings talks about visualization: "I visualize before each game, whether it be the night before or on the way to the arena. I pre-play the game and visualize each player approaching the net shooting from the outside and doing what he does best. I, in turn, see myself making those saves, controlling rebounds, and jump-starting the fast break. So when the whistle is blown and the ball is dropped in the real game, I've already faced this team and beaten them. I find this technique helps build my confidence and concentration."

Gee Nash of the New York Saints talks about ball handling: "A minor goalie can improve his ball-handling ability very easily by having a ball in his stick at all times during practice when there are no shots being taken. Aim for spots on the net or the boards when the play is in the other end in practice. Another way is that when goalies are doing passing drills in practice, always have the players running at game speed so there is no adjusting period for the goalie once the game begins. All in all, PRACTISE! PRACTISE! PRACTISE!"

Dallas Eliuk talks about screen shots: "More and more today there are screen shots. In fact, most outside shots are scored these days from screen shots where a shooter shoots around a defender. So a goaltender must stay alert and be ready for any type of shot: shooters are shooting around and over players more and they catch and shoot with a quick release where there is no wind-up."

Gee Nash talks about goaltending fundamentals: "A minor goalie can improve his stopping ability by always practising the basics. If they have trouble in a certain spot on the net then take a round of shots to that area until it becomes an easy save. Go back to the basics; use tennis balls if a goalie is scared of the ball at the beginning. Also make sure the goalie is well padded to prevent injury, which will enhance his stopping ability and his confidence of not getting hurt. Coaches should always make time in practice to work with their goaltenders."

Bob Watson of the Toronto Rock talks about getting mentally ready to play: "After the last warm-up, I take several deep breaths to relax myself; when totally relaxed, I visualize myself making saves, controlling rebounds, and making good passes. It is important that I keep all my thoughts positive, which is sometimes easier said than done."

Gee Nash talks about saves with the body and stick: "When I was young, in order to make myself a better goalie, I used to practise when I was not with my team. I practised five times a week with my team and would work with my stick every day after scheduled practice. For top-corner shots, I would take round after round of shots to the corners and I practised my lateral movement from side to side.

Dallas Eliuk talks about padding: "I feel wearing too much padding hinders a goaltender's movement, ultimately hindering one's development."

Gee Nash talks about the toughest saves: "The toughest save to make in the NLL is probably when the opposing team is on the power play and the pointman on the top of the power play looks as though he is going to shoot and then passes down to the opposite crease. It is tough because I am already committed to his long shot and I have to react fast to the opposite side of the net and I know there is at least one less person on defence to knock it down due to the penalty. But it feels great when I am able to make this type of save."

All-star goaltender Dallas Eliuk of the Philadelphia Wings comments on passing: "The ability to pass accurately and quickly in the NLL is important for a goaltender. But don't sacrifice ball possession with an ill-advised breakaway pass. Too often goaltenders try to throw the 'Hail Mary' pass or 'Hope' pass more often than not where the breaking player is covered. If the pass is missed, the opposition has another 30 seconds of possession."

Chapter 12

Practising Team Offence and Defence

• •

• •

A game that involves five players plus a goaltender on each side of the ball requires team cooperation. Successful lacrosse teams work together, each individual player displaying his or her greatest skills within the structure of the team's offence or defence.

All offensive and defensive systems are team systems, and I discuss the specifics of these systems — that is, the way teams play the game, either offensively or defensively — in Chapters 14 and 15. This chapter sets the foundation for understanding how a team works together so that it can successfully run its offensive and defensive systems.

How the Players Fit In: Roles and Positions in Team Offences and Defences

The offence is made up of two creasemen, two cornerman, and a pointman. The two creasemen start play low in the corner area of the floor. One creaseman is a right-shot who plays on the left side of the floor, and the other creaseman is a left-shot who plays on the right side of the floor. Now, this may sound complicated, but think of it this way: in lacrosse, players play with their sticks facing into the middle of the floor. Thus, a left-shot player on the right side of the floor has his stick positioned closest to the centre of the floor, and closer to the goal. This positioning also allows left-shot players to turn their body sideways to take the hits, slashes, and cross-checks to protect the ball in their stick.

The two cornermen, a right-shot and a left-shot, play above and behind the creasemen. They may start from this position, but they could end up anywhere on the floor really, depending on the flow of the offence and where their teammates are on the floor. Their best bet is to stay on their own side of the floor so that they can always be an instant threat to shoot when receiving the ball.

The pointman's position can be either behind the cornerman on his proper side of the floor or in the middle of the floor. He can start in the middle, but after the passing and cutting begins, he can cut, pick, or stay where he is for a return pass.

Lacrosse is not an equal opportunity game. Players must know their roles (passer, scorer, picker, screener, loose-ball player). If a player wants to shoot in a game, he must prove in practice that he can score with at least 25 percent of his shots.

The creaseman's role

The creaseman is like a forward or a winger in hockey or soccer. He tries to get out in front of the fast break and get down the floor as quickly as he can. He positions himself at the crease until any possibility of a fast break or odd-man situation has been eliminated. When the break is over, he now has the option of staying low on the offence or coming up and setting a pick against the cornerman's defender. He is usually one of the fastest players on the team.

On any missed shot, the creaseman's job is to go after the loose ball if he has a chance to get it. If he can't get it, he can delay the opposition's break by pressing the ballcarrier or trying to steal the ball from him. Or he can go to the bench if he is in a system that replaces offensive and defensive players on the fly, that is, an *offence–defence* system.

The creaseman scores on a breakaway after obtaining a loose ball while on defence in the defensive zone, from a pass from a teammate, or from a long breakaway pass from the goalie. The creaseman must be able to get down the floor very quickly either from the bench or out of the defence. Therefore, he must have a great ability to catch the ball while running down the floor at top speed. He must also have great ability to score on the run, either straight on at the goalie or cutting across close to the crease. Finally, he must be able to run plays such as the pick-and-roll and then have the ability to catch the ball in traffic and score in tight.

The role of the creaseman is quite different in field lacrosse than in box lacrosse. Creasemen in the field game (also called attackmen) are the most stationary players on the field, planting themselves in front of the crease and simply dunking home feeds. Size is a creaseman's greatest attribute in field lacrosse, with speed probably the least important.

The cornerman's role

The cornerman is usually the quarterback-type player who starts the offence and handles the ball while on offence, that is, he's the player you want to play through. He starts at the top of the offence and is always a threat to shoot long or go one-on-one. He is a great long-ball shooter, yet can cut inside and score. His options, if he doesn't shoot or go one-on-one, are to wait for a pick by a creaseman, to pass off and cut for a return pass, to hang back at the top of the offence for a return pass, or to set a pick for a teammate. He also is designated as the defensive safety on any shot at the net, either going all the way back to protect his own net or running to the bench to get a defensive player on the floor.

The pointman's role

The pointman's role is similar to a cornerman's role except that whichever side he is on becomes the strong side of the offence, that is, the side with three offensive players. A good pointman is always a threat to score and he knows which of his teammates has the best chance of scoring should he pass the ball. He can also pass off and clear out to the opposite side of his pass or he can pass to a cornerman and run a pick-and-roll with him. Finally, he should have great anticipation as to when to get back on defence.

Practising a Team Offensive Philosophy

The primary objective of an offensive team is to score. The score can come from defensive pressure, defensive steals, defensive hitting, loose balls, fast breaks, breaks off the bench, or from a set offence. It really doesn't matter, as long as the team scores.

A secondary objective for an offensive team is to keep itself in position to defend against the abrupt change of possession. These objectives are discussed in this section.

Know the playing lanes

The lacrosse floor has three playing lanes: the two outside lanes and the middle lane. Within these lanes, each offensive player has certain limitations. For example, the cornerman should not run the ball up the middle lane, but rather stay in the outside lane near the middle lane. Generally, players shouldn't stand in the middle of the zone on offence, leaving it open for long shots from the point or cuts inside to receive a pass.

Keep it simple

In general, a team should try to run a very simple offensive system. Try to avoid fancy and complex plays, instead running with simple concepts that do not take much time to set up.

Keep things fundamentally sound. Remember that the key is not what you do but how you do it. Make good crisp passes. Constantly run the floor to keep your opponents moving. Know your teammates' tendencies. Keep moving — with and without the ball.

Good execution and timing on your plays comes from skill with sound fundamentals. The two best things a player can offer on offence is a perfect pass and help to set a teammate in the clear with a pick or screen.

Balance freedom and structure

Freedom to move with the ball is an effective tool in lacrosse. It often can lead to a one-on-one scoring opportunity. However, it can also lead to selfish play and grandstanding, keeping other offensive players out of the flow of a game.

Try to maintain a balance by allowing appropriate freedom within a structured or disciplined system. You may want to set goals so that your team aims for 50 percent one-on-one plays and 50 percent team play.

Giving players too much individual freedom usually means that lacrosse is being played out of control. You want to be aggressive on offence, but with patience and control. You want to keep moving and cutting rather than constantly forcing plays and shots. Constant movement not only leads to more open scoring opportunities but also wears down the defenders.

Attack! Attack!

Attack the opposition and keep them off-balance before they get a chance to attack you. Any offensive action will get a defensive reaction; by attacking on offence, you're more likely to be facing a defence that is a split second behind you. And attack the defence from all points on the floor.

An aggressive offence is usually going to be met with an aggressive defence. You'll be taking shots both from around the perimeter and from the middle of the floor. You'll have defensive players coming at you from all angles. You cannot be afraid to get hit. And you *will* be hit, especially when you cut into the middle lane, the prime scoring area. Because the bottom line on offence is to get the ball in the middle of the defence, you're going to see aggressiveness right back at you from that defensive middle trying to protect its goal.

Focus on good shot selection

It stands to reason that if the primary objective of an offence is to score, then the number one way to achieve that objective is to maintain a high shooting percentage. Players must know what a great shot is! To get high percentage shots requires having discipline when taking shots, which reflects a team attitude.

- ✔ Do not show off or be selfish with the ball when shooting.

- ✔ Pass up a so-so shot and pass to a teammate who has a better shot.

- ✔ Shoot smartly. If the goalie is not giving you anything to shoot at, shoot at the top corners or bounce a shot at him to try to mix him up.

- ✔ Get the goalie to move. Cut across the floor and then shoot back. Make a lot of cross-floor passes to keep him moving. Or just take bounce shots beside his legs.

- ✔ Take only good shots, in your range and on your own side of the floor.

Your shooting rule should be that you cannot shoot when an opponent's stick or body is in front of your shot. The exception is when the defender backs off from the shooter, so that you can use him for a screen shot. (For more on shooting fundamentals, see Chapter 9.)

Practising a field offensive philosophy

With more space to work with, one-on-one play in field lacrosse serves as more of a starting point for offences than in the box game. And that translates into more of an emphasis on team offence and defence. More often than not, field lacrosse funnels into a six-on-six game in the offensive attack area, making it similar to basketball. The player with the ball tries to dodge by his man, draw a slide from another defender (when a defender leaves his cover for another player), and then find an open teammate. This serves as the beginning of most offensive plays — teams employ a host of different sets involving more than two or three players. Offensive possessions are generally longer and more calculated, with more set-up and coordination. It is rarer in field lacrosse than it is in box for a player to take a shot without beating his defender.

REMEMBER

Offensive mistakes that drive coaches crazy

Help your coach avoid premature greying by staying away from some of the following offensive no-nos:

- **Poor ball handling:** Remember that opponents are always stick-checking, trying to steal the ball. A ballcarrier's highest priority is to protect the ball at all times.

- **Unforced turnovers:** Losing the ball when not under pressure, badly thrown passes, or dropped passes are equally maddening. Take care with passing and catching.

- **Too much passing:** Some players spend too much time looking to make the perfect pretty pass rather than looking to go one-on-one to beat their defender or looking to shoot. As long as their shooting percentage is good, the greatest players are those who are known for their ability to beat a defender and score, not so much their ability to pass and get assists. Now don't get me wrong here. Seeing the floor and the ability to make a perfect pass into a teammate's stick for a score is naturally important, but it's secondary to scoring in a team's offensive weaponry.

- **Unable to set a pick:** In this day and age, players have to know how to set a pick on a pick-and-roll as well as how to come off a pick. This play is so effective in a team's offensive scheme that it has to be an automatic play between two teammates. The most common mistake is to come off the pick looking to pass rather than looking to shoot. The play is designed to free up an offensive player for a clear shot on goal.

- **Know your cuts:** Successful offensive systems require precise timing (see Chapter 14). Some players don't have the proper timing on their cuts, either cutting too early, when the ballcarrier is not ready to pass, or being cross-checked out of a cutting opportunity. Keep working to make cuts happen, to collapse the defence, and to just wear the defenders out.

- **Get back on turnovers:** Another major area that drives coaches crazy is when a team is scored upon during a breakaway. Players have to know who the defensive safety is when they go on the floor. On any shot, players need to be ready to react back down the floor to take away the breakaway, rather than admiring the shot.

The most popular offensive formations in field lacrosse are the 1-3-2 (with one player behind the net) and the 2-2-2 (putting two players in front of the crease). Another set, the *invert,* is becoming more popular, especially against teams with dominant *long sticks* (defencemen). Inverting means teams switch and move their *middies* (midfielders) behind the goal and push the attackmen out in front. This forces the long sticks, who most often defend the attackmen, out in front of the goal and away from the area where most of the offence is created. Because long sticks are so much tougher to play against (due to the length of the stick and the fact that all they play is defence), a large part of offence in field lacrosse involves trying to move around so that the player with the ball is going against a player with a short stick.

Building the Team Offence through Drills

This section suggests a few drills that your team can practise to help establish a team attitude when on offence.

- ✔ **1-on-1 offence multiple drill:** The player with a ball and being defended executes a give-and-go play by passing to the coach and cutting for a return pass and shot. The same player then goes back to his proper side of the floor and with the next set of partners sets an up pick-and-roll and because he is the picker, he rolls to the net for a pass and shot. The same player then comes back and sets a cross pick-and-roll with the same set of partners and again because he is the picker he rolls to the net for a pass and shot. This time he remains in the corner area to receive a down pass by the ballcarrier and a down pick.

- ✔ **1-on-4 "clog-the-middle" cutting drill:** You have a passer on one side of the floor. All the cutters are on the other side of the floor. Put four defenders in the middle of the floor to clog it up. The cutters, one at a time, cut through the middle of the floor for a pass but must dodge around the defenders who push the cutter with football-blocking dummies, with their hands, or with their sticks held upside down.

- ✔ **2-on-1 give-and-go and go drill:** Form two lines, one offence and the other defence, on the side of the floor. In the first option, the first ballcarrier makes a cross-floor pass to a lone passer on the opposite side and then cuts to the ball. The defender denies or tries to stop him from cutting with a slash and then lets him go for a pass and shot. For the second option, the next defender denies or tries to stop him from cutting and once he cuts, the defender cross-checks him across the floor as he cuts to the ball for a pass and shot. The cutter cuts in front of the defender who plays token defence. The passer must pass to the cutter while the defender is pushing on him. The final option is the cutter cuts backdoor behind the defender. Teach the cutter to relax on receiving a pass on a cut and to hold his stick ready to receive a pass. How to get in the clear? The cutter can cut instantly or he can take the defender down the side of the floor and then cuts hard to ball.

- ✔ **2-on-2 pick-and-roll on the ball drills:** Stress to the ballcarrier coming off the pick to look to shoot right away or go one-on-one rather than just looking to pass to the picker. If the picker gets open right away, pass to him for a close-in shot. Don't make flat passes to the roller; make it a short rainbow pass. If the switching defensive player fires out on the ballcarrier immediately, he goes the opposite way the pick is set and cuts backdoor. After the ballcarrier cuts outside the pick, some teams like to step or pop the picker back for the pass rather than rolling him to the net. Some players like to come up the floor and fake the up pick-and-roll and then quickly cut into the middle of the floor for a pass.

✔ **2-on-2 screen on the ball drill:** The cornerman passes down and sets a down screen for the creaseman on his side of the floor. He fights to get an inside position on the defender to stop him from switching. The man who sets the screen pops back after the cutter passes him for defensive safety.

✔ **3-on-3 pointman drills:** These are set plays for the pointman at the top of the offence. He usually starts the drill and initiates the offence at the top of the offence.

- **3-on-3 pointman cross pick-and-roll on the off-ball side drill:** Pointman passes to either cornerman and runs to the opposite side and sets a cross pick-and-roll for the other cornerman.

- **3-on-3 pointman down pick-and-roll drill:** Pointman passes to the cornerman and runs a down pick for the cornerman on the opposite side of the floor. Creaseman on that side of the floor just stays on the crease.

- **3-on-3 pointman give-and-go drill:** Pointman passes to either cornerman and cuts for return pass down the middle.

- **5-on-5 pointman double drill:** Pointman passes to cornerman who passes to creaseman and they both set a double screen for the creaseman. On the double screen, the top screener reads the play and comes back on defence.

✔ **3-on-3 defensive safety drill (full-floor):** The drill consists of three lines. Two of the lines play 3-on-3 live at one end; on the shot, two defenders stay on floor while one defender runs to bench for a cheater off the bench. The three former offensive players react back accordingly. The new offensive team gets one shot. After a shot by the new offensive team, the play is over. Now the new offensive team brings the ball up against a new defensive team.

Practising a Team Defensive Philosophy

A good defence stresses a team concept, that is, five defensive players playing as one. A team-oriented defensive system helps players perform as one. Players are able to anticipate the movements of their teammates. In this kind of team-focused and disciplined system, players are more likely to be where they're supposed to be and doing what they're supposed to do, rather than freelancing wherever the action is.

Within this defensive system, your team is trying to take away the strength of your opponent. Rules on defence can improve your chances of success, but against certain teams, your system needs to be flexible enough to make adjustments during the game.

> ## Team defence in the field game
>
> A key to playing defence in field lacrosse is using space as a buffer with the offensive player. Overly aggressive defencemen are easily burned. With no walls, you need to try to force the player with the ball away from his strong hand. For example, if a player is right-handed, force him so that he is going left, even if that's toward the goal. Sliding (that is, picking up the open man) is the most important part of team defence in field lacrosse. Slide packages can be complex, involving more than two players.
>
> With long sticks looming at the other end, it's uncommon for a field goalie to simply launch a clearing pass downfield. Clears are more deliberate, involving multiple steps as defencemen move the ball out of the defensive area past pressuring attackmen. Goalies need to communicate with their defencemen where the attackmen are and how to move the ball up the field.

A solid team defensive philosophy centres around placing your most talented defensive players in key positions, matched up with key personnel. For example, you may logically want to have your faster defensive players at the top of the defence, ready to switch down to help out as quickly as possible. But you also need to consider matching up your quick defenders with the opposition's quick offensive players to stop them from scoring, as well as matching up by size, your big defenders with the opposition's big offensive players.

You should realize that defensive rules alone do not get the job done; knowing how to play defence alone does not get the job done. It is the force of the personalities of players and coaches that determines the quality and intensity of defence — that, and the guidelines discussed in this section.

Communicate on the floor

This is probably the most important rule for defence: Players must talk to each other on the floor. Communicating helps to get rid of any defensive indecision about who is guarding whom and, at the same time, builds team cohesion. Here are some of the things that you need to communicate while playing defence:

- Let your teammates know when you're defending a certain player; call out, "I've got number 4," when picking up a check.
- When an opponent shoots, call out, "Shot!" to let the other defenders know so that they can look to see what happens to the shot.

Defence is an attitude

The key to defence in box lacrosse is having the right defensive attitude: aggressive, mean, being physically tough, intimidating, irritating, and downright ticking people off. It may help you to think of defence as a stormy day with lightning and thunder. When picking up your check, give him a solid slash or cross-check as he comes into your defensive zone to let him know what kind of game he is going to be in for. Play this type of aggressive defence to get the ball, to run, and score. Set a goal to score at least 25 percent of your goals off solid defensive play.

To play good defence, a defensive player needs about 75 percent attitude and 25 percent skill. Attitude can make up for lack of skill. If you do get beaten because of weak technique, an aggressive attitude can still help you recover by pursuing the ballcarrier or cutter and preventing him from scoring.

✔ If you spot a loose ball, call out something like "Loose!" This call warns the rest of the defenders to look for it.

✔ When you gain possession of the ball, let your teammates know that it's time to switch from defensive to offensive mode. Call out something like "Ball!" to encourage the rest of the defenders to break for a breakaway or to run to the bench to let offensive players on the playing surface.

✔ When you move over to help out a teammate, let him know that you're there. Call out something like "You've got help left" to let your teammate know — usually the one who's defending the ballcarrier — that he really has help.

✔ Likewise, if you need help, such as on a pick or a defensive switch, seek it. Call out something like "Pick left" and then, if necessary, "Switch" or "Stay" depending on whether you're going to switch checks because of the pick.

The flow of the game will dictate many more opportunities for you to communicate on defence. Remember that in an effective defensive system, communication is just as important as playing ability. Constantly remind yourself to talk to your teammates during a game; in fact, make sure that you remind yourself out loud, not just inside your head. At least then your teammates will hear you say something! And remember to talk during practice sessions as well, which will only serve to help you remember to keep on talkin'.

Pressure the ballcarrier by cross-checking

It doesn't matter what style or type of defence you play, if you can't stop the ballcarrier, you're going to have a long season. Stopping the ballcarrier is the foundation behind all defences. So having the right technique is extremely important.

The basic defensive stance is taking what is called a *position of readiness,* which means staying down on your opponent by keeping your knees bent, staying balanced by taking a wide stance, keeping your back straight, and looking at the ballcarrier at his chest rather than at the ball or his stick. Your stick should be held at chest level with your arms bent ready to explode out at the ballcarrier.

Naturally, you want to be between the ball and the net to stop penetration, but your position should also *overplay* him, that is, keep your body slightly off-centre from your opponent, trying to force him to the boards or sideline.

In this position, you can best pressure the ballcarrier: be a pest, cross-check his body, and slash him on his stick; don't just wave your stick in the air to try to intercept a pass. Force the action; create defensive pressure — be the aggressor — to stop his movement toward the net. Remember that once you cross-check the ballcarrier, you really are pushing him away from you, creating a gap between you and the ballcarrier. If you do not quickly fill this gap by moving out on the ballcarrier, he will use you as a screen and shoot around you.

 In the NLL, players are always trying to get the ball off the ballcarrier by using a wraparound check, slashing, or poking, increasing their chances of being beaten or getting a penalty. Referees are unpredictable regarding the slash: at one point in a game, they will call it; at other times, they will let it go. So consider your chances and the consequences as you make your defensive moves.

Force the ball

Your team defensive strategy should be to force the action, that is, always be aggressive against the opponent so that you try to dictate where the ball is going rather than the offence dictating it. When you force the action, you force the ball; by playing an offensive player a certain way, you may be able to get him to pass to a less-skilled shooter or to shoot from an angle that's not his best shot. This section suggests some ways to force the ball from various points on the playing surface:

When the ball is at the top side of the zone

When the ballcarrier is at the top side of the offensive zone, play the ballcarrier straight up, that is, evenly between him and the net. This play gives him two options: pass to a cutter across the top or pass to a cutter to the outside of the floor. Your goal in forcing the ball in this situation is to take away the first option; the ballcarrier's strongest move is the pass to the cutter across the top for a shot.

A defensive strategy that forces the ballcarrier to the boards or to the sideline gives him only the second option, the weaker of the two. Once the ballcarrier is in an outside lane, try to keep him in the *alley,* the lane between the defender and the side of the offensive zone.

When the ball is halfway down the side of the floor

In this situation, you want to force the ball back into the middle, where the defensive help is. When the ballcarrier starts to move down the side alley, you should follow him to the halfway point in the alley. Before that point, you want to keep the ballcarrier in the outside lane; after that point, however, he's getting a little too close to the net for your comfort.

When the ballcarrier reaches that halfway point, you should force him — and the ball — back toward the middle of the floor, where your defensive teammates are. The defensive strategy here is to encourage the help to come from the top down, not from the bottom up. If the help comes from a defender closer to the net, his check will cut backdoor and make it easier for the ballcarrier to pass to him for a close-in shot.

When the ball is in the corner

When the ball is low in the corner area, you want to force the ballcarrier back into the middle; again, this is where your help is. If you're beaten to the outside when in the corner area, your defensive teammate will have to come over from the off-ball side to help with the ballcarrier, who now just passes across to his teammate for an easy goal.

Dan Stroup and Chris Gill, both with the Vancouver Ravens, love to cut outside around the crease and shoot to the far side of the net.

Defend picks: To switch or not to switch

In today's game in the NLL, players switch on almost every pick. Switching on defence means exchanging checking assignments with a teammate during the play of the game. Switching occurs when two offensive players come close to each other where one tries to interfere with the other's defender in order to force the defenders to switch defensive assignments. One reason why picks are used so much is that, if they work, they create a moment of indecision for the defence or they create a gap for the ballcarrier to shoot or go one-on-one.

The first thing you do, even before the picker gets to set the pick, is to stop him from setting the pick as he goes to set it. You can do this by cross-checking the picker and pushing him out of the way so that you don't get tied up with the picker. By getting tied up, you create a screen for the ballcarrier, which gives him a number of options, including moving toward the net for a more open shot or passing to an open teammate.

How to defend a pick? First, you must anticipate being picked before it occurs. The job of the defender on the picker is to verbally warn you that you're about to be picked by calling out "Pick left" or "Pick right." Then you can jump out hard at the ballcarrier, rather than waiting for him to come to you. Or if you do get picked, you can go to him hard to fill the gap created by the pick.

When you hear your teammate calling out an upcoming pick, you can neutralize the pick by stepping back and switching checking assignments with your teammate. It is important on this switch that you, as the defender on the ballcarrier, get on the inside position of your new check, that is, between your new check and the net, and play his body to prevent him from receiving the pass as he rolls to the net. If you can't get the inside position, you may try to hook the picker's stick under your arm or grab his sweater so that he can't get away. On second thought, this move is illegal, so I shouldn't recommend it. (Just don't get caught by the referee.)

If it is a poor pick, you don't need to switch with your teammate; you can instead stay with your own check by fighting or sliding through the pick and staying even with your opponent. In fact, when you get past the picker, you can show yourself to the ballcarrier at an angle to force him back to the boards. Be aware, though, that the ballcarrier may fake to go one way and then go the opposite way off the pick as an element of surprise.

If you don't switch, the defender on the picker should call "Stay" to let you know that you're not going to switch. He can even show himself to the ballcarrier while still staying with the picker just to slow the ballcarrier down and to help you out.

Defend screens on the ball side: To switch or not to switch, part 2

A screen takes place when the ballcarrier is in the corner area, and his teammate on the same side of the floor has set a screen by leaning on his check, clamping his stick over the defender's stick, and getting the inside position on the floor. The ballcarrier reads this play and tries to use this screen to "rub" off his defender.

To defend against the screen, the defender on the screener must stay between his check and the ball. He plays on the ball side, or top side, of the screener, clamping his stick over the screener's stick; he definitely does not stand behind

What's the difference between a screen and a pick?

A *screen* is when an offensive player ties up his own defender so that the ballcarrier can rub his defender out of the play.

A *pick* is when an offensive player cross-checks the ballcarrier's defender to set him in the clear.

the screener. Now if the ballcarrier beats you, as the defender, in the corner area and goes to the net, your teammate is in a position to leave his screener and stop the ballcarrier. But if the ballcarrier comes out of the corner to use the screen, your teammate (the one defending the screener) can move around behind the screener, to the other side, or even stay in the front, to get into a position to switch and jump out at the ballcarrier aggressively as he comes off the screen. When this happens, you can switch defensive assignments, going to the screener who may try to roll to the net.

If the ballcarrier coming out of the corner can't get close enough to the screen to rub his check out of the play, the defenders just stay with their checks.

Never let an offensive player hold your sweater when on defence. Either knock his hand down or cross-check his hand. Also, never get tied up on defence by pushing a player out of the way or by cross-checking a screener as it may put you out of any position to help.

Maintain floor position

When defending on the off-ball side of the defence, your defence should form a *flat triangle.* You're at the apex of the triangle (toward the centre lane), and the ballcarrier (up top) and your check (in the outside lane) form the base of the triangle (see Figure 12-1). It is called a flat triangle because you play off your check slightly and toward the ballcarrier to be in a position to help.

If you play a *deep triangle,* where you're closer to the net, with your check and the ballcarrier at about equal distances from you, you're protecting the net more than playing your check and watching the ballcarrier. In this situation, your check could cut very easily for a pass and shot. And in the flat triangle, you should always keep your opponent in front of you, never playing him even, or parallel to the net, as he could fake up and cut behind you for a quick pass and shot. If your opponent goes behind you on a backdoor cut, always assume that a pass is coming his way and turn and play his stick hard.

Solid team defence related to the position of the ball suggests that if your ballcarrier passes the ball, you should move to the level of the ball immediately

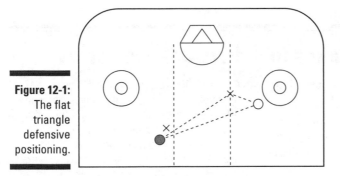

Figure 12-1:
The flat
triangle
defensive
positioning.

and then adjust your position according to your check. You're now in a position ready to collapse, help, and rotate, especially from the top of the defence.

The final rule for positioning is that the defence moves before the offence moves on any movement of the ball.

Building the Team Defence through Drills

This section suggests a few drills that your team can practise to help establish a team attitude when on defence.

- **2-on-1 defending the pick-and-roll on the ball:** In this drill, you can put the defender on the ballcarrier first to learn to step back when being picked, or to fight through the pick if it's a poor pick, before re-establishing pressure on the ball. Then, you can put the defender on the picker who must call out "Pick" to the imaginary defender and jump out on the ballcarrier. The next progression is to let the offensive player go one-on-one against the defender when he jumps out.

- **4-on-4 shell drill to teach defensive positioning:** This is a great drill to do during every defensive practice. First, get the offence to stay stationary and move the ball around. After the defenders have taken the proper position regarding their checks and the ball, the offensive players without the ball can move to get in the clear; the ballcarrier cannot move. Practise several scenarios with each drill, including moving with and without the ball, using and not using picks or screens, penetration or no penetration, and shot or no shot.

- **3-on-2 help-side defence drill:** Break the four-on-four drill down into a three-on-two situation. The ballcarrier tries to make a cross-floor pass to the two-on-two on the off-ball side with offensive players remaining stationary. Then the offensive players can interchange, move up and down the side, try to cut to the ball for a pass, and work a pick. The defenders work to defend against each offensive scenario.

Defensive mistakes that drive coaches crazy

Improve your team's defence by not making defensive blunders:

✔ **Pressure the ballcarrier:** It's really interesting as a coach that I am constantly asking players to pressure the ballcarrier. All they seem to want to do is stand in front of the ballcarrier and either just watch him or wave their sticks in front of his to delay a pass or look to intercept a pass. Instead, pressure with cross-checking and slashing, giving yourself the best chance to avoid getting beaten by the ballcarrier faking a pass or a shot, then cutting around you.

✔ **Defend the pick-and-roll:** All you have to do to defend the pick-and-roll is to warn your teammate that a pick is coming. Speak up! If you don't, both you and your teammate will end up trailing the cutter who is wide open for the pass.

✔ **Close to the net, defend in front of your opponent:** A basic offensive play is when an offensive player stands in the middle of the floor, in front of the net, waiting for a pass. Many defenders play behind him and try to cross-check him out of the way. However, the offensive player can just lean on his defender, equalizing the defensive pressure and putting himself in a "relaxed" position to catch the ball and turn to shoot. The best way to defend this situation is to play on the ballside of the opponent, clamping his stick with yours. This way you are in a position to help your teammate on the ballcarrier if he gets beaten, plus you can deny the pass to this offensive player very easily by just playing his stick with yours.

✔ **4-on-4 defending screens on the ball or off-ball drill:** Defending the off-ball screen, the top offensive player passes outside to a teammate, and then sets a screen for the bottom offensive player by tying up or getting inside position on his defender on the way down. The defender on the screener must be ready to switch onto the cutter coming off the screen. He does this by not getting tied up and fighting to get inside position on the screener so that he is in a position to fire out on the cutter.

You can also work this drill on the ballside of the floor with the ballcarrier passing down to the creaseman and then trying to set a screen on his defender as he looks for a phony return pass. The ballcarrier comes out of the corner area looking to use the screen. The defenders play the screen accordingly.

✔ **3-on-2 half-floor defensive drill:** A group of five players rotate in and out of the defence and offence. Two defenders try to stop three offensive players from scoring for ten seconds, or until they drop the ball. Give one group of two defenders five opportunities to stop the offence. This drill stresses aggressive and intense defensive play, communication on the floor, concentration and anticipation, helping out a teammate and recovering or rotating totally, and working on defensive coordination.

Chapter 13

Becoming a Better Lacrosse Player — Physically and Mentally

● ●

In This Chapter

▶ Defining the physical and mental challenge of lacrosse

▶ Getting in shape — and why

▶ Starting your workouts with stretching

▶ Conditioning schemes for lacrosse

▶ Gaining quickness and flexibility

▶ Increasing strength with weight training

▶ Getting mentally ready to play

● ●

*T*o play lacrosse successfully, you need physical qualities, such as strength, endurance, quick-as-a-cat agility, flexibility, and quickness. In this chapter, I show you how to improve these qualities and how to get into shape to be a better lacrosse player (hopefully, so you'll stay injury-free — injuries can make or break a season).

I may be biased, but I think lacrosse players are among the fittest athletes in the world. They must have speed and quickness, plus strength in the upper body to take all the pounding in a box lacrosse game, whether it's a cross-check, a body check, or a crunch into the boards. You should do your best to be in game-ready shape when your team gathers to start workouts for an upcoming season. These training camps don't always focus on getting into shape; instead, they concentrate on skills and team play.

Here are a few more things to keep in mind as you get in playing shape for lacrosse:

✔ **No rest for the weary, so train to minimize weariness.** The nature of a lacrosse game consists of endurance running, short bursts of speed, stop-and-start running with high intensity, and a lot of body and stick contact thrown in, with only brief rests on the bench while waiting for your next shift.

✔ **Practise sprint marathoning.** Lacrosse players have to run short bursts of speed over a long period of time, so players have to train for both types of running.

✔ **Even a flat surface has its ups and downs.** In a lacrosse game, if you're in shape, you feel like you're running downhill; if you're not in very good shape, the game feels like drudgery, and you feel like you're running uphill.

Being in game-shape includes a mental challenge for lacrosse players. You should be able to stay in the "zone" that encourages great performance. This chapter discusses getting ready to play mentally, but here are a few tips to get you started:

✔ **Be positive.** Lacrosse is, after all, a game, and your mental attitude toward it should be a positive one. Remember, too, that it's easy to stay positive when you're winning; the tough part is staying positive after losing or after making mistakes. It's all part of the lacrosse learning curve.

✔ **Accept the challenge.** Look forward to each upcoming game, to the challenge of the opponent (both your team's opponent and any particular individual opponent you have in mind), and to the fundamentals of the conflict ahead.

✔ **Plan for success.** Show me a lacrosse player who anticipates that each game will be a good game, and I'll show you a successful lacrosse player.

✔ **Use your nervousness.** You should try to calm and quiet your mind before the game. However, it's also okay to feel a little bit nervous (but not overly so). Use your nerves to help you get physically energized and ready to play; let your mind keep things loose.

✔ **Have fun.** Lacrosse is a game. Enjoy yourself.

The result of these good feelings is that you get into what is called the *zone*. Being in the zone means that you play alert and can anticipate things before they happen — all the activity around you seems to happen in slow motion. Your mental focus is totally absorbed in playing the game and blocking out all distractions. You play with self-confidence, and you're emotionally controlled. Being in the zone helps you play the game effortlessly, and you react more by instinct than by rote.

Understanding the Benefits of Top Physical Condition

Being in great shape allows you to perform at the highest level your body (and mind) can. Here are a few reasons why you should strive for top physical conditioning:

- ✔ **You get in top physical condition to prevent injuries.** Injuries are part of lacrosse; you *will* get hurt at some point. Whether it's a cut, a skinned knee, a muscle pull, a broken arm, or a sprained ankle, whether it's inside the boards of a box lacrosse arena or on the grass of a field lacrosse surface, you *will* get hurt. How often you get hurt and how fast you recover depends a great deal on what condition you are in.

  I have played all my life and have never had a major injury. I really believe that I've avoided serious injury because of the way I've looked after myself — eating right, stretching all the time, getting plenty of sleep — with a little help from plain, old good luck. Of course, I have had broken noses from cross-checks; a neck injury (probably a concussion) from running head-first into the boards; numerous leg injuries involving knees, ankles, and shins; and many cuts around the head area. But being in good shape prevented the really serious stuff, and also helped with a quick recovery when I did get hurt.

- ✔ **You get in top physical condition to improve your lacrosse performance.** If you are in top physical condition, you can improve your speed, increase your ability to take a hit, become more agile, react quicker and run faster, and play longer at maximum efficiency.

- ✔ **You get in top physical condition to help make you mentally tough.** When you start to tire in your conditioning drills, that is when you start to push yourself more.

When considering mental toughness, remember that your team has to play together as one, so mental toughness as part of top physical conditioning is a team goal as well as a personal one. When working on conditioning, make sure that all players reach the goals set for your team on any particular day. If one player falls behind, everyone goes again.

Stretching to Be Your Best

As with any physical conditioning, your best workout is only as effective as your best pre-workout stretch.

Stretching helps to reduce strains, sprains, spasms, and muscle tears when muscles are tight and inflexible. Stretching also helps to prevent injuries common to running, such as pulled muscles, shin splints, ankle sprains, hamstring pulls, pulled groins, and Achilles tendonitis (also known as an Achilles heel — an inflamed heel cord).

Stretching before and after practices and games will keep you flexible — it reduces muscle tension by increasing your range of motion, which makes you a better lacrosse player.

Stretching correctly and consistently

Before you stretch, it's a good idea to warm up a little with a light jog, some skip rope, bike riding (stationary or road), running backward, or even enough carioca to work up a sweat. (*Carioca* is a sideways running exercise that requires you to cross-step laterally up and down the playing surface.)

You should conduct your stretching sessions in just about the same way every time you work out. Work your larger muscles first before moving on to your smaller muscles. In other words, start with your back, hips, hamstrings, groin, and quads (calf, ankles, and feet), and then follow up by stretching your shoulders, arms, wrists, and neck.

When you stretch, you should hold the stretch in a fixed position for a sustained period of time — try for 20 to 30 seconds. You want to avoid bouncing up and down when stretching; save any movement for the practice or the game.

When stretching, you should feel a mild tension or a moderate burning sensation in your muscles, but no pain. If you feel pain, your body is telling you to stop.

Stretching exercises for lacrosse

Any kind of stretching is a good habit to get into before working out with your team or before a game, and some stretching methods are especially helpful for getting ready for lacrosse activity. This section introduces these drills.

Back stretches

Whether you're playing on the hard indoor surface of a box lacrosse arena or the (relatively) soft grass of a field lacrosse surface, your constant running will put some strain on your back, not to mention the convoluted body positions you may end up in as a result of a cross-check or an awkward shot on goal. Here are some good stretches to get your back limbered up for practice or a game.

- ✓ **Rollover:** From a lying-down position, bring both your legs together over your head and back. (You'll want to be lying on your back, of course.) Keeping your legs straight, and your arms on the floor, try to touch the floor with your feet.

- ✓ **Pretzel stretch:** This activity works on your lower back. Sitting upright, place one hand on the floor behind you and rotate your head and shoulders toward that hand. Then cross the leg on that side over your other leg. Pull the knee of that leg across your body with your free arm until you feel the stretch in the hip and torso of your lifted side.

- ✓ **Lying gluteal stretch:** Another exercise for your lower back, this one starts with you lying on your back. Bend one knee and pull it toward your chest until you feel a good stretch in the lower back area.

Leg stretches

Because lacrosse requires constant motion on your part (unless you're weighted down with the goaltender's pads), stretching your legs in preparation for this constant motion is critical. These stationary exercises are a good start.

- ✓ **Side-to-side leg swings:** Stand so that you face the boards. Swing one leg at a time from one side of your body to the other. You'll likely want to hang on to the boards for balance, as you'll be swivelling your legs through the hips. Work on this exercise doing ten repetitions per leg.

- ✓ **Forward-to-back kicks:** Stand so that you're parallel to the boards. Swing one leg at a time, forward and back, not using so much thrust that you risk kicking off your shoe. Remember that you're just warming up here. Again, you'll want to hang on to the boards for balance and work on ten repetitions per leg.

- ✓ **Sitting leg stretch:** Sit on the floor with both legs straight and together (in a pike position, for you diving enthusiasts). Bring your chest to your knees and hold for 20 seconds. This exercise stretches the backs of your legs as well as your hamstrings.

- ✓ **Straddle leg stretch:** In a sitting straddle position (that is, legs flat on the floor and forming a V), slowly bend forward from the hips toward one foot. Keep your head forward and back straight, bring your chest to one knee, and hold for 20 seconds. Then move to the other leg. Stretch until you feel tension in your hamstrings.

Hamstring and quad stretches

These leg-stretching exercises are designed to loosen up and improve the flexibility of your calf and thigh muscles.

- ✓ **Sitting hamstring stretch:** In a sitting position, bend one leg, bringing the sole of that leg's foot to rest on the inside and upper part of your straight leg. Lean slightly forward, bringing your chest to the straight leg, and stretch the hamstring of the straight leg. Hold stretch for 20 seconds.

✓ **Standing hamstring stretch:** In a standing position, put one leg up on a bench in a straight position, bring your chest to the knee of the straight leg. Hold stretch for 20 seconds.

✓ **Standing hamstring and calf stretch (iliotibial band stretch):** In a standing position, cross one leg over your other leg and then slowly bend, moving your hands down toward the ankle of your back leg. Hold stretch for 20 seconds.

✓ **Stork stand:** For this quad stretch, stand on one leg, balancing yourself by holding on to a wall, grab one foot near the toes, and pull your toe toward your buttocks. Stretch for 20 seconds.

✓ **Quad sit:** In a sitting position, sit on both legs and lean back. Hold for 20 seconds.

✓ **Hurdler's stretch:** For your quads and hamstrings, start in a sitting position. Put one leg straight and one behind you and slowly lean back to stretch your bent leg's front thigh, the quad. Hold for 20 seconds. Then slowly lean forward grasping the straight leg's foot to stretch your straight leg's back thigh, the hamstring. Hold stretch for 20 seconds.

✓ **Achilles stretch:** This exercise works on your calf muscles. Stand a little away from a wall and lean on it with your hands, bending your front leg and placing your back leg straight behind you. Slowly move your hips forward until you feel a stretch in the calf of your straight leg. Keep heel of the straight leg on the ground. Hold stretch for 20 seconds.

Abdomen and groin stretches

These stretching exercises will improve your flexibility, which can come in handy when you reach for loose balls or create an awkward shot opportunity.

✓ **Crunches:** This exercise stretches your abdominal muscles. Lying on your back with your knees bent, pull yourself up into a sit-up position, holding briefly a 45-degree angle to the floor before lying back down.

✓ **Sitting straddle stretch:** For the groin and hamstring areas, you start in a sitting straddle position and slowly lean forward at the hips bringing your chest toward the ground until you feel a slight pull in your groin and hamstring area. Keep your back straight and hold this stretch for 20 seconds.

✓ **Groin sit:** Sitting with your knees flexed and your heels together, press your knees toward the floor with your elbows. Stretch until you feel tension in the inner thigh or groin area for 20 seconds.

✓ **Forward lunge:** Also for the groin and hamstring, this exercise starts from a standing position. Lunge forward by placing one foot forward, and then push the hip of your straight leg forward. Switch legs and repeat. Hold for 20 seconds.

Stretching for speed during and pre-season

Some stretching exercises can be targeted to certain activities as well as providing your body with an opportunity to loosen up and prepare for a workout. Here are a few exercises to help you increase your running speed for a game:

✔ **High knee marching:** In this drill, you try to improve your high knee drive. When you accelerate during a game, you need a high knee drive. Drive your knee upward, thigh parallel to the ground, keeping your feet moving in rapid fashion. Try this drill for 20 yards with a marching or skipping motion.

✔ **High knee with straight leg reach:** With your legs straight, run while trying to extend stride length. Keep your legs straight and your

knees locked, pushing back off the ground. Focus on driving forward off the ground. Try this drill for 20 yards.

✔ **Heel kicks:** Run 20 yards aggressively, focusing on how rapidly your feet move to touch your buttocks with your heels. Keep your toes pointed, try to keep your upper leg from moving, and run with a slight forward lean and proper arm action.

✔ **Shuffle:** Across a 10-foot-wide section of the floor, focus on lateral movement and low hip strength. If you work on keeping your centre of gravity low, you can change direction more quickly.

Stretching head and shoulders above the rest

Really designed to loosen up your neck and shoulders, these exercises work well for reducing tension — physical and mental.

✔ **Shoulder stretch 1:** Wrap one arm around in front of your neck as the other arm presses the elbow back. Hold for 20 seconds and then switch arms.

✔ **Shoulder stretch 2:** Reach over your head and down the back with one arm as the other arm presses down at the elbow. Hold for 20 seconds and then switch arms.

✔ **Shoulder stretch 3:** Reach straight backward with both your arms and press both upward toward your back. Hold for 20 seconds.

✔ **Neck stretch:** Stretch neck side to side. No rotation.

Running for Top Physical Conditioning

You have to run both long and short distances in lacrosse because of the nature of the game. All that running requires you to stay in running shape with long-distance conditioning, sprint conditioning to increase speed, and endurance training. This section offers advice for this kind of training. While you can run for game-shape conditioning at any time during the year, long-distance and endurance training are best reserved for the off-season or during pre-season training, and conditioning for speed is ideal for in-season workouts.

Off-season and pre-season conditioning

A typical off-season lacrosse program may include a 120-minute workout for total conditioning: 30 minutes of stretching, 30 minutes of weight training (strength training), 30 minutes of distance running (aerobic activity), and 30 minutes of sports activity (basketball, floor hockey, lacrosse).

Long-distance and endurance conditioning

Long-distance running is what you do first to build up a base for the cardio-vascular part of the game. By building up your cardiovascular system, you can recover quickly from tiring so that you can run, rest, and then quickly go again. Usually, a good long-distance run lasts from 12 to 15 minutes. Because running is a high-impact exercise, try to run on a soft surface to reduce any potential knee and back problems.

Endurance, or interval, training is good for the off-season and pre-season because you can stop and start in the midst of an extended workout. Here is an example of an endurance-training set:

- **Inside single-line run:** This is a 10- to 12-minute run around the perimeter of an arena. If you're working out with a group of teammates, you can add a sprint element by making sure that the player at the back of the line sprints to the front of the line after each lap.

- **Outside one-mile run:** Record your times for this shorter long-distance run so that you can gauge your improvement. Under 6 minutes is a fast time; around 7 minutes still offers a high-fitness workout. A good average time is around 8 minutes.

- **Outside one-and-a-half-mile run:** Do another long-distance run and aim for between 9 and 10 minutes. Anything under 12 minutes is good.

- **Outside two-mile run:** Keep this run under 14 minutes for a good workout. Remember to record your personal times.

- **20-metre shuffle run:** This is a good run to close an endurance workout with. Find a 20-metre-long space, indoors or outdoors, and wind down with some back-and-forth shuffle runs.

Endurance training gets you in the best shape possible for training camp. Training camp is no longer the place to work yourself into shape. To make a team today, you have to be in shape going into training camp to impress the coaches.

Sprint conditioning

Speed is in the genes; you either have it or you don't. But you can increase speed to a certain degree. Here are a few different programs to increase running speed during the off-season:

- ✔ **Weight training:** To develop leg strength for longer strides, work out with squats, leg curls, leg extensions, leg presses, dead lifts, and step-ups.

- ✔ **Resistance training:** Also for leg strength (and longer strides), workouts may include running uphill, running up steps, running in water, running with weights, and running with a partner in tow.

- ✔ **Over-speed training:** To develop stride frequency, that is, to increase the number of strides in your sprint, try running in sand, running on a treadmill, sprinting on a gradual downhill slope, and running while being towed with a stretch cord.

- ✔ **Plyometrics:** Also for stride frequency, jumps, hops, and bounding exercises are resistance exercises that work to contract your muscles more quickly, increasing your power.

In-season conditioning

Beyond lacrosse games and practices, your in-season training regimen should focus on increasing efficiency — efficiency in endurance, efficiency in speed, and efficiency in transitioning between the two. The primary way to achieve maximum efficiency in your workouts is with the correct form.

- ✔ Relax your torso, shoulders, hands, and jaw.

- ✔ Lean the upper body slightly forward but don't bend at the waist.

- ✔ Swing your arms without crossing the midpoint of the body. The faster your arms move, the faster your feet move.

- ✔ Keep your head upright and relaxed, focusing straight ahead.

- ✔ Move your feet in a straight line, not inward or outward.

- ✔ Drive your lead leg out and up, not just lifting it upward. Snap your down leg back beneath your hips with full extension. You want a pushing action off the balls of your feet; don't run on your toes! Your body is better at pushing than pulling, so make a pushing action with your feet against the ground.

To increase speed efficiency in a lacrosse game, stress short strides to begin with, starting with running on your toes and the middle of your foot, and then once in the open floor, generate more speed by opening up your stride. You run faster by increasing your stride length and moving your legs faster.

Endurance, or interval, training during the season can be tailored to your lacrosse practices. Focus the workouts on simulating lacrosse game conditions, that is, going for short intensive spurts of activity before a period of rest. Box lacrosse players play in shifts and each shift requires continuous bursts of speed over short distances with little recovery time.

The shorter your work period, the higher its intensity should be. Therefore, with shorter work periods, increase your rest or recovery period.

Following are some examples of efficient interval training sessions for endurance, power, and speed:

- ✓ **Interval endurance training:** Run 400 yards in consecutive 40-yard increments. This workout is relatively light (about 60 percent maximum effort) and should be done in 60 to 70 seconds. Your rest period should therefore be about 180 seconds, about a 1:3 work-to-rest ratio. Complete three repetitions.

- ✓ **Interval power training:** This drill increases endurance for repeated high-speed sprints and is performed with 100 percent maximum effort. Run a 40-yard sprint within 6 seconds. Your rest period will be 30 seconds, a 1:5 work-to-rest ratio. Complete eight to ten repetitions.

- ✓ **Interval sprint training:** Sprint up and down the playing surface for 40 to 45 seconds at 75 percent maximum effort. (This workout simulates the time and game speed of an average lacrosse game shift.) Rest for 120 seconds, about a 1:3 work-to-rest ratio, before starting your second of five repetitions.

Thoughts on conditioning program during the season

How long is a lacrosse shift? The average lacrosse shift is between 50 and 60 seconds, possibly 45 seconds for a fast-breaking team. How long should the players rest between shifts? If you play three lines, players will go on the floor every third shift (1 work: 2 rest). So try to relate your training to these variables.

Make the training demands slightly greater than in game situations. Hard practice days should be followed by easy practice days or days off during the season. A hard practice should not be done on the day before an important game. To increase speed, use a stopwatch, which makes everyone faster. Have players race against time or race against another player. You should be interested in a player's time from one end of the floor to the other.

Remember: Recovery from a hard day or a game can take 24 to 48 hours.

The beauty of interval training is that these variables can be changed to your age and level of conditioning. Keep the distance a constant, but you can vary the time of the run and rest.

Conducting conditioning drills during in-season practices

All in-season drills should focus on keeping players in game-shape throughout the season. This outcome is best achieved with continuous movement during practice, rather than extra conditioning after practice. During the season, you should avoid conditioning after practice because players may hold back during practice if they know they'll be expected to run later. Try motivating your players: If they run an all-out effort during practice, there will be no conditioning after practice.

But if you do run conditioning drills during in-season practices, here are a few tips to keep in mind:

- ✔ **Go all-out.** All running drills are at full speed and use the full length of the floor.

- ✔ **Set goals.** Let your team know how much they are expected to run, as well as the number of quality workout repetitions that are expected. Or set a time limit for completing certain drills.

- ✔ **Toss a ball in the mix.** Players run the hardest when a ball is involved in the drill. That is why the best way to prepare for playing lacrosse is to scrimmage.

- ✔ **Mix things up.** Try to change the style, intensity, and order of drills conducted during practices or your players will get bored.

- ✔ **Create a challenge.** Make your drills challenging and competitive. Your players are on the team for a reason — they want to succeed in a competitive environment. Try to make your practices almost as rewarding in that way as an actual game.

Conditioning drills without a ball

Not every drill needs to have a ball to be successful (though you'll still want your players to have a ball while running them). Here are a few drills to run during in-season practices that may be a blast for your team:

- ✔ **Sprints down and back:** Run five sprints from one end of the floor to the other, adding one sprint if any player comes in over a predetermined set time. Use three groups of players — fast, medium, and slow — with target times for each group.

- ✔ **Suicides down and back:** Suicide runs have three stages: groups of players start at one end of the floor and run to the first centre line and back, then to the far centre line and back, and finally to the far end boards and back. Use three groups of players — fast, medium, and slow — with target times for each group. Let your players know ahead of time how many repetitions they'll run, adding one for each time a player comes in over a predetermined time.

- ✔ **Relays down and back:** Line up three or four lines along one goal line, giving one stick to each group. Each player in a group runs down to the far end boards, touches the boards with the stick, and runs back to hand the stick to the next player. Again, let your players know how many repetitions will be run.

- ✔ **Variety run:** This drill incorporates four separate styles of running. In the end, each player will run the length of the floor and back twice. Set target times for each player.

  1. Run length of floor.

  2. Run backward back to other end.

  3. Zigzag through cones to other end.

  4. Run length of floor chasing loose balls rolled to them.

Conditioning drills with a ball

Here are some drills to run that are guaranteed to have a ball — though your players may not be too thrilled:

- ✔ **2-on-0 run and pass:** Pair up players to run the length of the floor while passing the ball back and forth. Each player should call out the receiver's name when passing, and each pass should be thrown after no more than two steps with the ball. The goal is to keep the ball moving forward, that is, passing in front of the other player and not behind or short of the receiver.

- ✔ **5-on-0 run, pass, and shoot:** Line up five players across one goal line. The players run down the length of the floor and back together, passing the ball from one player to the next. When the line reaches the faceoff circles in the offensive zone, the player that controls the ball shoots. The drill continues until every player shoots at least once.

- ✔ **Shooting and breaking out on a loose ball:** Roll a ball into a corner of the boards and send a player after it. The player runs the ball down to the other end of the floor and shoots on the goalie. Alternate left-hand and right-hand shots, switching sides when every player has run the drill at least once.

- ✔ **Mini-games:** As an alternative to running or other conditioning drills at the end of an intense practice, stage brief (three- or four-minute) games without line changes.

Improving Your Quickness and Agility

Quickness comes into play when you take a speedy first step with which you are able to beat your defender and explosively go by him. This first quick step is important because it can get you past your defender or create space between you and your defender to be able to take a shot or make a pass.

If you have average speed, however, you may be able to beat your defender because of your agility, your flexibility, and your ability to change direction quickly. You can set up an opponent by making him think you are going one way by your body language and instead you fake and go the other way. This kind of flexibility can cause your defender to lean one way while you make your offensive move the other way, again creating an opening for a shot or a pass.

Quickness and agility are critical to defensive play as well. A quick defender is able to react to offensive movement, possibly catching up to an opponent who has beaten him. Agility and flexibility on defence can combine with defensive smarts to anticipate when an offensive player may try and beat you to the punch.

This section offers some quickness and agility drills to improve your offensive and defensive games.

Offensive quickness and agility drills

These drills work on your footwork and foot speed, skills required for quick and agile movement on the lacrosse playing surface.

- **Faking:** While jogging around the arena, take short, quick steps in an opposite direction. Push right, step left, and then push left, step right.

- **Pivoting (for a left-shot player):** Fake right with your right foot, step inside with your left foot, pivot (or spin) on your left foot while pulling your right foot over your left foot, and then go left.

- **Pivoting (for a right-shot player):** Fake left with your left foot, step inside with your right foot, pivot (or spin) on your right foot while pulling your left foot over your right foot, and then go right.

- **Agility obstacle run:** Run up and down the floor through and around cones. You can add faking drills to this run as well.

- **Sprints:** Set up a cone about 12 feet from the end boards. Run back and forth from the cone to the boards, touching the boards with your stick. Run in 30-second repetitions.

✔ **Agility square:** Start in a corner and run up the sideboards for a pass, making a one-on-one move across the top of the zone. Then after a pass, make a V-cut to the crease area to set a cross pick before rolling back to the original corner for another pass.

Defensive quickness and agility drills

To improve footwork, most defensive drills deal with lateral action, footwork, communication, and quickness. Make your drills short, quick, and hard.

✔ **Footwork:** Some examples of footwork drills are running backward (up and down the length of the floor), carioca (step-over runs facing the side boards up and down the length of the floor), and forward and backward cross-over runs.

✔ **Wave drill:** The team reacts to the direction in which the coach points. Your reaction motions should be step and slide down and back or drop-step and slide across. Work on keeping your knees bent and on maintaining a proper defensive stance.

✔ **Shadow drill:** With a partner, one player mirrors the other for ten seconds. This drill can be a non-contact drill (ballcarrier moves side to side and can't beat the defender) or a contact drill (ballcarrier works defender, but can't beat him).

✔ **Defensive square drills:** To work on lateral motion, agility, and quickness, place four cones to mark a square that equals the distance a player would move during a game. You can run this drill clockwise or counterclockwise. Do four repetitions or target a set time.

• Facing the same direction at all times, backpedal, shuffle, sprint forward, and shuffle from cone to cone to complete a square.

• Starting in the top-side corner, shuffle down to the first cone in a defensive stance (facing the boards). Open your stance and shuffle across to the next cone (facing the goal). Turn and run up the side-boards to the third cone, changing to a shuffle for the last two steps. Close out the drill by shuffling back across to the original cone.

• Starting in the middle of the square, run to a corner and backpedal back to the middle. Repeat to all four corners. You can run the same drill with sprints or slides back and forth from middle to corner.

Weight Training to Get into Top Physical Condition

Strength is one of the keys to success in modern lacrosse, and strength can best be developed through a properly organized weight-training program. Players are hit into the boards going after loose balls; they are cross-checked hard across their upper body and arms to stop them from going to the net; they are slashed by a lacrosse stick to steal the ball; they are stopped from cutting into the middle of the floor; and they are required to sprint to the other end of the floor to score. In all these situations, weight training will help players improve their performance by increasing their endurance, their flexibility, their agility, their running speed, and their overall physical strength. Besides improving all of these qualities, weight training helps to prevent injuries.

Ten weight-training pointers for an efficient and effective off-season program

What you do during the off-season determines what you do during the season, and a solid off-season training program should include weight training. As with any training that you take on, keep a record or chart to gauge your progress, as well as to motivate you to greater heights. For more information about training with weights, check out *Weight Training For Dummies* (published by Wiley Inc.).

1. **Weight training works on the overload principle.** You demand a muscle to do something it doesn't want to do by increasing the amount of weight or increasing the number of repetitions that you can do.

2. **Repeat consistent repetitions.** Start with enough weight to do about eight reps each set, working your way up to ten reps.

    Repeat each exercise eight to ten times working with 75 percent of your maximum weight. After you can complete ten repetitions without straining too much, increase the weight. It is important to work with weight that is best for you — not too heavy yet challenging enough to make you work.

    Maximum weight is simply the most weight you are capable of lifting for a single repetition of a given exercise.

3. **Train in sets.** You may want to start with one set, and then progress, working up to three sets. Some people recommend one set to total fatigue. A set is doing one type of exercise for eight to ten reps.

4. **Maintain consistency in your order of exercises.** Start with the largest muscle groups first, such as your shoulders, back, abdomen, chest, quadriceps (upper leg muscles), and calves, and then work with the smallest muscle groups, such as shoulders, arms, and ankles.

5. **Lifting with proper form is important in strength training.** The technique must be correct, slow, controlled, and smooth. Concentrate on your form and don't cheat, such as arching your back when bench pressing for more leverage or bouncing or swinging the weight when doing arm curls. Lift weights up in two seconds (positive) and lower weights down (negative) in four seconds.

6. **Breathe consistently.** Some people recommend no scheme to breathing when lifting weights, but just don't hold your breath. Some recommend you breathe in while raising the weights or working the muscles and breathe out while you lower the weights. Whatever you choose to do, do it the same way every time.

7. **Raise and lower the weight through a full range of motion.** This maintains or increases flexibility, which is so important for prevention of injuries.

8. **Take time between exercises.** In a weight-training program, if you're working on endurance, cut down your recovery time to 15 to 45 seconds between exercises, or even no rest. If you're working on strength, rest for one to two minutes between exercises.

9. **Maintain a consistent training schedule.** During the off-season, you can train three times a week on alternate days. Your muscles need time to recover and grow. An alternative that some players practise is to train six days a week by working the upper body one day and the lower body the next day.

   During the season, you can train two times a week to maintain if you have the time, but be careful, because rest is important during the playing season.

10. **Manage your training time.** Players should spend no longer than 45 minutes (for endurance training) to one hour (for strength training) in the weight room. It's a good idea to work in teams so that one member can be a spotter, and each of you can push the other. There will be times you won't want to work out, but you'll do it because your partner wants you to.

A basic weight-training program with free weights and machines

This section offers some standard weight-training exercises that you can start with for both the upper and lower body.

- ✔ **Crunch (builds abdominal muscles):** Lie on your back, knees bent, and feet flat on the floor with your fingers lightly touching your ears. Slowly curl your torso until your shoulder blades leave the floor. Hold this position a few seconds, then lower slowly back down to the mat.

- ✔ **Bench press (strengthens chest muscles):** Lie on an exercise bench with knees bent so your feet are flat on the floor, grasp the barbell from the rack with your hands slightly wider than shoulder width, slowly lower it to your chest, and then press the barbell up until your arms are fully extended.

- ✔ **Military press (develops shoulder muscles):** Sitting at the end of the bench, grasp the barbell, and plant your feet firmly on the floor. Lift the weight over your head and rest it on the back of your shoulders; push the bar up to arm's length, and then lower it to the starting position and repeat.

- ✔ **Bicep curl (builds bicep muscle):** In a standing position, hold the barbell with an underhand grip, allowing it to rest against your thigh. Slowly bring the bar up to your chest, bending your elbows but keeping your upper arms motionless against your sides. Hold the bar against your chest and then slowly lower it to the starting position.

- ✔ **Lat pulldown (strengthens back muscles):** Grasp the bar at the lat-pull-down station of a weight machine with your hands 36 inches apart, and then sit down, allowing your arms to extend overhead. Pull the bar down slowly until it touches the back of the neck right above the shoulders, and then return to the starting position.

- ✔ **Squat (for quads and buttocks):** In a standing position, grip a barbell and place it across your shoulders, behind your head. Holding the bar and placing your hands shoulder-width apart, squat slowly down until your upper thighs are parallel to the floor, and then return to the original position. Make sure you keep your head up and your back straight.

- ✔ **Leg curl (strengthens hamstrings):** Sit in the curl-machine placing your heels on top of the footpad. To get support, hold onto the front or side of the machine. Curl your legs, that is, bring your heels toward your buttocks, and then slowly let the weights come up back to the original position.

- ✔ **Leg extension (for the quads):** Sit in the leg-extension exercise machine with your feet under the footpad, raise the weight stack until your legs are parallel to the floor, and return it to starting position.

Eating and sleeping your way to game-shape

What you eat and how you sleep affect the way you play. Good nutrition alone is not enough to produce a winner, but poor nutrition may be enough to keep you from being a winner. Athletes must eat a balanced diet daily. Recovery is also critical to help you restore your energy. And the best recovery starts with a good night's sleep. Following are a few eating and sleeping tips to keep in mind to help you achieve your best on the lacrosse field:

✔ Keep hydrated. Water has more impact on performance than any of the food a player eats. The biggest mistake that players make is to wait until they are thirsty to drink. You should drink throughout the day whether or not you're thirsty. Drink a considerable amount of juices, water, or sports drinks before, during, and after a lacrosse game or practice. Aim for eight glasses of water each day.

✔ Eat a simple, balanced diet that leans to the low side in fat content and to the high side in carbohydrates. (Carbohydrates help you increase endurance.) And stay away from junk foods.

✔ Eat and drink every two hours whenever possible. Aim for four to six meals per day, but eat lightly, for example, three moderate-sized meals plus two to three snacks each day. Eat more frequently, but in smaller portions.

✔ Try for eight to ten hours of sleep every night, especially during the season. As well, don't underestimate the value of a nice catnap. During the playing season, short naps (10 to 15 minutes) will make you feel energized and refreshed.

Mentally Preparing for Lacrosse

Because lacrosse is such a physically demanding game — whether it's the quick turns and body-banging of a box lacrosse game or the endurance and stamina required for a field lacrosse contest — the focus of this chapter has been appropriately on physical readiness. However, being ready to play lacrosse takes more than just physical strength. As in any sport, mental toughness is more than just a hackneyed cliché; it's a requirement.

How you mentally approach lacrosse — whether it's your approach before a game or before a practice — is an important factor in how well you'll play. For some players, preparing mentally may mean little more than going over a checklist of emotions and expectations before a game.

✔ Do I have the proper attitude or outlook?

✔ Do I feel optimistic?

✔ Am I ready to have fun?

✔ Am I calm and composed?

> ✔ Am I self-confident?
>
> ✔ Am I alert and totally focused?

Other players, however, may need some additional help to prepare mentally for a game. This section discusses a few approaches.

Goal-setting strategy

By setting long-term personal goals, or *outcome goals,* you can become more self-motivated. For example, you may want to be recognized as the best player or the best defender on your team or in your league. If you are motivated to do your best to achieve this goal, you can get mentally ready to play more easily. Outcome goals can also help you get over the rough spots that every player faces during a long season; short-term disappointments are overcome by long-term personal goals.

These long-term outcome goals, of course, are nothing more than a whole bunch of short-term goals strung together. Your short-term goals may be performance or behaviour goals; either way, you're setting a bar for yourself for the outcome of a game or practice. For example, a short-term performance goal may be to score two or three goals in a game. As well as competing against your opponent, you're competing against yourself and the achievement of your short-term goals.

You may want to have your players create a personal plan so that they are aware of the goal-setting strategies to help them prepare to play.

Relaxation strategy

Athletes often fail to achieve their best performance because they are too tight, anxious, or stressed out. Of all the human emotions, nervousness is the greatest enemy of achievement. There is no way to eliminate pressure situations; they will always be there because they are a natural part of a lacrosse game. If you are prepared to play, however, the game will not be a stressful situation and you will have "good pressure" as a result. Good pressure heightens your senses, makes you more focused and motivated, and helps you play to your maximum potential. And understanding your response to that kind of pressure is one of the best ways to relax in preparation of a game.

> ✔ **Relax with a proper attitude:** You create your own pressure by the way you look at a situation and by what you say to yourself about it. Play down the importance of the outcome of a game. Approach each game as a welcome opportunity for success and challenge rather than as dreaded threats. You get "good pressure" if you look at the game as an opportunity to feel the joy of playing a great game against a worthy opponent.

Your anxiety level rises if you put a life-or-death price tag on the outcome of a game. Yet, in reality, no loss or setback from a "game" will ruin your life.

✔ **Relax by tightening and relaxing your muscles:** Proper deep breathing and muscle-relaxing exercises help you to feel loose and calm, to relax your muscles, and to energize you. This strategy involves just tensing and relaxing your muscles, which help your muscles loosen up. Some players like to shake their arms especially to feel relaxed. You could also tighten and loosen your grip on your stick until you feel the level that is just right.

✔ **Relax with deep breathing:** A small amount of arousal and pre-game excitement are healthy and necessary to get you ready to play a game. But how do you know if you are too excited? Breathing is the first step to recognize your level of arousal. So before the game, check out your breathing. Because stress influences breathing, be aware of short, shallow breathing. Focus instead on inhaling slowly and deeply through your nose, filling your lungs and diaphragm as completely as possible. Then focus on your exhalation as relaxing any muscle tension in your body, letting the air out slowly through your mouth. It is the exhale that relaxes you and reduces stress, which in turn increases performance.

Relaxation can help during a game as well. "Give it all you got" is one of sports real myths; in fact, giving it all you've got usually leads to tension, stress, and anxiety, slowing down your decision-making skills and hindering your performance. As you perform in a game, relax. A relaxed body and mind are characteristic of all great players.

Visualization strategy

Visualization should always be a part of mental preparation for every lacrosse player. There is a direct correlation between the mind and the physical body. You visualize in your mind how you want to play in the upcoming game and when you have that in your brain, the physical body just seems to take over. You visualize in your mind before the game seeing yourself playing a perfect game. You want to visualize success, such as beating your defender, scoring a goal, or stopping your opponent's goal scorer. The more real the experience in your mind, the more effective your performance will be. Visualization works because it acts like a practice or dress rehearsal before the game. So when the time comes for the real game, you have a sense that you have already done this before.

Most players who visualize, imagine all the good things that can happen in the game. But the top players also visualize all the bad things that can happen and how they will handle them. Jim Veltman of the Toronto Rock says about his mental preparation: "I do a lot of my pre-game mental prep the night before a game. I'll think about things that I want to do on the floor and think about our team's game plan that we went over in practice. In the dressing room before a game, I try to get a sense of the team's mental state and think about ways to get our team focused before a game, either by providing verbal encouragement or relaxation comments or by showing my concentration by example."

Self-talk strategy

What do you say to yourself before a game? Is it positive or negative, or do you not talk to yourself at all? To get into the correct playing mental zone you have to be positive, you have to think you can do it. The good lacrosse players know that if they don't learn to control their thoughts, their thoughts will control them. Self-talk is basically the skill of replacing a negative inner voice that hurts your performance with a positive inner voice that will help you perform better. If your thoughts are positive and focused, you will increase your performance state. Positive self-talk helps you get into the zone by making you feel good, feel optimistic, focus on your performance, feel confident, feel energized and alert, and feel calm and physically relaxed.

If you want to be a good player, you have to learn to play hurt, play when fatigued, and play when you don't feel like it. Great players talk themselves into playing their best when they feel their worst.

You can also use self-talk to relax yourself. If you feel you are trying too hard or tensing up, just say to yourself something like "relax," "just let it happen," "just let it flow." You can even talk out loud, or give yourself a pep talk. For some players, talking out loud seems to help more than just talking in their heads. The speed and tone of your "voice" is as important as what you say. Talking rapidly with a harsh tone will tighten your muscles. Talking slowly and in a low tone can relax you. Some players also find that talking to the opposition helps them to stay relaxed.

Controlling-your-emotions strategy

One player gets upset over a bad call and comes out on his next shift playing brilliantly. Another player might get upset over something and retaliate. Both players get upset, yet one handled it well, and the other didn't. Know your "hot buttons" — what gets you upset and makes you lose your temper. Hot buttons can hurt your performance because powerful negative emotions weaken your decision-making ability. You may not make the hot button go away, but you can learn to cope with the situation. Instead of allowing the situation to control you, you can control the response you choose. The best way to deal with getting upset is to be prepared for it. A self-control strategy is to make a list of adversities and visualize how you will react to them.

Have you ever seen a perfect game? There will always be setbacks, adversities, and mistakes in any game and in any season. By planning ahead and anticipating problems, you will feel confident that you can handle any unexpected situations. Think about all the things that could go wrong and imagine how you would handle them. Problems could happen before the game, in a hotel room or at home, on the bus, in the arena, just before the game, while warming up in the arena, as you step on the floor for warm-up, during the game, or at the very end of the game. So the trick is to expect the unexpected and try to prepare for it.

Focusing strategy

Some players walk around before a game in a trancelike state. What they are doing is focusing on their performance and thinking about the game. When you focus, you force everything out of your mind except your preparation and your performance to minimize as many distractions as possible before the game. You have to focus to avoid the invasion of self-defeating thoughts, such as worry, doubt, and fear, and to enter the game with your own positive thoughts.

- **Focus on what you are doing.** You must focus your attention on your performance rather than on any desired outcome. You must focus your attention on what you can control, which is your performance, rather than on things you can't control, such as winning. Just think about doing your best and losing yourself in your performance.

- **Don't force concentration.** Mental preparedness includes being in tune with what is happening on the floor and fitting into the flow of the action. When in this zone, you just let your focus happen. If you try too hard to focus, your performance deteriorates, especially when things are going badly: you think too much, you start to force things to happen, you play uptight and end up getting yourself into more trouble.

    When a player is playing well, he is not really thinking about anything; he is just doing. Bob Watson of the Toronto Rock says: "I don't want to try too hard because I will tense up. I just say to myself, 'Let it happen.'"

- **Focus on the positive.** You'll perform better by thinking or focusing on what you have to do rather than on what you don't want to do. If you think negatively, such as "I'm not going to throw the ball away," that thought of not committing an error focuses your mind on committing the error, thereby directing the body to do just that. If you focus positively, such as "I'm going to hit my teammate's stick high and outside," that thought helps your mind to concentrate on a relaxed, positive focus, your teammate's stick.

Establish a pre-game routine

Jitters and butterflies will always be there before a game; if not, you're in trouble. Nervousness keeps you alert, but it could result in nervous exhaustion if you do not learn how to control it. You need a pre-game routine to help you relax before a game, to get rid of nervousness and butterflies, and to help you energize if you are not in a ready state to play.

It is important to keep the same pre-game routine for every game; this same-approach method prevents panic if things start going wrong. You have to have a ritual — a warm-up routine to take control of your mental state and get rid of any negative distractions and thoughts. For example, what can happen before a big game? Players panic and change their approach to the game. The major cause of failure in the big game is altering your routine. You must establish your own pre-game routine that feels comfortable for you and then stick to it, no matter what happens!

So what is your routine? Do you take a nap? Do you eat a certain pre-game meal? Do you get dressed in a certain order? Do you never wash your socks and underwear until the end of the season? Do you have a special pre-game warm-up? Well, if you don't have a routine, get one. Are these idiosyncrasies, habits, good luck charms, superstitions, rituals, or just eccentricities? Call them what you will, they work. Some players like to be quiet; others like to be loud, joke around, and be chatty. Some players like to seclude themselves and listen to quiet music; others like to listen to loud music. Some have a plan to keep busy right up to game time to keep them from getting nervous. Some have developed a ritual of putting on their equipment in a certain order. Others just get dressed quickly and put on their equipment in any order. Some like to energize by doing physical exercises such as push-ups, jumping, skipping, or stationary biking. Some like to relax by doing deep breathing and muscle relaxation. Then there are others who want to watch the video of the opposition to look for habits and weaknesses. Some players go through the mental preparation strategies of relaxation and visualization, imagining their best game in their mind. Others do self-talk to get themselves ready to play by telling themselves how they want to feel and play.

Jim Veltman of the Toronto Rock talks about pre-game routine: "I do not like to get to the arena too early. If I do, then I spend some time in the arena seats and think about the game and our team. When I arrive at the arena about a couple of hours in advance, I get dressed in this order: shorts; old minor lacrosse jersey under my equipment; socks; shoes; shoulder pads, arm guards, and kidney pads all in one gear that I put on like a suit jacket with four clips in the front; game jersey; helmet; gloves; and stick."

✔ **Block out distractions.** To stay mentally alert during a whole lacrosse game takes full concentration. You have to work at it to shut everything out and dismiss all stray thoughts from your mind except what you have to do. You cannot have any momentary lapses, so you must play as if every loose ball, every one-on-one confrontation is important. You must concentrate at not letting your mind wander.

Jim Veltman of the Toronto Rock was once asked how he blocked out the crowd of thousands of rowdy fans that regularly attend Rock home games. His response? "What crowd?"

✔ **Focus on the present moment.** Concentration is the ability to focus all your attention on what you are doing in the present moment, not what happened two plays ago, and not what is going to happen in the next two minutes.

How can you concentrate for 60 minutes in a game? Here are some comments from some NLL players: "I play only 1 minute, 60 times." "I stay focused in the present moment by taking 'one shift at a time.'" "If I focused on the whole game, the mere thought of such a task would distract and fatigue me, so I focus in-the-moment."

Energizing strategy

If you feel tired or low-key before a game, what can you do? If you're feeling sluggish or fatigued before a game, you likely have some nervous pent-up energy. Physical activities can get the circulation going and pump yourself up; try jumping up and down, skipping, or stationary biking. You may find that these physical activities will wake you up and make you more alert. You get energy by using energy. You can listen to upbeat music to get yourself energized; try listening to music while you visualize or breathe or practise some other mental preparation. Whatever the activity, your goal is to get your heart pumping and excited for the upcoming challenge.

Part IV

Coaching Lacrosse: Winning Strategies

"Let's see - I'll need some children's aspirin for my players and some sedatives for their parents."

In this part . . .

If you're a lacrosse coach, especially a new one, you need to know where to look for advice on building your team, preparing them for a game, and motivating your team. This part offers all that and more. You can read about how to decide on a style of play for your offence, defence, and specialty-team units. And when your systems don't work, I offer some tips about how to adjust strategies during a game, or at any time during the season. Finally, I've added a great chapter about coaching kids that will be useful to both coaches and parents.

Chapter 14

Developing Your Coaching Philosophy for the Offence

*Y*our most important decision as a lacrosse coach is to determine what type of system to run. By system, I'm referring to a style of play that best fits your offensive and defensive strengths, such as a fast-paced, up-and-down style of play or a slow-it-down, physical style of play. The decision comes down to creating a system around the strengths of your players or forcing your players to adapt to your system, no matter what.

The good coach is one who can adapt his system to his players' talents rather than forcing his players to play his system, though you'll find exceptions. Jim Bishop, one of the greatest lacrosse coaches of all time, coached only one way, and that was to fast break (see "Breaking Out on the Quick: The Fast-Break Offence," later in this chapter for more about the fast-break offence). His players had to adapt to his system rather than him adapting to them. Nevertheless, you may be able to create a team as the NLL teams do, that is, go out and find players that fit the particular system that you're most comfortable coaching.

This chapter doesn't make the system decision for you, but it does help you understand what your options are.

Understanding the General Principles of Lacrosse Playing Systems

The good teams have a system they believe in whether it is an offensive running game, an offensive slow-down game, an aggressive-type defensive game, or a contain-type defensive game. The most important point is to have a system, rather than allow a freelance style of play where players do whatever they want. Even if your team has a disciplined playing system, you can also be ready to adapt your system to fit the special skills of some of your players or adjust your style of play based on the strengths or weaknesses of the opposition.

Coaches know that players win games, but the system gives them the opportunity to be successful. The system gives coaches the chance to be flexible so that their best players are in the best possible position to succeed.

Defining lacrosse playing systems

The following list runs through the basics of some of the most popular playing systems for lacrosse. You may come across some different systems or some variations of what is included here, but these styles of play are the ones you're most likely to face during the majority of your games.

- **Running offence:** This offence tries to establish a game pace that will keep fans' heads turning as if at a tennis match. Running offences look to get the ball quickly up to the offensive end to take advantage of defenders who are slow to join them or are slow to come off the bench. In this way, running offences may give themselves a non-penalty-created player advantage (say, three-on-two or two-on-one). Running offences thrive in a high-scoring game. You may also hear this style of play referred to as a fast-break or a run-and-gun offence.

- **Slow-down offence:** Quite the opposite from a running offence, a team that runs a slow-down offence is trying to create a game tempo that sees players almost walking up and down the playing area. These offences usually recognize that they don't have the players to outrun their opponents into their offensive zone, so they focus on taking their time and setting up a play in the zone that plays to their strengths, for example, by overpowering defensive players. Slow-down offences love the low-scoring games.

- ✔ **Aggressive defence:** An aggressive defence is one that is constantly trying to create turnovers or loose balls. Defenders in this style of defence are usually looking for ballcarriers to cross-check or offensive sticks to slap at, trying to get their opponents to lose possession or make a bad pass or shot. Depending on a defence's ability to play this style, these defences may give up many goals when their aggressive play leads to overplaying mistakes, or they may create a number of goals when the offence becomes frustrated with the physical nature of play.

- ✔ **Contain defence:** This style of defence concentrates on defenders who can keep their opponents contained in the areas of the zone that are least vulnerable to good shots. Contain defences focus on player positioning rather than the physical play of more aggressive defences.

Keeping the system simple

As a coach, you should try to have a vision, an idea, or a system of exactly how you want your team to play and how you want your team to work within that style of play. Don't be vague about the system to your players; tell them exactly what you want from them so that they can be successful within your system.

Your best chance for this success is to keep your system simple, organized, and part of your personality.

- ✔ Simplicity gives players the freedom to focus and stay in the present moment while they perform, giving your players the best chance to make great plays. Also, by keeping your system simple, when it comes time to change the game plan, you can modify these simple plans more quickly and easily than complicated ones.

- ✔ Organization helps players know where to go and what to look for when looking for guidance about an element of your system. Whether it's in the form of a game or practice plan written out on the dressing-room chalkboard or a two-inch-thick binder complete with set plays for any game situation and tips about what to eat before a game, your players will always know there's a place to look to alleviate any confusion.

- ✔ Developing a system that reflects your personality can become almost a motivational tool for you and your team. As noted earlier, Jim Bishop is well known as a coach that adheres to a fast-paced style of play; it's become part of his coaching personality. When your coaching personality is known and respected, it may also be feared, giving your team a bit of a motivational advantage.

Systems help players to perform as a team. In a disciplined system, players know where they're supposed to be and do what they're supposed to do. In a disciplined system, the players can anticipate more quickly because they know what is going to happen before it happens.

Setting Up the Offence

The main goal of an offence is to set up a player so that he has a good shot on net with the best chance of scoring. How you go about achieving this goal is the crux of this section.

Teams get scoring chances using a number of offensive weapons, such as the following plays that help offensive players get in the clear for good shots:

- ✔ The long pass up the floor from the goalie to a breaking player or a player coming off the bench
- ✔ The odd-man situation that comes from a fast break off the bench
- ✔ Going one-on-one against a player whose team is still in defensive transition
- ✔ From set plays such as picks, give-and-go, and screens
- ✔ From a motion-style offence that involves players passing and cutting continuously until someone is open for a shot on goal

Playing to your strengths on offence

Coaches can design offensive set plays and then teams can practise them for hours, but the true execution on offence depends more on the players' abilities than on the actual play itself.

As a coach, your first job is to analyze the talents of your players and how they fit into your offensive scheme. Find out about your players' offensive strengths: Look for the shooters, the passers, the catchers (especially those who seem to grab any ball out of midair no matter how many other players are around), the players who are best at going one-on-one, the ones who can pick-and-roll, and even the aggressive players. By knowing your players' strengths, you can create an offence to complement them.

But no matter what type of offensive system you run, you have to have offensive balance. You need an inside-shooting game, with players who are not afraid to cut into the middle for a pass and shot, knowing that they will get hit. You need an outside-shooting game to draw the defence out of the middle.

You need players who can go one-on-one, cut and catch the ball in traffic, and execute the pick-and-roll. Look to fill these roles first before you design a simple offensive scheme; no scheme will be successful without players to fill these roles.

Besides knowing their strengths, you should position your players on offence at spots from which you think they are most likely to score. This positioning is usually determined by the players' skills, abilities, size, strength, and quickness.

Establishing your offensive formation

What kind of offensive alignment do teams set up in? In box lacrosse, the choices you have are a strong-side offence, with three players lined up on one side, or a 1-2-2 alignment, with the pointman at the top of the zone.

The strong-side formation is one that works especially well for running offences (see Figure 14-1). You can create a great deal of player movement off this set, having your three strong-side players alternate in and out of the centre of the zone, looking for an opening for a pass or a shot. One example is the *weave* play, where you start the ball on the strong side of the offence and pass and cut on the inside of the defensive alignment continuously. This play gets some movement in your offence.

Figure 14-1:
This strong-side formation sets up offensive player movement from the left side of the zone.

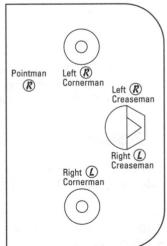

The 1-2-2 offensive alignment helps your offence maintain floor balance and defensive safety (see Figure 14-2). In the 1-2-2, your pointman determines how much energy the players on the floor have and then decides which side to attack from. At the beginning of a set play in this alignment, the pointman stays at the top of the offence but can move anywhere within the zone once the offence starts. Note that the pointman's movement out of this alignment often transitions to a strong-side alignment, with him positioned as one of the three players on the strong side.

Figure 14-2:
From a 1-2-2 alignment, the point-man can pass to his left cornerman and set a pick for his right cornerman, staying in defensive position for a possible giveaway.

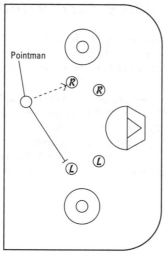

The most common offensive field formations are the 2-3-1, 2-2-2 (invert), and the 1-3-2 (see Figure 14-3). In these formations, the first number represents the number of offensive players that are set up behind the crease.

Executing your offensive system

Ed Comeau, the offensive coach of the Toronto Rock, offers the following keys for running your offensive system effectively, no matter which offensive system you run.

✓ **Always know where the ball is.** All offences are designed to score a goal. You can't score if you don't know where the ball is.

✓ **Know where your defensive man is.** Often, a player is open but doesn't realize it because he's lost track of the player defending him.

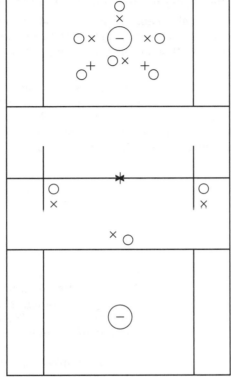

Figure 14-3:
The 1-3-2
alignment is
a common
formation
for a field
lacrosse
offence.

✔ **Recognize mismatches.** Set your bigger offensive player against a smaller defender, and then give him the ball.

✔ **Stay balanced.** Keep your offensive players balanced within the zone, such as three to the right and two to the left, or maintain a nice balance of players high in the zone and low in the zone. Also, keep good spacing between players.

✔ **Shoot!** If you have a shot, take it. You want to take more shots than the opposition. But make good decisions.

✔ **Cut through the middle.** Run everybody hard through the middle of the floor; it creates a lot of confusion. Chances are that when you run three or four players through the middle and none of them receive a pass, the fifth player through will be open for a pass and shot.

✔ **But don't park it in the middle.** Keep cutting because you want to keep the middle open. On a cut, if you hit the midpoint of the floor and don't receive the ball, go back to your own side.

✔ **Keep the ball low.** Pushing the ball low toward the goal is harder to defend. You can start your offence from up top, but run that offence low.

✔ **Cycle passes through your pointman.** Though you constantly want to push the ball low, not every attempt is going to result in a shot. Reverse the ball back to the top rather than make cross-floor passes so that you can reset and try again.

✔ **Freelance with structure.** Use some ball possessions to allow players to do their own thing, without any set plays. You're asking your players to find out what the defence is doing and then exploit it. The structure comes with watching how a defence reacts and then asking your players to freelance with the stronger set plays in your playbook.

Attacking the Zone Defence with a Zone Offence

The reason you play a zone offence is that your opposition is playing a zone defence, usually in a 1-2-2 or 2-1-2 alignment (see Chapter 15 for more information about defensive alignments). Typically, zone defences are played at the minor level only; as the level of play improves, you'll see more man-to-man defences. The NLL plays exclusively man-to-man defence.

You can use your opponent's choice of defence as a motivating tool for your team. Tell your players that the opposition is playing a zone defence because they can't play you or guard you man-to-man. Now your players feel good about attacking the zone because they know why they are playing against it.

Box lacrosse features three basic zone offences:

✔ **Motion:** This passing-centred type of game gives players the freedom to do whatever they want within your zone offence guidelines. This type of offence allows your players to take what the zone defence gives them.

✔ **Continuity:** This zone offence focuses on running through the same offensive concepts over and over until a seam in the zone defence opens up to create a scoring chance.

✔ **Set plays:** Your zone offence should have a few special set plays that you can run when your normal offence (zone or otherwise) becomes stagnant. The set plays force ball and player movement.

Because playing a zone offence is more of a reactionary strategy dictated by what the defence gives you, this section starts with a brief look at the strengths and weaknesses of a zone defence.

Understanding why teams play zone defence

In minor lacrosse, you're likely to run into zone defences most of the time because a zone defence is easy to teach. You tell a player to play in a certain area of the floor and not to move out of that area.

However, coaches also know that opponents don't like to play against zone defences because they have to attack them a little differently than a man-to-man defence (where each defender is assigned an offensive player to cover). Following are a few of the advantages of going with a zone defence:

- **Forcing the tempo:** Zone defences change the tempo of the game because the offence tends to hurry its shots more against a zone defence.

- **Creating easy-scoring chances:** Defenders in a zone defence are taught to break up the floor after an opponent's shot, hoping to set up a fast-break opportunity, which forces the faster and better offensive players to play at the top of the zone to defend against the breakout.

- **Compensating for poorer defensive players:** Some teams play zone defence to hide their weak defenders. These players are usually put at the back of the zone (toward the net), where they'll see less action.

- **Neutralizing the stars:** In a man-to-man defence, one great offensive player or a solid two-man offensive game stands a better chance of beating you than in a zone defence. A zone defence forces all five offensive players to work together rather than letting the best players beat their own defenders.

Recognizing the weaknesses of zone defences

The major weakness of playing a zone defence is that it doesn't teach young players how to stop an opponent with the ball one-on-one, which is what the higher levels of lacrosse are all about. Following are a few other weaknesses of the zone defence that you may be able to exploit:

- **Too much ball watching:** A zone defence is set up so that all defenders can see the ball. However, they can sometimes get so caught up with watching the ball that they sometimes forget about the offensive player in their zone area, who can cut and receive a pass and shoot.

- **Too little movement:** Because a zone defence is not active, players can fall asleep in the zone. Defensive players in the zone may play flat-footed, so they don't move as quickly as they would when they're playing on the balls of their feet defending an opponent man-to man.

- **Too much reliance on the stick:** Zone defenders tend to stick-check rather than cross-check, often getting beat on a wind-up fake shot.

- **Don't fall behind:** If the zone defensive team gets behind in a game, it's hard for them to catch up, because their style of play encourages the offensive team to play more deliberately to protect their lead. However, watch out when a zone team gets ahead in a game; the zone team seems to get stronger with every possession of the ball.

- **Poor transition:** Most zone defensive teams want to play five-on-five lacrosse. To do so, they have to get back quickly to get set up. If they don't get back in time, they get mixed up trying to play some players man-to-man and other players in a zone.

Grasping zone offence principles

Running a successful zone offence requires a number of skills, but they all seem to play off the one critical component: patience. Because a good zone defence offers few scoring opportunities per possession, your team needs to show an ability to wait for the best opening to get the best shot.

- **Be patient:** A zone offence team needs to practise patience when attacking the zone defence. As defensive players have a tendency to fall asleep in a zone defence, the zone offence must constantly move players and the ball through the zone to make it react and collapse. Zone teams want you to shoot the ball quickly, so stress to your team to take their time, keep their poise, and with patience in attacking the zone defence, they will end up getting a good shot.

- **Align in the gaps:** Zone offence players have a tendency to go and stand right beside the zone defender, making it very easy for him to do his job. What a zone offence player should do instead is to align himself in the gaps of the zone, that is, between two defenders, to create indecision about who should defend him (see Figure 14-4).

- **Move the ball:** By moving the ball from side to side and "around the horn" (around the outside of the zone), you stretch the zone from one side to the other. Swinging the ball around the zone quickly creates openings in the zone defence through which players can cut.

    Another result of moving the ball around is that when a player receives a pass, he can set up his defender quickly by faking a shot, freezing him, and then going around him for a real shot.

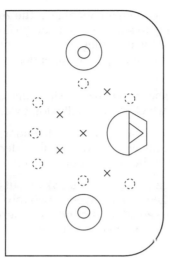

Figure 14-4:
A good zone offence fills the gaps between defenders, as in these possible floor locations.

✔ **Move the players:** To be effective against a zone defence, you want to make it move, stretch it out, and make it shift. Defensive players will move and stretch and shift when they see a great deal of ball and player movement. When offensive players cut through the zone defence, the defensive players have to collapse into the zone to defend those cutters. When those defenders collapse, or shift out of their assigned area, another offensive player can fill that gap and attack the net.

The worst thing your players can do against a zone defence is to stand still; nothing will happen and the zone defence will win the battle. When a player cuts, another player should move to the area just vacated by the cutting player. When a player passes, he should cut, giving the receiver another option for the next pass. Cut backdoor, that is, from behind the zone defence where the defensive players will have a hard time seeing a cut. And cut while running in a circle rotation on one side of the floor where you may have two to three players cutting one right after another.

✔ **Ballcarrier must penetrate:** By going one-on-one or penetrating the zone, the ballcarrier is more likely to draw two defenders. When the ballcarrier penetrates the gaps, he's trying to make the zone defence shift. If the shift includes two defenders, the ballcarrier should be able to dish off the ball to an open teammate.

✔ **Attack from the side of the offence:** Because it can be easier to stop the ballcarrier when the ball is at the top of the offence, attack from the side of the zone defence. Get the ball low into the corner or to the sideboards, and then pass it back out and around the zone to stretch the zone defence down and back up. You keep the defence moving and reacting to the ball and any moving players, creating openings for attacking the net.

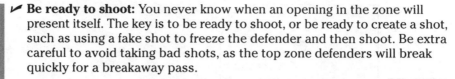

✔ **Be ready to shoot:** You never know when an opening in the zone will present itself. The key is to be ready to shoot, or be ready to create a shot, such as using a fake shot to freeze the defender and then shoot. Be extra careful to avoid taking bad shots, as the top zone defenders will break quickly for a breakaway pass.

A goal scored by a good outside shot will make a team come out of the zone into a man-to-man defence, which they usually don't want to play.

✔ **Defend the defenders:** On any shot, watch for zone defenders breaking out to take a fast-break pass from the goalie. When a defender takes off, your offensive players at the top of the zone should also take off.

You may be able to take advantage of defenders breaking out by looking to grab long rebounds. Consider keeping a player or two toward the top of the offensive zone in case a missed shot rebounds out there. You may end up with the ball and a couple of overmatched defenders.

Running a Penetration Man-to-Man Offence

The penetration offence takes advantage of the skills of your best offensive players. Based on these players taking on their defenders one-on-one, this offence runs primarily through the ballcarrier, who is charged with shooting first, passing second, and asking questions later. Other offensive players have to create their own offensive opportunities by positioning themselves for rebounds, loose balls, or passes when the ballcarrier is double-teamed.

Knowing when to go one-on-one

With just about any type of offence, executing one-on-one takes precedence over other offensive manoeuvres. So it is with a penetration offence — a shoot-first mentality. Passing is a second option. The best time to attempt a one-on-one move is when you have a mismatch against the defence — that is, your offensive player is quicker or bigger than his defender. When no mismatch exists, your offensive players need to rely on guile and fakes to try to create a mismatch, sending your opponent off balance.

The better vantage point for going one-on-one is from the side of the floor, in the outside lane. From the side, once your offensive player beats his defender, he will end up in the middle of the floor for the best shot. You should start your one-on-one play on the proper side of the floor so that you end up shooting from a high percentage spot, keeping in mind whether you're sending in left-shot or right-shot players.

To beat a defender, you must do so immediately; unless you're setting up a pick, hanging on to the ball while waiting for a chance to beat a defender slows down your offence. If the ballcarrier beats his defender and another defender helps, your ballcarrier has a teammate who can take a pass or can run a backdoor cut for a close-in shot.

The ballcarrier must keep his stick moving all the time (*cradle*) when he has the ball. He must protect his stick with his body by turning his body sideways. And he must keep his feet moving, unless he is setting up his defender to take a pick so that he can roll off him.

Opening up penetration with outside shots

When playing a team that plays a less aggressive defence, your players may find it difficult to beat a defender one-on-one. A less aggressive defender tends to stand back from the ballcarrier to protect against such one-on-one penetration moves. To combat this style of defence, you need strong long-ball shooters.

Good long-ball scorers complement your best one-on-one moves. When you show the defence that you can score consistently from the outside, they will play your ballcarriers tighter to try to take away the long shot. Their defence becomes more aggressive, and your offence has a better opportunity to beat defenders inside. Conversely, if you show that your ballcarriers consistently beat defenders inside, the defence will play more loosely to protect against penetration, opening up space for your outside shooters.

Running set plays for a penetration offence

Set plays for this offence should create space for your best one-on-one ballcarriers. You create space by clearing out the four other offensive players. *Clearing out* involves positioning the offensive players without the ball to one side of the floor so that your ballcarrier can initiate a one-on-one play from the opposite side of the floor.

Mix up your set plays. When teams fall behind during a game, they may have a tendency to panic and resort solely to one-on-one plays and nothing else. Make sure to include other set plays, such as the pick-and-roll or give-and-go, so that the defence can't anticipate what your offence will run.

Mastering the Motion Man-to-Man Offence

The motion offence is just the opposite of the penetration offence. In the motion offence, you look to pass first, and then go one-on-one or shoot second. This offence is designed for passing the ball and cutting. No matter what offence you run you must have cutters going through the middle of the floor. Some teams are afraid to cut because they may get hit; the better defensive teams don't let cutters cut across through the middle of the floor *without physical contact*.

However, you can't run a successful offence without any movement; your players will simply just stand outside the defence and look to shoot long. You must cut to collapse the opposition's defence. The offence must dominate the middle of the opposition's defence. However, you can pass around the outside of the defence, waiting for a teammate to get open.

Passing to keep the offence in motion

Quality passing is critical to an effective motion offence. The idea behind the offence is to keep the ball moving until you can get it to the offensive player with the most ideal shot at goal or the best match-up to go one-on-one. Encourage your team to take pride in its passing; emphasize simple, unforced passes.

The quality of your passing determines the quality of your shots. So keep in mind these tips: Before every pass, keep your attention on the business at hand, that is, focus on your pass and your target; before receiving a pass, keep your eyes on the ball; and be ready for the pass, knowing what you are going to do with the ball before you catch it.

Here are a few other things to keep in mind as you work with your team on passing in the motion offence.

✔ **Pass early and often:** The qualities that determine a good passing team include players with good passing skills, a team-oriented offensive system (as opposed to one that centres around one or two great players), and players with an unselfish attitude about giving up the ball early. By passing early, you're giving the receiver the best chance to do something with the ball; by holding on to the ball too long before passing, you give defenders a chance to anticipate where the ball will go.

✔ **Pass to the creaseman:** The pass to the crease must be made for a purpose, not just to make a pass. The pass to the crease does not move the defence much, so if you do make the pass, make sure that the creaseman is in a position to go one-on-one. Also, the passer must cut to look for a return pass; the creaseman, if he can't go one-on-one, must run the ball out of the corner to either look for another one-on-one opportunity or to pass across to the off-ball side.

✔ **Pass to get the offence going:** There are passes that result in a score, and passes that get things started. The pass before the pass that leads to a score is very important. If you start your offence with a bad pass, the next pass will also be bad, a chain reaction that usually leads to your team not having the ball. If a player receives a bad pass, it is important that he pauses before throwing the next pass so that your team can regain some purpose and composure in its offensive set.

Passing to move the defence

You want all your players involved in passing because it makes it harder for the defence to stop you as a team. By moving the ball quickly, and keeping everybody moving, your players are trying to make it hard for the defenders to guard them, which can lead to good things happening offensively.

When you pass the ball, you force the defence to react, usually by moving or shifting in the direction of the ball; therefore, every pass counts. You want your players to pass the ball around the outside of the defence in a U-shape formation, either passing down to the crease or back up from the crease, with some cross-floor passes thrown in. By changing the ball from one side of the floor to the other with cross-floor passes, you not only move the defence but also move the goalie, all the time looking to get the ball into the middle of the defence.

Moving without the ball

As I note at the beginning of this section, passing skills are just one element of a good motion offence. The second critical element is your team's ability to move without the ball. Chapter 8 offers some suggestions for your players to help them understand the importance of moving — with or without the ball. In this section, I share some coaching tips for you to stress with your team — specifically, in a motion offence, what options your players have when they're not in the process of passing or receiving the ball (Figure 14-5 demonstrates a few of them).

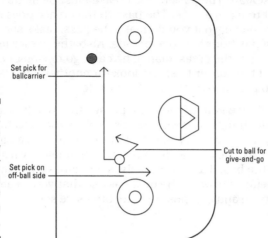

Figure 14-5:
Just three
of many
options for
moving
without the
ball on
offence.

Set pick for
ballcarrier

Set pick on
off-ball side

Cut to ball for
give-and-go

✔ You can cut to the ball for a give-and-go.

✔ You can go and set a pick for the ballcarrier.

✔ You can go and set a pick on the off-ball side.

✔ You can run off a pick set by your teammate.

✔ You can go and set a screen for your teammate on your side of the floor.

✔ You can run off a screen set by a teammate.

✔ You can V-cut to get open for a pass.

✔ You can stay where you are to stay out of the way of a developing play.

✔ You can clear out for the new ballcarrier. You must create the right spacing on the floor to make the team better.

Cutting through the middle

Players must cut through the middle with the idea that their defender cannot stay with them (see Figure 14-6). They must cut with the stick ready to catch rather than just going through the motions. I've always measured the toughness of a player by the number of times he catches the ball cutting through the middle! The toughest battles are getting shots in front of the net or in the middle of the defence. By passing and cutting through the defence, you force the defence to react and move, and they start to wear them down.

Figure 14-6:
Keep your players constantly running through the middle to force the defender to follow.

If a player cuts through the middle and does not get a pass, he should stop at the centre and V-cut back to his own side. A V-*cut* is simply a move where the player turns around and heads back to the position where he started; you don't want the player looping back from the centre (I guess that would be a U-cut); rather, he should make a sharp redirection, heading back in the general direction of where he came from, thus creating a V. After the V-cut, the player can be an instant threat for a pass or another cut, or he can circle the net. You'll be amazed by how many times a player can get open just by running around the net. The point of all this movement in and out of the middle is that you don't want players standing in the middle of the floor and clogging it up; you want to keep the middle lane clear for additional cutters.

Getting open for a pass

Unless a defender literally falls asleep, your players have to work hard to get open. (Okay, not literally — figuratively. If a defender literally falls asleep, make sure the ballcarrier doesn't trip over him on his way to the net.) Most of a player's time on offence is without the ball, so use it wisely.

When running the motion offence, make sure that your ballcarriers don't spend all their time looking to pass. When a ballcarrier does so, he's no longer an offensive threat. The ballcarrier has to be a threat to score or go one-on-one, no matter what type of offence a team is running. A problem with running the motion offence is that some players play too far outside of the defence so that they don't get hit. They are sometimes afraid to cut into the middle, afraid to set a pick, and afraid to go one-on-one. Always coach that your players keep moving and working to get open for a pass. In any offensive scheme, but especially in the motion offence, getting open keeps the flow of play moving and increases your chances to score.

Setting picks: Forcing the defence to create openings

Sometimes a defence can help your players get open. If a tough defender overplays your best scorer, then as a coach, you must call for a pick on the defender. This strategy may force the defender to switch assignments, with your scorer checked by a weaker defender. Or the defence may not switch, choosing to double-team your scorer, leaving a teammate in the clear.

Picks and screens are a great way to help your teammates get in the clear. By getting a ballcarrier in the clear, you give him an open shot. Remember that an open shot comes when a player has time to shoot without a defender interfering with the stick.

When setting a pick, make sure that your players set a good solid pick and do so immediately so that the defence can't figure out what play you're running. They need to make body contact with a teammate's defender that may force the defender to switch (see Figure 14-7). Once the ballcarrier passes the picker's shoulder, he should push off on the defender and roll to the net for a soft pass from the ballcarrier (see Figure 14-8).

Figure 14-7:
Setting an up pick against a defender.

Figure 14-8:
The picker rolls to get open for a pass from his teammate.

For the pick to be legal, the picker must be stationary. However, when setting the pick, a picker is allowed to use his body or to cross-check and push off on the defender when he rolls to the net.

With its larger playing area and its higher number of players, picks and set plays are just as important, if not more so, in the field game. Many field plays are designed to exploit the long-stick defenders.

Running the give-and-go play

This play is the quintessential motion offence set play; it requires crisp passing and quick cutting. It works best when a defender adjusts — even slightly — to the direction of a pass. In a give-and-go play, an initial ballcarrier does both the giving and the going. He passes the ball to a teammate, typically in about the same area of the zone, and then cuts toward the goal hoping to take a pass from that same teammate. When it works well, the initial ballcarrier's defender relaxes or follows the initial pass just enough so that the ballcarrier can break ahead of his defender toward the net.

Figure 14-9 shows a give-and-go play where the cutter is the initial ballcarrier, and he breaks outside quickly before heading for the net for a return pass and shot. When you pass the ball, the next move is to fake or take one step to the boards when your defender reacts, and then plant your outside foot and push off explosively and cut sharply to the ball or net. You can ask for the ball by keeping your stick up and out, even shaking your stick hard to indicate that you want the ball.

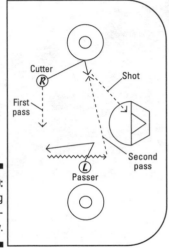

Figure 14-9:
Diagramming
a give-and-
go play.

When executing the give-and-go, you have the option of cutting in front of a defender or cutting *backdoor,* that is, going behind the defender. Your players have to anticipate how a defender is going to react and then decide what move to make. The best option is to cut in front of the defender because your player can receive the pass and still be in a good position to shoot, even if the defender is right beside him. If your player is being overplayed or when the defender tries to cheat to intercept a cross-floor pass, the backdoor cut becomes available for a pass and open shot.

Running the pick-and-roll play

Another game situation that works well in a motion offence, the pick-and-roll is a kind of give-and-go, but with the defender instead of the ball. An offensive player, the *picker,* gets in the way of the ballcarrier's defender so that the ballcarrier can create some space for a shot or pass. The picker then rolls to the net for a pass from the ballcarrier and a close-in shot. In this "give-and-go," the ballcarrier "gives" the defender, and the picker goes.

The pick-and-roll play creates chaos and indecision for the defence, plus it creates a gap for the ballcarrier, who has three options:

✔ Shooting coming off the pick

✔ Going one-on-one off the pick

✔ Passing to the picker (who I guess could also be called the roller, having already set the pick)

When setting a pick, you *will* be cross-checked. But don't let a defender stop you from setting it; if you get tied up with him, stay where you are and let the ballcarrier read it as a screen and make his cut off the screen. If the defender fires out on the pick at the ballcarrier, you can then cut backdoor.

Running Set Plays in Your Man-to-Man Offence

Running set plays does not really work well as an offensive system on its own. Instead, you may call set plays during games in which your better players are not handling the ball as much as you'd like, or your players may be holding onto the ball too long and not moving efficiently enough. The most common set plays in lacrosse involve only two to three players.

No matter the reason for running a set play, you want to maintain some parameters for how your players should execute the play.

✔ A well-executed one-on-one move takes precedence over any set play that you call for.

✔ Teach your players to call a set play on their own during a game. They can either make a real call during action on the floor, or they can suggest a play while sitting on the bench.

✔ If a set play doesn't work, your players should know to return automatically to your regular offensive system, such as the motion offence.

✔ Consider running two set plays: a real one on the strong side and a decoy play on the off-ball side.

When running set players, your offensive players need to play alertly and intelligently because you want them to read the defence, that is, anticipate what they may do so that your players can execute the called play. By reading the defenders, your offensive players can react efficiently when a defender doesn't play the way your set play anticipates. Instead of ending up with a *broken play,* one that doesn't reach its conclusion, you may end up with an improvised play that nevertheless leads to a score.

The following list offers a few set plays that you can try with your team. These plays are designed for the strong-side alignment, and each play includes an introduction setting up the play, as well as tips for what you should ask your players to do.

- ✔ **Up pick-and-roll:** The main play here is at the top of the offensive zone when the creaseman comes up the floor and sets a pick for the ballcarrier.

- ✔ **The ballcarrier:** To make this pick-and-roll work, stress that the ballcarrier face his defender or turn sideways and receive a cross-check while he waits for the pick. When coming off the pick, he should look to shoot right away or go one-on-one, and not fade away or look to pass. One option is to cut outside to the boards and then back in to the middle for a shot. Another option is to pass to the picker, who has rolled into the middle of the floor for a pass and close-in shot. A third option becomes available if the defender charges him quickly on the switch, in which case he should cut across the top of the floor for a long shot.

- ✔ **The picker:** Make sure that the picker doesn't pick directly at the defender's back but instead more to his back-leg side, preferably his blind side. Stress that the picker get his whole body on the pick, not just an arm and shoulder, and then stay with the defender until the ballcarrier passes his shoulder. He must keep his stick parallel to the floor so that he can cross-check or push off on the defender. And remind him to roll so that he's always facing the ball with his stick ready for a forward pass.

- ✔ **Cross pick-and-roll:** The cross pick-and-roll (see Figure 14-10) is one of the great plays in lacrosse, and nobody executes it better than Colin Doyle and Kim Squire of the Toronto Rock, and Tom Marechek and Jake Bergey of the Philadelphia Wings.

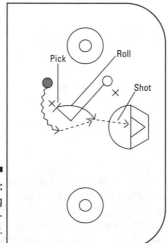

Figure 14-10:
Diagramming a cross pick-and-roll play.

Playing defence on offence: Preventing a breakaway

In the NLL, all teams send players quickly off the bench for the long pass after a change of possession. If your offensive players are watching the ball on a shot, they *will* get beat, and you definitely don't want to lose because your players aren't getting back on defence. But who should you send out after the shot to defend the breakaway?

The *defensive safety,* or the first player back on defence to prevent a breakaway, is the player who ends up in the pointman's position on the shot. The cornerman who is on the opposite side of the floor from the shot runs back second.

The first player back must play the opposing player coming off his team's bench, not the man going off the floor. He should not run down the middle of the floor, but instead run (not backpedal) closer to the bench side so that he can stick-check the player's stick when he comes on the floor. When you think a pass is coming to a breakaway player, keep your back to the passer and play the breakaway player's stick, watching his eyes. Avoid turning around and going for the steal, or you could get beat.

Other offensive players have a role in stopping breakaways as well. When the creasemen realize that they've lost possession of the ball on a missed shot, they should look for the passer and try to pressure him into making a bad pass down the floor. And the best way to defend against breakaways is to take high percentage shots, that is, shots that have a better chance to get past the goalie into the net.

Note: One of the big differences between the field game and the box game is that after a field player shoots, the offensive players hang around the net in case the ball goes wide and past the net. Remember that the field endline is actually 15 *yards* behind the goal. If you're coaching a player who's played a lot of field lacrosse, stress that he immediately look to play defence after a shot, not try to grab a loose ball in the 15 *feet* behind the box goal.

- ✔ **The picker:** Try to set *cross picks* — that is, running a crossing pattern through the middle and up toward the ballcarrier — for long-ball shooters so that they can cut across the top of the floor for their shot. The play is executed in the offensive end when the creaseman or picker comes up the floor at an angle to set a pick on the ballcarrier's defender's body but on the inside side of his body. Remember after picking, the roller must roll so that he is facing the ball with his stick ready for a soft, lobbing, forward pass.

- ✔ **The ballcarrier:** After the pick, the ballcarrier cuts across the top of the floor for a good long shot. Another option is to pass to the picker, who is rolling toward the net for a pass and close-in shot. A third option occurs if the defender charges him quickly on the switch, so he can go the opposite way and cut to the boards for a shot.

- ✔ **Down screen:** This screen play is designed to create a close-in shot for a shooter. The shooter works off his teammate's screen to try to get to an opening in the defence for a shot.

✔ **The screener:** The cornerman is the screener, and he starts the play by passing down to the creaseman and then cutting to the net slowly as if he wants a return pass so that his defender stays beside him. When he hits the middle of the floor, maybe slightly off-centre, he stalls just long enough for his teammate to run his own defender into the screener, creating the opening for the shot. Make sure that the screener gets the inside position on his own defender and clamps his stick over his defender's stick, making it hard for the defender to switch to the shooter. After the screen, the cornerman pops out toward the top of the zone for defensive safety purposes.

✔ **The shooter:** After receiving the pass and while the screen is being set, the creaseman cuts out of the corner looking to rub his defender out of the way by cutting close to the screen. As soon as he goes by the screen, he's looking for a shot.

The difference between the pick and the screen is that when you set a pick, you're interfering with your teammate's defender. When you set a screen, you're interfering with your own defender.

Breaking Out on the Quick: The Fast-Break Offence

A *fast break* is when the ballcarrier runs the ball up the floor over the offensive line before the defence has a chance to get back and set up their defence. A fast-break offence is designed to create odd-man situations and an easy score. But running the fast break is not just frenzied chaos; it's more like organized chaos.

You want to break quickly in an organized manner from your own end and run down the floor creating an odd-man situation at the other end from which you can get a good scoring opportunity. When running the ball up the floor, the ballcarrier must look to attack the net so that he forces a defender to commit to him — that is, to choose to defend the ballcarrier rather than another offensive player on the fast break — and then he can pass to an open man. If the defender doesn't commit to your ballcarrier, he may have an open shot on goal or, if another defender has joined the fray, he may just peel off to the side of the floor looking to pass or set up the offence.

Too many fast-breaking teams can get bogged down by the pace of play dictated by a slow-down team, and they end up simply jogging the ball up the floor rather than running full-out. For most teams, it's easier to slow a game down than speed it up. To keep your team focused on running, stress the quick outlet pass by the goalie and the hard and fast breakout by the ballcarrier.

Fast breaking down the field

Fast breaks in field lacrosse are different from box lacrosse. As a defenceman or midfielder brings the ball out of the defensive end, three attackmen and three opposing defencemen are waiting at the midfield line. The most important part of the fast break is for the attackmen to take advantage of whatever lag time exists (a split-second usually) between the ballcarrier and whoever is defending him. This is when the offense can exploit a numbers advantage.

Attackmen must know exactly what to do when their teammates clear the ball and how to best prepare for the incoming players. Common drills involve running different scenarios over the midfield line — one player bringing the ball up with no one trailing, two players with one trailing, three with two trailing, and so on. These drills help prepare the attackmen to know how to react and the midfielders know how to proceed when charging into the offensive zone.

Also, to prevent your team from being unduly influenced by a slow-down team, reward players that run at full speed at any point during the game, including pushing the ball up the floor, scooting off the bench to join play, or even dashing to the bench to be replaced on a line change.

Assembling your fast-break personnel

The fast-break offence works especially well when you can play everyone on your team. The more players that you send out running at full speed, the better your chances of wearing down the opposition. (If you're familiar with football, compare the impact of your fast break on the defence to the impact a big strong running back has on a defensive line: After 25 or 30 carries, the defensive line is just too plum wore out to stop the running back.) You also need to set a team objective to be one of the best-conditioned teams in the league (see Chapter 13 for more about conditioning for lacrosse).

To run a fast-break offence, look for players who play with quickness, aggressiveness, and tenacity. The fast-break offence places less emphasis on bigger, more physical players, and it has a place for the little guy. When building your fast-break team, look for players with speed rather than size, and then press, press, press. You can find more about defensive pressing in Chapter 15.

Ideally, your cornerman should start the fast break, either by running the ball up the floor into the offensive end or by passing it to a breaking teammate. He must protect the ball up the floor at the same time that he's seeing the positioning of his teammates and their defenders.

Don't limit your fast-break offence to just those few seconds that it takes for the ballcarrier to run the ball down the floor. If your team doesn't score off the fast break, you still want your players to emulate the pressure and intensity of the fast break in its half-court offence. Constantly attack the net. Keep players moving and cutting, looking for an opening or a breakdown on defence. And you also want players who are daring and aggressive on the defensive end. Because of the pace of play that you want, your fast-break players have to play both ends of the floor; aggressive defenders lead to turnovers and loose balls and more fast breaks.

Steve Toll of the Toronto Rock says about fast-break lacrosse: "Transition is a huge part of lacrosse, but when breaking, don't leave early and don't let your offensive man score. Anticipate the play and go hard up the floor. To become the best you have to want it. Lead your team by example."

Running team fast-break drills

When building your team's fast-break offence with drills, stress passing and catching on the run, and stop the drills when you see too many players making poor decisions under defensive pressure. You'll play the full floor in most drills, but you can teach drills in one zone only. Your drills may be most effective if you make them competitive, assigning rewards for successful drills. Here are a few fast-break drills that you can work on with your team.

- ✔ **Single-line drill:** A good drill for a warm-up, it uses two lines of players, each one with a ball, on one endline. Place three sets of stationary passers on each side of the floor: one at the top of the faceoff circle along the sideboards, another at the centre of the floor, and the third at the defensive line on the sideboards. Each player runs from the endline, making three passes along the way, one to each of the stationary passers, from whom he also receives a return pass. After the third return pass, the player shoots at the goalie (see Figure 14-11).

- ✔ **2-on-0 down-and-wait drill:** Another good warm-up drill that uses two lines of players (right-shots and left-shots) behind the endline, with just the right-shots carrying a ball. Two players at a time, one from each line, run down the floor, passing back and forth two or three times before taking a shot at the other end.

    Variation: Change this drill to a down-and-back drill, running the length of the floor and back before taking a shot.

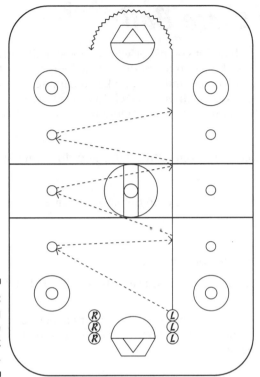

Figure 14-11:
Diagramming
the single-line
fast-break
drill.

✔ **1-on-0 breakaway-pass-from-goalie drill:** This drill allows your goalies to work on the passing and timing of throwing a long outlet pass. Run this drill regularly because long-passing may be difficult for a goalie to practise on his own.

Variation: Run this drill for short outlet passes, which your goalie will use to get the ball quickly to a fast breakout player. You can run this drill in practice, perhaps with an assistant coach, while working with the rest of the team on the other end of the floor.

✔ **2-on-1 half-floor teaching drill:** Keeping this drill in just one end of the floor allows you to stop the drill at any time so that you can teach players what to do and where to go on the fast break. Two offensive players start from centre floor, and one defender plays the middle lane of the offensive zone. The offensive players have four seconds to create a shot on goal.

Variation: Start the drill with an outlet pass from the goalie to one of the offensive players, or run it as a three-on-two drill.

Battling for the Loose Ball

How important are loose balls? If you never win the loose-ball battle, you'll never have the ball with a chance to break down the floor for a fast-break opportunity. Or you'll miss opportunities to make an easy score off a missed shot and rebound. It's not too much of a stretch to say that loose balls are the key to victory. If your team outplays your opponent in collecting loose balls, you will win the game.

Jim Veltman of the Toronto Rock offers these five keys for winning the loose-ball battle:

- ✔ Anticipate where the ball will end up before it becomes loose.

- ✔ Get to the loose ball first by going at full speed.

- ✔ Know your options before scooping the loose ball up, whether it's an outlet pass to a teammate or a breakaway with the ball in your own stick.

- ✔ If you get to the ball first, spread your legs to shield the ball from your opponent.

- ✔ If you get there behind your opponent, hit his stick just before he attempts to pick up the ball and hope the ball passes by him, giving you a chance to pick the ball up.

After you get possession of the loose ball, you have a few options as far as what to do next. You can tuck the ball into your body to protect the ball. You can pass the loose ball back to your goalie, if you're in your own defensive zone. Or you can pass it to the closest available teammate. If you can't pick the ball up cleanly, knock it back to your goalie or to a teammate.

Gaining possession of a loose ball

The following list offers a few of the game situations during which loose balls become available:

- ✔ Recovering a rebound off a missed shot
- ✔ Stealing the ball from the ballcarrier
- ✔ Forcing the opposition to take a bad shot
- ✔ Forcing the opposition to make a bad pass
- ✔ On any faceoff

Now, trying for the loose ball in these situations and actually gaining possession of it are two very different matters. The balance of this section offers some tips and tricks to better your chances of picking up a loose ball.

Scooping is not just for dog owners

The scoop pick-up is probably the most common pick-up in lacrosse because it's so fast and simple. Other moves include the *trap-and-scoop* (covering the ball with your pocket and then scooping up the ball) or the politically incorrect *Indian pick-up* (placing the backside of the head of your stick over the ball and knocking the ball with the side of the frame while turning the head of your stick over), but you usually don't have time to try these fancier, less-effective moves.'

The scoop pick-up is basically making a shovelling motion with your stick while picking up the ball. Once you get the ball into your stick, make sure that you protect the stick by pulling the stick in close to your body and then start to cradle immediately to make sure that you have the ball.

When going after a loose ball, bend your knees, stay low, keep a wide stance, and bend over to protect the ball. You should always have two hands on the stick, with your top hand near the throat and your bottom hand at the butt or end of the stick. And remember to keep this butt end low to the floor to make it easier to scoop through the ball.

Steve Toll of the Toronto Rock says about picking up loose balls: "When I go after a loose ball I get low, keeping two hands on the stick. Once I have the ball, I raise my head quickly to find out what's going on."

Positioning for the pick-up

When you go after a loose ball with an opponent beside you, get your body between the ball and your opponent. With this positioning, you can use your body to shield the ball from your opponent while you pick it up. After you get in front of your opponent, you may want to slow down a bit, maybe even backing up slightly so that you can prevent your opponent from slashing at your stick as you try to pick up the loose ball.

Attacking all loose balls

The way you approach going after a loose ball could be the difference of two goals: a possible goal for your team and a possible goal for the opposition. So don't take it casually; instead, attack loose balls aggressively rather than wait for them to come to you — watching versus attacking is the difference of possession or lost of possession.

Rather than going after a loose ball, some players just cross-check their opponent from behind — they're lazy, selfish, and not too swift. Plus, this move usually results in a penalty for cross-checking from behind. (See Chapter 4 for more about lacrosse penalties.)

Turning the loose-ball battle into a team reunion

Don't be the only player to go after a loose ball. Your team stands a better chance of picking up a loose ball if you're consistently meeting one or more of your teammates at the ball. By outnumbering your opponent, you can more easily gain possession of the loose ball.

With two or three teammates around a loose ball, you may be able to use one or two players to fend off opposing players so that the best ballhandler can pick up the loose ball and do something with it.

Working on loose-ball drills

You can work on these drills on your own or with friends or teammates. Although you want to remember to keep both hands on the stick in a game situation, practising with one hand may help you become more confident with stick control. Try alternating your pick-up move between hands.

In all these loose-ball drills, you should face the direction of the ball, whether it is stationary or rolling. However, the best loose-ball drills usually occur during team scrimmages, because obtaining a loose ball depends less on technique and more on persistence.

- **1-on-0 pick-up drill:** This drill has several variations. You can work on picking up a stationary ball. You can bounce a ball off a wall, simulating a ball coming of the end or sideboards, and then pick it up. Or you can have a friend roll a ball toward you for a pick-up.

- **Loose ball with partner drill:** Standing side-by-side, one partner rolls the ball and the other chases it. You should roll the ball in different directions to simulate a loose ball from a faceoff, which is often unpredictable.

- **5-on-0 rebound-off-the-boards drill:** Five players line up at centre. The first player rolls the ball off the boards hard. The next player in line attacks the ball when it hits the sideboards, retrieves the loose ball, and then bangs it off the boards for the next player.

  Variation: One player rolls or shoots all the balls, one at a time, and the players at centre attack and pick up the ball before returning to the roller.

- **1-on-1 teaching progression for picking up loose ball:** This series of drills starts with positioning for a loose ball without sticks. When you start using sticks and a ball, you'll need a coach or teammate to roll the ball to begin each progression.

  - First player boxes out opponent along the sideboards. Neither player has a stick.

- Defender tries to push the offensive player into the boards. The offensive player has to be low, anticipate getting hit, and lean back into defender.

- Both players now have sticks. While the offensive player tries to pick up a loose ball, the defender leans or pushes against him with his hands or body.

- Defender can only stick-check the offensive player, who attempts to pick up loose ball. Defender starts behind offensive player.

- Defender starts from a half-step behind the offensive player, who attempts to pick up the ball.

Chapter 15

Coaching Defensively

· ·

· ·

*T*he main objective for any defence is to stop the opposition from scoring, or at least to force them to take bad shots. And whether it's a stay-in-your-area zone defence or an aggressive and pressuring man-to-man defence, a secondary objective for the defence is to create a change of possession so that its own offensive team can get the ball and score.

Playing defence is combative and aggressive, but that doesn't mean that defences should be designed to find out who can give the biggest hit or who can intimidate the other team. You want to develop a defence that's physical and tough but also smart enough to avoid bad penalties from over-aggressive play, such as hitting from behind, charging a player, or slashing a player.

This chapter focuses on the two primary defences that you'll likely use in minor lacrosse: the man-to-man defence and the zone defence. I also share a few drills that you can use to develop your team's defensive philosophy.

Going Head to Head: Playing a Man-to-Man Defence

In lacrosse, the unsung heroes are the great defenders who shut down the offensive stars, or who at least make it tough for the stars to score. If you don't have a great defence, you will not be successful in lacrosse. In the NLL, the first-place teams generally boast the best goals-against statistics, and not necessarily the best goals-for stats. The common perception is true: The offence may win games, but the defence wins championships.

Your defence should be the cornerstone of your team. With a solid defence, your team can be competitive game in and game out no matter how your offence performs. And a solid defence starts with solid defenders, the kind of players who can take on an offensive player on his own and have some measure of success in preventing him from scoring. These defenders are the foundation you need for a successful man-to-man defence.

Recognizing the types of man-to-man defences

A man-to-man defence is different from a zone defence in that you assign individual defenders to check individual offensive players, by following them around wherever they go in the defensive zone. A zone defence places your defenders in assigned spots in the defensive zone, areas that they are responsible for covering.

However, variations exist in how you play man-to-man defence, whether it centres on the ball or on individual players or some combination of both.

✔ **Ball-oriented man-to-man defence:** I believe that to play great team defence, each defensive player must know where the ball is at all times. If you're a ball-oriented defensive team, your players focus more on where the ball is than where their opponents are. However, defenders still have to keep track of the players they're defending, which presents the primary challenge with this type of man-to-man defence: With the great ball movement and skills of today's player, it's hard to focus on the ball and also follow your man.

To play this style of man-to-man defence, you have to stress maintaining an open stance, looking down the floor, and keeping your eyes on both your off-ball man and the ball by looking between them so that you can see both of them at the same time. To play this ball-oriented type defence, you need good pressure on the ball, which admittedly is hard to do with the ball moving so quickly and accurately. Without pressure on the ball, your defenders who are playing the off-ball opponent are susceptible to cross-floor passes to the player they're defending for a quick shot, or quick cuts by the offensive player to the ball.

✔ **Man-oriented man-to-man defence:** If you are a man-oriented defensive team, you must stress a closed stance — belly-to-belly — to keep your eyes on the opponent even to the point where you stay with him more than helping out. In this system, players don't always know where the ball is, and they are susceptible for picks and screens, so they end up trailing the play rather than anticipating and staying with the play. If the ballcarrier beats his defender, his defensive teammates are not looking for the ball and are not in position to help him.

✔ **Combination man-to-man defence:** A combination type of defence gives the ball and the opponent equal importance (see Figure 15-1). This defence is the primary one played in the NLL. When a player defends an off-ball opponent, he should play in a closed stance, staying with him while looking slightly over his shoulder to find out where the ball is. When your players know both where the ball is and their opponents are, they are better able to anticipate the next offensive move: Which offensive player will make a cut? Who will set a pick for a teammate? Who will receive a pick? Who will stay and wait for a return pass? Anticipating an offensive player's next move is half the battle on defence.

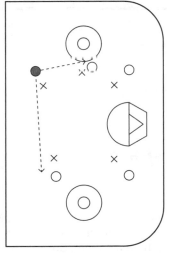

Figure 15-1:
Combination man-to-man defence keeps pressure on the ballcarrier and helps deny possible passing lanes.

The difference in this defensive scheme is that, although a player defends one person, as does each of his teammates, they are still looking to help. (See "Helping: To rotate or not to rotate" later in this chapter.) No matter what defensive systems you play, if you have defenders who play strong on-the-ball defence, you're going to be in great shape every game.

Playing both ways in the man-to-man defence

Believe it or not, a team needs offensive defenders and defensive defenders on their defence. To be successful, a team needs to score goals from their five-on-five offence, from their breaks off the bench, and from their defence. It really helps a team when its defensive players can run the floor and score rather than just run the floor and pass off.

"I have 11!"

The easiest way for a player to know his defensive assignment is to have him call out his opponent's number and point a stick at him. This simple practice helps keep everybody mentally in the game and removes indecision about who is covering whom.

In addition to knowing who is defending whom, each player must know who has the ball. Get your players on the bench to yell out to their teammates who has the ball. The hidden ball trick is not just a baseball move!

You want to build a man-to-man defence that can initiate an instant offence from steals, loose balls, forced turnovers, and missed shots. These situations can lead to easy fast-break goals, and they take a great deal of pressure off your five-on-five offence. Players who can play both ways, offence and defence, are a tremendous asset on any team.

Applying pressure in the man-to-man defence

The man-to-man defence is a very aggressive, pressuring defence. Most man-to-man teams want to put the opposition under continuous pressure by aggressively cross-checking or slashing the ballcarrier. But where should you start applying this pressure?

The obvious answer is to start applying pressure when the ballcarrier enters his own scoring area. But when the ballcarrier is not in a scoring area, he can still pass the ball to a teammate who is in a prime scoring area. Now you have to defend a ballcarrier who is a threat to both score and pass. So the obvious answer may not always be the best answer, meaning that you have to rely on your players to decide how to play a ballcarrier, based on what they know about his offensive strengths and weaknesses.

Scary, eh? But that's where your preparation as a coach comes in handy. By attending other games, watching game films, and doing research on your opposition, you can tell your players exactly what the opponent's strengths and weaknesses are.

You should still encourage your players to cross-check the ballcarrier to slow him down, or to try to steal the ball from him. Aggressive cross-checking and slashing can often pressure the offence into making mistakes and turnovers. However, if your players try to force a turnover, they risk enabling the ballcarrier to dash past his flailing defender on the way to the net. But if you don't put pressure on the ball, the opposition will pick you apart with their passing.

Forcing defensive action to get an offensive reaction

Players in a man-to-man defensive system are daring and aggressive. They will take calculated risks and instigate action by attacking on defence. They do not play conservatively or cautiously. They are dictating the pace of play.

This type of defence does not want to react to the offence by guessing where the play is going or waiting to find out what the offence is going to do. The man-to-man defence attacks the offence before it has a chance to attack the net. For example, when the ballcarrier is at the top of the offence, the defenders should try to force him toward the sideboards.

This defence wants to make the offence do something by taking it out of its comfort zone, that is, what they hope to accomplish offensively. When the offence reacts to the defence's aggressiveness, the defence is in a better position to anticipate and out-think what the offence is going to do before they do it.

COACH TIP

Maintaining your advantage in the ring, or rather, on the floor

When I'm coaching an aggressive and pressuring man-to-man defence, I like to compare my team to a small boxer taking on a big boxer in the ring. Size won't help them knock anybody out, so they have to keep moving and jabbing to wear down the bigger opponent.

In an aggressive man-to-man defence, you want to apply relentless pressure throughout the whole game to wear the opposition down. You'll wear them down physically and mentally and force them into mistakes with your constant defensive pressure. If you're fortunate enough to have a defensive team that includes both quick *and* big players, you can add explosive hitting to your repertoire. Your players will be quick enough to recover when they take themselves out of position to deliver a hit.

Concentrating to get the job done

How many times have you seen a defensive player fall asleep for just a split second only to have a non-ballcarrier cut for a wide-open pass and shot with the defender trailing behind him? Or a ballcarrier faking one way and then going the other way when the defender bites on the fake? An alert defender can avoid these situations.

One of the most important qualities that the great defenders have is that they never get caught off-guard. Certainly, defensive players who play on the off-ball side may have a tough time staying alert when they have to concentrate on both their man and the ball. However, the best defenders have a great ability to focus on the two things at once. And defending the ballcarrier means concentrating on more than just the ballcarrier. Your defender has to be aware of players picking him or the ballcarrier coming off a screen.

Helping: To rotate or not to rotate

Rotating is simply helping out a teammate who has been beaten by the offensive player he's covering. But you can also use some planned rotation, where any or all of your five defenders can rotate to play the ball or the moving offensive players.

A total full rotation, that is, all five defensive players rotating, happens only in the ball-oriented type defence, because your players are following the ball as it moves around the offensive end of the floor. In a man-oriented or a combination-type defence, rotation occurs generally in a helping situation. Ideally, your defence will have such great defenders that they'll never get beaten, and you won't need any rotation at all.

A man-to-man defence is not successful if only individual defenders keep their own man from scoring; it has to keep the other *team* from scoring. Helping out is critical to a man-to-man defence because usually a good one-on-one offensive player can beat a good defender — he knows where he's going. Man-to-man defence works best when defenders help each other. Decide how and under what situation you want your defence to rotate.

- ✔ You may choose to stress that no ballcarrier should be allowed to go directly to the net without a defender attacking him to try to force a pass instead of a shot. In other words, don't let a ballcarrier take an uncontested shot.
- ✔ Defensive help can come from the top of the defence down, from the bottom of the defence up, or from the off-ball side over. You should dictate where the help should come from based on the quickness of your defensive team on the floor.

✔ Some defences choose not to rotate at all in certain situations. For example, the Toronto Rock of the NLL likes to keep their defenders closest to the net with their opponents all the time. By preventing their bottom defenders from rotating, they try to minimize the number of close-in shots attempted.

Where does the beaten defender go after a teammate has rotated to help him? The typical move is for the defender to rotate opposite the direction in which the ballcarrier passes.

Rotating against a motion offence

Here is a sample rotating progression against a motion offence, one that passes the ball around the zone (see Chapter 14 for more about the motion offence). Figure 15-2 diagrams each step of the progression.

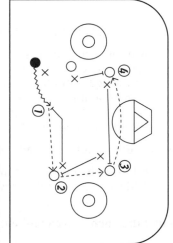

Figure 15-2:
Defending against a motion offence.

1. **Rotate when ballcarrier from top corner cuts inside.**

   If a defender in the top area of the floor is beaten by the ballcarrier into the middle of the floor, help comes from the off-ball top defender sliding over. If the ballcarrier sees the defensive pressure coming across, he may pass to a cornerman on the side of the floor where the help came from.

2. **Rotate on pass across to cornerman.**

   To help his teammate who rotated across, the bottom off-ball defender may leave his check to come up and pressure the new ballcarrier, who now may pass down to the creaseman on his side of the floor.

3. **Rotate on pass down to creaseman.**

   The off-ball bottom defender now rotates across the floor to check the creaseman who just received the pass.

4. **Rotate on pass across to creaseman.**

   And to make the rotation complete, the offensive creaseman, on seeing the bottom defender coming across, may pass to the other creaseman, but one of the off-ball top defenders has now rotated down to pressure the creaseman on his side of the floor.

Rotating against a penetrating offence

Here is a sample rotating progression against a penetrating offence, one that passes the ball around the zone (see Chapter 14 for more about the penetrating offence):

1. **Rotate when ballcarrier cuts inside from the top.**

   If a defender in the top area of the floor is beaten by the ballcarrier into the middle of the floor, help comes from the off-ball top defender sliding over. In this rotation, the defenders have a good chance of recovering back to their original man.

2. **Rotate when ballcarrier from the top area cuts to the outside.**

   If the ballcarrier keeps penetrating down the side and cuts in between the two side defenders, the ball-side bottom defender has to leave his man to help stop this penetration. On drawing the bottom defender, the ballcarrier then passes off to his now-open teammate on the crease who is cutting backdoor to the net. The rotation is: The bottom off-ball defender is ready to come across to defend the creaseman.

3. **Rotate when ballcarrier comes out of the corner area and cuts inside.**

   If the defender in the crease area is beaten to the inside (the middle of the zone), the top defender on the ballside slides or rotates down to help on the ballcarrier.

4. **Rotate when ballcarrier comes out of the corner area and cuts outside.**

   If the defender in the crease area is beaten to the outside or to the crease area, help comes from across the off-ball bottom defender with the off-ball top defender sliding down to take away a possible pass to the crease.

Using the man-to-man defence in game situations

The rest of this section about the man-to-man defence suggests a few ways in which this style of defensive play can help your team against certain offensive situations.

Defending the off-ball pick-and-roll

Most teams switch defenders when the offence executes an off-ball pick or screen (see Figure 15-3). To prevent a pick or screen, however, off-ball defenders must play between their man and the ball, not between their man and the net, which is a perfect setup for a down screen. If an offensive player cuts and tries to get the inside position on his defender so that he can set a screen, the defender must not let this happen as he won't be in a position to switch to help his teammate being screened. The defender should instead move down with the screener evenly, staying between his man and the ball.

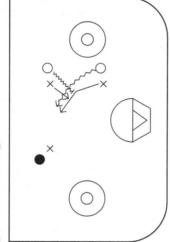

Figure 15-3:
Switching to defend against the pick.

Defending a player standing in the middle of the floor

Some offensive players love to stand in the middle of the floor, waiting to receive a pass and then take a shot. To defend this play, some defenders try to cross-check or push the offensive player from behind and out of the way; this only serves to create a good screen for the ballcarrier to shoot around. A good offensive player can also just lean and relax on the cross-checker to neutralize the defender, receive a pass, turn, and get a shot off.

To counter a player who stands in front of the net looking for a pass, a defensive player just has to stand beside him, playing between him and the ball, and playing his stick by clamping his stick over the opponent's stick. Now the defender is in a position to help a teammate if a screener tries to rub him out of the play.

Defending the give-and-go play

The give-and-go is one of the best plays in lacrosse; it's simple to execute because all the player does is pass the ball and cut. Ideally, the cutter wants to beat his defender by a step so that he gets into the clear for a pass and shot.

Or he can cut in front of his check and lean into him as he receives a pass and while he gets his shot off.

To defend this play, the defender shouldn't wait to find out what a passer does after passing. Instead, when the ballcarrier passes the ball, the defender drops to the direction of the pass and toward the middle of the floor, called *jumping to the ball*. The defender is trying to maintain his position between his opponent and the ball. He doesn't want to end up behind or beside the offensive player when he cuts. By stepping in the direction of the pass, the defender has a good chance of getting in front of the cutter, getting the inside position, forcing the cutter to go backdoor, and then reacting by playing his stick hard. If the cutter does get inside position on the defender, stress that the defender just slash his stick hard assuming that a pass is coming.

Defending penetration by the ballcarrier

As noted previously, a good offensive player can beat a good defender almost any time, which is why your defenders need to help each other. However, if you establish a defensive goal that says that nobody penetrates between two defenders, you'll stand a decent chance of winning the penetration game.

The standard man-to-man reaction to offensive penetration is called *help and recover*. It's a two-man game in which a defensive player *helps* a teammate who has been beaten while staying in position to *recover* should his own opponent end up with the ball. On the recovery back to his opponent, the defender has to close out quickly.

Closing out is running back to the new ballcarrier (the helper's previous check), staying down in a defensive stance, shuffling the last two steps, and coming at an angle to force him to the boards and stop him from going to the net or from taking a long shot. Stress to your defenders to cross-check the ballcarrier when they go to help, rather than stick-check, especially when closing out on great offensive players. If they gamble for the ball by stick-checking, they'll come up out of their defensive stance and will become vulnerable to getting beat.

Defending the odd-man situation

At some point during a game, probably even at several points during a game, your defenders are going to be outnumbered by attacking offensive players. Here are some coaching tips for defending these odd-man situations in a man-to-man defence:

- **Defending the 2-on-1:** The first man back on defence should stay in the middle of the floor until the ballcarrier becomes a scoring threat, at which point he attacks him hoping to force a bad pass. His goals are to protect the net first, stop the ball second, and force a pass third. Another option is to play a cat-and-mouse game, where he fakes to go after the ballcarrier to force a pass but stays in the middle to be ready to move to the other offensive player.

- **Defending the 3-on-2:** The two defenders who get back on defence play in tandem formation, one behind the other. The top defender plays the ballcarrier while the back defender plays behind his teammate and between the other two offensive players. When the ballcarrier passes to his breaking creaseman, the back defender pursues the pass and pressures the new ballcarrier, while the top defender drops down to the side opposite the pass to defend against a pass to the other creaseman. If the original ballcarrier does not pass, the top defender drops down with his teammate and plays between the two off-ball offensive opponents, forcing the ballcarrier to attempt a long shot or wait for the rest of his teammates to reach the offensive zone and set up a play.

- **Defending the 4-on-3:** The three back defenders play a triangle zone defence. The rotation is the same as against the three-on-two, and the keys are to pressure the ball and rotate in the opposite direction to where the pass goes.

- **Defending the 5-on-4:** The four defenders play a box zone defence and rotate as against the three-on-two.

Defending the Zone

Two basic types of zone defences are employed in lacrosse: the 2-1-2 and the 1-2-2. The only differences between these two alignments are how they start out and match up against the offensive alignment. If the offence starts with an offensive player at the top of the offence, the zone defensive team plays a 1-2-2 zone defence, with the "1" player of the 1-2-2 matching up against the top offensive player. If the offensive team overloads one side of the floor (the strong-side alignment), the zone defensive team plays a 2-1-2 zone defence, with the "1" player staying in the middle of the zone. Except for this distinction, the guidelines for playing these defensive systems are the same, so the balance of this section applies to both alignments.

Some teams like to change to a zone defence just to change up the defence and give the offence a different look and try to change the tempo. Other teams change defences each time down the floor to create some confusion and hesitancy with the offence.

Understanding the zone defence philosophy

The zone defence is designed to take away the opposition's inside game and force outside shots, which are easier for the goalie to handle. This defence works best against offensive teams that don't play well together: they haven't yet developed as a team; they aren't great at passing; or they have players that prefer to go on one-on-one and don't want to give the ball up.

You can play zone defence and still apply the kind of pressure that you'd normally find in a man-to-man defence. To do so, you play the ballcarrier man-to-man within the zone; for example, the top defender in a 1-2-2 defensive alignment covers the ballcarrier. When applying pressure in a zone defence, try to force the ball to the outside of the defence or all the way to the boards. If the ball goes inside the defence, the zone defence acts as backup protection as the defenders sag inside to try to force the ball back out. You also want to pressure or force every shot by having a stick bothering the shot.

The 1-2-2 zone defence looks especially like a man-to-man defence — at least until the first pass when the top defender drops into the middle to plug up any gaps (see Figure 15-4). The four perimeter players are responsible for an area of the floor rather than for an offensive player, so the defence divides the floor into quarters. In this setup, when an offensive player goes from one area to another in the zone, the defender in the vacated area does not follow.

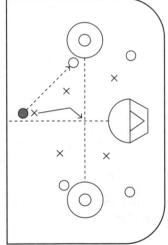

Figure 15-4:
On the pointman's first pass, the top defender moves to the middle of the zone defence set.

The following list includes some critical elements to any successful zone defence. Work with your players on these actions in the defensive zone:

✔ **Adjust:** When playing a zone defence, defenders must remember to adjust. The defenders have to constantly change and make adjustments during an offensive set, depending on the position of the ball.

✔ **Talk:** Defenders must communicate with each other. The back defenders (closest to the goal) are usually designated as floor generals because they can see most of the defensive zone. The middle defender in a 2-1-2 alignment must also talk to get rid of any indecision by top defenders.

- **Pressure the ball:** The closest defender to the location of the ball must pressure the ball to stop the offence from moving it around easily. This element also helps keep all your defenders alert and in the game, as they always have a task to do as soon as the ball enters their area of the zone.

- **Stop any penetration:** Nobody penetrates between two defenders. This rule is important for helping out between defenders.

- **Move with every pass:** On every pass, all five defenders must move, even if it's only a quarter-turn of the body to get a better view of the ball without losing sight of the offensive player in that area of the zone. By stressing universal movement on *every* pass, your defence will be in better position before the offence adjusts to the new ball position.

- **Follow the cutter:** If an offensive player cuts, the defender goes with the cutter until the cutter crosses over to another defender's area of the zone. On the cut, make sure to cross-check the cutter or deny him a pass

  If the new defender doesn't pick up the cutter, you can't leave him alone to wait for a pass and an open shot. The initial defender should stay with the cutter, with an eye to any activity in his own area of the zone, until the new defender finally picks up the cutter.

- **Protect the net in the middle:** The middle defender always stays between the ball and the net. Even when the ball goes back to the top of the offence, the middle defender remains between the ball and the net while playing the top offensive player.

- **Protect the middle against a strong-side offensive set:** When the ball is on the strong side (the side with three offensive players), and the ballcarrier is in the middle of the other two offensive players, the top ball-side defender must play him. If you play the middle defender in this situation, you're leaving the middle vulnerable to an open shot by a cutter from any position on the floor. You don't want the middle defender to play against any offensive player except at the top of the zone or when a teammate has been beaten.

- **Back up the middle against the weak-side offence:** If the ball is with a player on the weak side (the side with two offensive players), the two defenders on that side match up with each of them. The middle defender acts as a backup in this situation, protecting the middle from any cutters.

Homing in on the ballcarrier with a double-team

Although you can double-team an offensive player in any defensive set (including man-to-man), the double-team is essentially a zone-like defensive play. On the *double-team,* two defenders double the ballcarrier — that is, they both defend the ballcarrier at the same time — while the other three defenders form a triangular zone that covers the rest of the floor, ready to help and rotate if the ballcarrier breaks through the double-team. Because one offensive player will always be open during a double-team, the defender furthest from the ball plays between the two offensive players closest to his area of the zone.

To initiate a double-team, designate certain colours to call out so that all defenders know to make the defensive switch. Following are some game situations in which I like to call for the double-team:

✔ When the ballcarrier turns his back to the rest of his teammates

✔ When the ballcarrier is a weak ball-handler who's less likely to handle the pressure, making him panic and turn the ball over

✔ To force the opposition's best player to pass the ball to a less talented teammate

The double-teamer — the player who leaves his own offensive assignment to join another defender — should usually come from the strong side of the defence, the side with three defenders on it. If the ballcarrier is on the strong side of the defence, the defender beside the defender checking the ballcarrier leaves his man to double-team. If the ballcarrier is on the weak side of the defence, the side with two defenders, the top defender on the strong side leaves his check and comes across to double-team the ball.

If the ballcarrier is on the weak side, but is with the creaseman, the top defender on the weak side drops down while the top defender on the strong side comes across. The other three defenders form a triangle ready to slide or rotate (see Figure 15-5). The defender creating the double-team should stick-check the ballcarrier rather than cross-check. If the ball is passed out of the double-team, the double-teamer rotates or drops opposite to the pass.

Figure 15-5:
In a double-team set, the three defenders not doubling the ball-carrier form a zone-like triangle to defend against the other four offensive players.

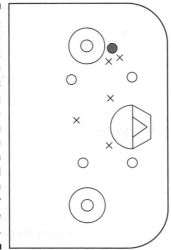

Recognizing a few other zone defences

You may be able to create your own zone defence that best suits the players on your team, but failing that, here are a few defences to try out in practice to find out how well your players adapt to them.

I call these sets *gadget defences,* and you should only use them as short-term solutions dictated by the game situation, rather than throughout the game.

- ✔ **5-on-5 rover defence:** This defence is a floating one-man zone defence. Put a defender in the middle of the defence to play a one-man zone. He picks out the weakest offensive player and pretends to play him, but in reality he is backing up the defenders who are playing man-to-man against the opposition's best offensive players.

  The Philadelphia Wings of the NLL like to play a floating one-man zone defence to stop the pick-and-roll executed by Colin Doyle and Kim Squire of the Toronto Rock. This one-man zone defender slides down into the middle of the defence to plug it up.

- ✔ **5-on-5 half-floor trap defence:** The rule in the NLL is that once the ball goes over the centre line, it cannot go back over it without losing possession. (See Chapter 4 for more about lacrosse rules.) Teams such as Toronto and Albany take advantage of this rule by looking to trap any out-of-control ballcarriers running up the floor over the centre line.

  One man defends the ballcarrier but allows him to cross over the centre line, keeping him in the alley near the boards. The trapper stays in the middle of the floor, looking to cut the ballcarrier off at the boards. The other three defenders drop into a triangle zone. The back defender in the zone on the ballside takes away the sideline pass.

- ✔ **1-plus-4 half-floor defence:** This defence is not used too much in lacrosse because you need time and practice to execute it properly. However, it's essentially the opposite of the rover defence mentioned above. You have one defender on the ballcarrier playing man-to-man while the other four defenders play a box zone.

- ✔ **Stopping a great player:** The one thing you don't want to happen as a coach is to have one player beat you. So you should have a few wrinkles that will make it difficult for a great player to play against you. One way is to double-team him and force him to give up the ball, as I mentioned earlier in this section. Another way is to assign a good defender to overplay him and try to completely deny him from receiving the ball. The tendency is to put your best defender on a great offensive player by matching size with size or quickness with quickness.

Playing a full-floor zone press

You can apply defensive pressure to the whole floor if you have the players to do so. The 2-1-2 full-floor match-up zone is an attacking-style defence that starts in your team's offensive end as soon as you lose possession of the ball. Its objective is not so much to defend against a goal or trap the ball, as it is to force turnovers. You can run this zone press all the time or periodically, or you can have a special line that comes in at certain times of the game to apply pressure.

You can use the press to control the tempo of the game against teams that try to slow the game down; a full-floor press speeds the game up by pressuring the ball and denying all passing lanes down the floor. The press works especially well against teams that switch offensive- and defensive-oriented players on and off the floor with each possession of the ball — the so-called offence– defence system. Applying the press here puts your defenders against your opponent's defenders, who usually can't handle the ball as well as the offensive players, are poorer passers than the offensive players, and if checked, have a tendency to drop the ball.

This press is a bit of a gamble. Occasionally, you are going to get burned and scored on in this set. So if you press, don't get upset if you're scored against.

Why not a man-to-man full-floor press? I tried to coach this type of press once and found that the pressing players got mixed up trying to find the player that they were supposed to defend with the obvious result that an opponent ended up wide open somewhere on the floor.

Setting up your zone-press alignment

Start your players in a 2-1-2 alignment and then have each player pick up the opponent nearest to their zone area. With this alignment, a player can think less about where to go before heading right to his position in the zone press.

For the press to work, your two front men in the press — the offensive creasemen — need to pick up their opponents quickly because their teammates will read off them to pick up the other offensive players (see Figure 15-6). The two back men in the press, an offensive cornerman and the pointman, should break quickly back down the floor so that nobody gets behind them. The cornerman on the strong side of the line slides into the middle of the floor and waits for an offensive player to enter his area of the zone. If he has no opponent in his area, he must then move up or to the side of the floor to find the next closest man.

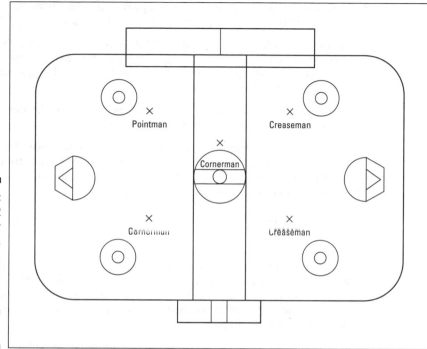

Figure 15-6:
The 2-1-2
full-floor
press calls
for the
offensive
creasemen
to press on
their end of
the floor.

If the offence clears the zone press and you get back into your defensive zone, make sure to switch assignments when you can so that you don't end up with a weak defensive player against a strong offensive player.

Assigning player duties in the full-floor zone press

The front defenders, the creasemen, are responsible for the following:

✔ Rebounds and loose balls on shots off the boards or off the goalie. Both creasemen go for possession of the loose ball. If one creaseman goes into the corner, the other creaseman backs him up.

✔ If the goalie makes the save and delivers an outlet pass to a fast-breaking teammate, one of the creasemen tries to delay the ballcarrier, taking time off the shooting clock and slowing down the push up the floor.

✔ If the opposition ballcarrier is quick, the creaseman shouldn't crowd him; instead, he should give him a cushion by taking a step or two away from him so that he doesn't get beaten. Putting tight defensive pressure on the ballcarrier encourages him to try to beat his defender; he sees it as a challenge, and if he's successful, he can break the press and speed up the offence.

✔ Try to force the ballcarrier to go in a particular direction. Force him to the boards and use the boards as an extra defender.

✔ Approach the ballcarrier under control; put pressure on the ball and try to steal the ball by stick-checking, keeping a safe distance back from the ballcarrier. Against a poor ballhandler, increase the pressure against the ball, trying to knock it loose.

✔ If the creaseman gets beaten, he should try to recover by catching up with the ballcarrier and running beside him.

✔ If the ballcarrier passes the ball over his head up the floor, the creaseman should drop to the level of the ball. The front defenders retreat to the line of the ball on any pass up the floor to help their defensive teammate who is now checking the new ballcarrier.

On the change of possession, the back defenders — the pointman and one of the cornermen — have these assignments:

✔ Get back on defence to the centre line and pick up the first opponent into their area, denying any pass down the floor. Watch for someone coming off your opponent's bench to try to break the press. If an offensive player heads for the bench after the possession change, watch the offensive bench door, not the player.

✔ On getting back, in the first few seconds, the back defenders must turn their backs to the ball to play their opponent's stick to cut off the deep pass. They must assume a pass is coming even if it isn't. Nobody goes by them in the clear.

✔ Once the back defenders have taken away the long pass, they must open up their stance and floor position to read the situation. They are now playing in front of their opponent, facing down the floor, and playing between the ball and this opponent.

✔ Cushion their checks; that is, defend tight enough to deny the long pass and loose enough to prevent an opponent from breaking back toward the ball to get into the clear. If his opponent attempts to break into the clear toward the ball, he should just stay in front of him and assume the ball is coming, playing his stick, and watching his eyes.

And finally, the middle defender positions himself between the two front and back lines of defence. He must quickly decide which side is the opposition's strong side and then pick up an opponent to deny a pass.

Running full-floor zone-press drills

When teaching positioning, show the whole situation first and then break the press down to off-ball side and ballside. Begin with drills where the ball starts with the goalie. The breakout team must first get into the clear and then try to get the ball down the floor. Stress that the press is used to create havoc, to force turnovers by pressure, to steal the ball, to force bad passes, to make the opposition run, to make the opposition play at a higher intensity level than it may be used to, and to delay the ball to kill time off the clock.

- ✔ **5-on-5 positioning drill:** The offence passes the ball up or across the floor with the pressing team reacting accordingly. This teaching drill has the ballcarrier run the ball through each pressing position on the floor, while you explain the different roles for the players in the press.

- ✔ **1-on-1 full-floor drill:** The ballcarrier runs the ball the length of the floor. The defender can stick-check, try to steal the ball with a slash, do an over-the-head check, or try a wraparound slash.

  Variation: Instead of playing the stick or trying for the steal, the defender tries to delay the ballcarrier or slow down the ball to use the clock.

- ✔ **1-on-1 press game:** Start with an outlet pass from the goalie to the offensive player. If the defender delays the receiver from getting the ball from the goalie, he gets one point. If the presser delays the ballcarrier for ten seconds from getting to centre floor, he gets two points. If the ballcarrier gets the ball over the centre line, he gets two points.

- ✔ **2-on-2 full-floor press drill:** Two defenders delay two offensive players, a right-shot and a left-shot, from running down the floor. The ball-side defender puts pressure on the ball to steal it or prevent a pass; the other defender plays his opponent to not allow him to catch the ball.

  After the two offensive players get the ball into the offensive end, they play a two-man game looking to score. After the score or missed shot, you can reverse roles and head down the other direction.

  Variations: Work up to three-on-three, four-on-four, and five-on-five drills, occasionally throwing in a player who comes off the bench.

Understanding the Field Lacrosse Defence

The outdoor lacrosse field has more space and that translates into an offence's increased ability to design more intricate plays and additional time to set up those plays around a team's best offensive player. This means that match-ups are tremendously important on defence. The defence's goal is to make sure that the long sticks (a maximum of four, three defencemen and a midfielder) defend the best offensive players. Offences try to evade the long sticks and draw them away from the ball, so this adds a dynamic element to defensive strategy.

With more space, offences can also more easily isolate the man with the ball against one defender. So in any sort of defence (zone or man-to-man), one or two defensive players may still be aggressively playing the ball. No field lacrosse defences are set completely one way — with everyone either on their toes attacking the offence or everyone packed in the zone ready to slide toward the ball. Most field defences use some combination, though a man-to-man defence is generally more aggressive than a zone.

Zone defences are most often used when defences are being dominated inside and/or off the dodge. Zones slow the pace of the game, forcing offences farther away from the goal and keeping players off the crease. Zones are generally more situational and used less often as the skill level of players increases. Field lacrosse zones are run exactly as they are in basketball, with players taking a space on the field and shifting as the ball moves. The most popular zone in field lacrosse is a 3-3 alignment, using four long sticks and two short sticks. The two short sticks play either up top or near the crease, the latter position is best against players who are more prone to dodging. If the offence plays with passers behind the goal, the defence should play long sticks there to apply more pressure on the passer's hands to keep them from passing out front. Use short sticks behind the goal to force players toward long stick slides before they can get an angle to shoot.

Checking is an important part of field lacrosse defence, but with the wider spaces, a defender has to be careful that he does not get beaten after throwing a wild check. An offensive player can easily skip by and get just the opening he needs for a shot on goal. Picks are important to watch out for as well; as with box lacrosse, communication is so important. Fighting through or switching men through a pick depends on the man you're covering and where your defencemen are. A crucial part of playing good team defence is making sure that your defensive teammates are aware of picks and screens and that offensive players are not overlooked.

Another important part of field lacrosse defence is *riding,* that is, slowing down a fast-breaking team on change of possession. After an offence loses possession, its three attackmen become full-court-press defenders (remember that attackmen are not allowed to cross over the midfield line). Offensive players must always be aware of the opposing defences trying to clear the ball. Turnovers and failed clears can lead to easy momentum-swinging goals.

Chapter 16

Calling On the Special Forces: Special Teams

. . . .

In This Chapter

▶ Revving up the offence with the power play

▶ Overcoming a player deficit with the man short

▶ Working on the faceoff

. . . .

*T*he most underappreciated part of the game of lacrosse is its specialty teams: the power-play offence and the man-short defence. If you have a great power-play offence that you can run when your opponent is down a player because of a penalty, you can score almost at will. If you have a great man-short defence that can keep an opponent's power play at bay, limiting the number of goals per shot attempts, you'll also be very competitive. In my opinion, the closest, toughest games are won by the specialty teams.

This chapter also reviews the strategies behind the faceoff, not necessarily its own specialty team, but certainly a game situation that stands on its own. And you may have players who specifically excel in the faceoff circle who you can consider specialty players.

Operating the Power Play

The power play occurs when an opposing player (or players) commits a penalty and is sent off the playing surface for (usually) a two- or five-minute period. That player (or players) is not replaced, so the non-penalized team has a player advantage for the duration of the penalty period (or until it scores a goal, in the case of the two-minute penalty). See Chapter 4 for more information about the rules involved in power-play situations.

Understanding the importance of patience on the power play

One of the key elements for players on the power play is patience. A lot of players feel they have to get the shot off right away or feel they better shoot because they may not get the ball back from their teammates. The main thing that the man-short wants to achieve is for their opponents to take quick shots. Quick shots are okay as an exception to the rule, usually when you use them as an element of surprise.

Take your time by reversing the ball around the zone or among the three top players of your power play. Unless you have a no-brainer wide-open shot, you never want to make one pass and then shoot, because the man-short players are usually in their best defensive position at the beginning of a penalty-killing situation, and they are alert and active. Also, the goalie is in his best position to see the pass and shot.

However, you don't want to just pass the ball and pass the ball and pass the ball and then shoot only when you realize you're running out of time. A great power play not only moves the ball but also moves the defensive players out of their alignment by penetrating or attacking the gaps (see "Mastering the keys to a successful power play" later in this chapter).

 Most field lacrosse penalties last 30 seconds or a minute — though three-minute penalties do exist — limiting your *man-up* (the field designation for power play) offence's ability to be patient. With the added space in field lacrosse, man-up units rely on set plays. Though penalty opportunities are few during games, most college teams spend as much time practising their man-up plays as they do their six-on-six offences. This is because in these often-elaborate offensive man-up sets, everyone has a role and execution is crucial to succeed in these extremely important scoring opportunities.

Aligning your players on the power play

The man-short defence is likely to be a simple box alignment: two players up top, two players down low. Your pointman should play at the top of the zone between the top two defenders. The standard practice is to line up your other players behind the defenders, not beside them. Players tend to gravitate to their opponent, which makes it easier for them to check your players.

The shooters stand outside and behind the two top defenders. By playing your shooters behind the two top defenders — in fact, by playing them almost equidistant from the top and bottom defenders — you may be able to create indecision by the man-short players. On a pass to a shooter, which defender will move to play him — the top one or the bottom one? With this slight indecision, your shooter may obtain that split second he needs to get an open shot or pass.

The creasemen also stand outside and behind their two defenders. The creasemen can choose to move in and out of the middle — in front of or behind the defenders — to create an additional passing lane. Figure 16-1 shows a standard power-play alignment.

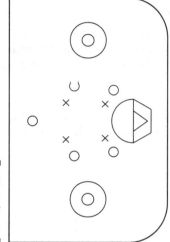

Figure 16-1:
The
power-play
alignment.

Singling out good "power players"

To be successful on the power play, your players must practise discipline. That is, they shouldn't take any retaliatory penalties, mouth off to the referee, or do anything else irresponsible that would negate the advantage. They also need to commit to being at practice all the time because the power play requires precise execution, which must be practised continually.

If a player can't or won't give you this kind of discipline, that doesn't mean you can't use him. But you probably don't want to waste your time with him on the power play. He can still play a regular shift for the team.

When selecting your man-up units for the field game, choose your team's top offensive players, regardless of position. An athletic midfielder may be able to get up and down the field and run on the first line, but a fourth attackman with more pure offensive skills to feed, shoot, and dodge will be more valuable to a man-up unit.

Quarterbacking the power play: The pointman

Your pointman is definitely the most important player on the power play. If you don't have a great pointman, you probably won't have a great power play. A great pointman's qualities consist of a great long-ball shot, usually overhand or sidearm; great passing skills with the ability to pass quickly and accurately; the ability to see the whole floor and read the defensive setup; and the ability to be decisive with the ball.

Here are the pointman's options during a power-play set (see Figure 16-2):

- ✔ Score with a long shot from the top.

- ✔ Follow passes to either shooter by taking a step toward his pass. He wants to make sure that the top two defenders remember that he remains an option and they continue to play between him and the shooters.

- ✔ Be ready to reverse the ball. If the shooter with the ball gives the ball back to the pointman, and the off-ball top defender comes over to play him, he just completes the reversal by passing the ball to the open shooter for a great shot. If the off-ball top defender stays where he is, then the pointman just winds up and shoots.

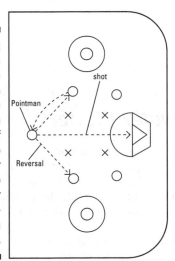

Figure 16-2: Being able to score from the top or reverse the ball from one side of the floor to the other are two options for the point-man on a power play.

Shooting and attacking: The shooters

Your two shooters (cornermen, in a regular set), left-shot and right-shot, play on each side during the power play and are your primary shooters from the side. They should be excellent shooters with the ability to hit the far top corner or far side of the net as their primary shot and the near side of the net as their secondary shot. They also have to be good passers who can dump a pass to the near creaseman or fire a level pass to the opposite side of the floor to the far creaseman or the other shooter.

The following are some of the options for the shooters in a power-play set (see Figure 16-3):

🖝 Always look to shoot first.

🖝 Step down in the zone and look to the net to remind the defence that he's a threat. When he steps down and in toward the middle, and the top defender doesn't follow, he can then cut inside for a shot.

🖝 Penetrate, and when a bottom defender comes after him, he can dump the ball to a creaseman.

🖝 Skip a pass across to the other shooter for a shot.

🖝 Look for a diagonal pass to a creaseman.

🖝 Reverse the ball back to the pointman. A good play for the shooter is to fake a return pass to the pointman, getting the top defender to play the pass with his stick, and then cutting inside the zone for a shot.

The shooters should not pass to a creaseman unless a bottom defender comes up after the shooter. You should limit your passes to the crease unless you have a clear chance to score.

Figure 16-3:
Two power-play options for the shooter are cutting down and in for the shot or dumping a pass to the creaseman when a bottom defender comes to meet him.

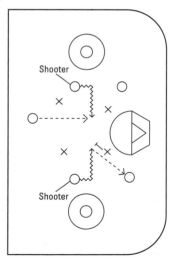

Gathering up the scraps: The creasemen

Your two creasemen, left-shot and right-shot, play near the crease and must have the ability to catch and shoot in one motion. They should have what it takes to score around the crease, such as the courage to step around in front of the net to shoot and a great touch or fake move that moves the goalie to get the shot they want. They also need to be great loose-ball players who are not afraid to get hit along the boards and still come up with the loose ball. They should be good passers, especially for short, level passes to the other creaseman, and they should be able to catch the ball in traffic.

Once he receives the ball, the creaseman has these options (see Figure 16-4):

✔ Step around in front of the net and shoot.

✔ If the opposite bottom defender comes across, pass to the other creaseman.

✔ Or, if the off-ball top defender is quick enough to rotate down and take away the crease-to-crease pass, the creaseman looks to make a diagonal pass to the opposite shooter.

✔ If he has no play, pass back to the shooter on his side of the floor.

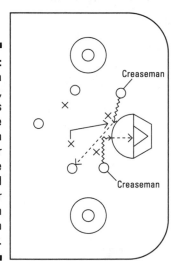

Figure 16-4:
During a power play, two options for the creaseman are to either turn to the goal and shoot or pass to an open shooter.

Taking good shots on the power play

As a coach, your power-play philosophy should be similar to your offensive philosophy in that you want to create an uncontested or clear shot. You don't want your players to force any shot with an opponent's stick in the way, or hurry a shot because an opponent is coming after you, or "bomb" your shots, that is, just shoot away at the net without looking for an open spot. Remember that you have two (or five or more) minutes in which to take advantage of your advantage — though the 30-second shot clock is still running. Stress to your players that they need to pick a spot for their best shot and take the time necessary to get that good shot.

Mastering the keys to a successful power play

This section includes the most important functions of the power play that you should make clear to your specialty teams. Remember, too, that by teaching your power-play offence these fundamentals, you're also reminding your man-short defence what to watch for from the other team when they're playing with a player disadvantage.

- ✔ **Decoy the first pass:** Try to fool the man-short players into thinking that you're going to attack from one side, and then reverse the ball and look to attack from the other side. Stress to your players that even with the decoy, as they swing the ball quickly to the other side, they should always look for an open shot.

- ✔ **Move the ball:** Swing the ball around quickly to get the goalie and the man-short players moving out of their positions. Too many teams slow the ball down while looking for a shot, giving the man-short players time to recover and interfere with a shot.

- ✔ **Make your passes count:** Practise throwing *shooting passes,* passes that the receiver can catch and shoot all in one motion. Have your players work together to get to know their teammate's best shooting positions; for example, if one shooter has a great sidearm shot, a shooting pass to him would be off to the side of his shooting arm.

  Also, try to avoid making predetermined passes, unless you're running a set play; instead, move the ball randomly, counting on your players to spot defensive weaknesses and get the ball to that area of the zone.

  Ed Comeau of the Toronto Rock says about passing: "If you can't pass accurately and quickly, you'll have a tough time getting a good shot away on the power play. The passes have to be shooting passes that go from stick to stick. Players should hold their sticks in the position from which they're going to shoot immediately, whether they need a wind-up or can just catch and shoot."

✔ **Be ready to shoot before you get the ball:** Encourage your top three offensive players to be ready to shoot before receiving the pass. That is, their sticks should be back, level to the floor, and their feet planted for a quick step into their shot. This ready position helps a player get a quick and accurate shot off as soon after he catches the ball as possible.

✔ **Penetrate:** Encourage your ballcarriers to attack the net for a shot. On receiving a pass, your shooters should look to penetrate the gap between the two top defenders. On penetration, if the top defender doesn't play the ballcarrier, he can just step into the gap behind him and shoot. If the bottom defender comes up to play him, he just dumps a little pass to the creaseman who is all alone for the shot. Two important things on this pass: The creaseman should not cut to the net until he catches the ball and the pass should be to the outside of the creaseman so that he can catch the ball and go to the net quickly.

✔ **Keep your players moving:** By moving the ball and moving your players, your power play can make the defence move or shift, potentially creating openings for penetration or shots. Don't resort to only passing the ball around the outside.

Running set plays in the power-play offence

Set a target for your power-play team to run a set play every third or fourth possession. You usually have your best chance of scoring on the power play without running a set play — the freedom that your players have to read what the defence gives them is usually your best offensive weapon. However, the occasional set play can give a lift to a power-play team whose ball and player movement has become stagnant.

Set plays against the box alignment

Here are a few set plays to try against a box alignment in the man-short defence. (See "Defending in a box: The man-short box formation" later in this chapter for more about this defensive set.)

✔ **Cutter play:** Sending cutters through the man-short can create confusion and chaos. The first pass of this play goes from the pointman to the shooter. The second pass goes back to the pointman who makes the third pass by reversing the ball to the other shooter. On that pass, the opposite shooter cuts behind the top defender on his side of the zone. After the cut, the creaseman on the cutter's side pops back into the shooter's spot to create a second passing option. This play works well against man-short teams who keep their bottom defenders with their opponents.

✔ **Swing play:** The pointman passes to the shooter on the side of the floor from which the play runs. The shooter passes back to the pointman who continues the reversal to the other shooter. When this shooter catches the ball, the off-ball creaseman cuts into the middle while the off-ball shooter slides down into the creaseman's spot for a pass and shot.

✔ **Diagonal play:** When you call this play, the creaseman on the side on which the play occurs moves behind the defender or out at an angle so that he creates a passing lane. Following a reversal sequence, the pointman passes to the shooter who then makes a diagonal pass to the opposite creaseman. The other option is that the pass can go directly from the pointman to the creaseman. If the pointman is a right-shot, he passes to the left-shot creaseman, his natural side to pass to.

✔ **Middle play:** This play calls for the pointman to cut down the middle of the man-short. You should run this play only periodically; it's a great surprise play to catch the man-short off guard. If the pointman is a left-shot, he passes to the right-shot shooter, who passes to the right-shot creaseman, who passes to the pointman cutting down the middle of the zone. If the pointman is a right-hand shot, reverse the sequence.

Set plays against the diamond alignment

The diamond alignment of the man-short plays three defenders (a point defender and two wing defenders) against the three top players in the power-play alignment. The fourth defender (the back defender) plays between the two creasemen in the middle of the zone, creating the fourth point on the diamond. (See "Diamonds are a defender's best friend: The man-short diamond formation" later in this chapter for more about this defensive set.)

To beat a diamond man short, look for diagonal passes, send cutters through the middle of the zone, pick defenders in the zone, and get the ball to the crease. In fact, the first play you must make is the pass to the crease so that you can read how the man-short zone reacts and rotates to this pass.

The pointman passes to the shooter who passes to the creaseman on the same side of the floor. After receiving the pass, the creaseman's first look is to make a cross-floor pass to the other creaseman or to make a diagonal pass to the shooter on the opposite side. The creaseman has to read the off-ball wing defender to find out how quickly he drops down to take away the cross-floor pass. If the defender is slow getting down, he can make the cross-floor pass to the creaseman. If he gets down quickly to take away the cross-floor pass, then he looks to make a diagonal pass to the opposite shooter. Another option on the pass to the creaseman is that he can just step around for a shot at the net if the back defender stays in the middle and does not rotate across to pressure the creaseman on his shot.

Here are a few set plays to run against the diamond man short:

- ✔ **Up pick play:** The off-ball creaseman sets an up pick (that is, picking him up toward the top of the zone) on the off-ball wing defender while the off-ball shooter drops to the crease for a pass and shot from the opposite shooter or creaseman. A great option to this play is available if the off-ball wing defender slides past the pick, so the picker steps to the ball in the middle of the zone for a pass and shot.

- ✔ **Top pick play:** To start this play, the left-shot pointman passes to the right-shot shooter. The left-shot shooter sets a top pick (toward the top of the zone) on the point defender while the left-shot pointman cuts to the left-shot shooter's position for a pass and shot.

- ✔ **Diagonal pass to crease:** The pointman passes to the shooter who returns the ball back to the pointman who reverses the ball to the other shooter. This shooter looks to make the diagonal pass to the opposite creaseman. Another option is that the right-shot pointman passes directly to the left-shot creaseman, his natural side.

Working the power play against a rotating man short

A rotating man-short defence changes back and forth from a box to a diamond alignment. (See "Rotating from box to diamond: The rotating man-short defence" later in this chapter.) Here are three basic guidelines for executing the power play against a rotating, pressuring man-short defence:

- ✔ **Don't take a hit.** Get your ballcarrier to back off when he's pressured so that he can make a perfect pass.

- ✔ **Pass the *opposite* way from where the defensive pressure is coming from.** Most players under pressure tend to force a pass to the area where the pressure comes from, which places the offensive teammate under similar pressure, potentially leading to a turnover.

- ✔ **Look first to make diagonal passes.** These passes will be through the passing lanes created by the rotating defence.

Drilling for successful power plays

Work with your team on these power-play drills, emphasizing ball movement, crisp passing, player movement, and other fundamentals of the power play as discussed in the "Mastering the keys to a successful power play" section earlier in this chapter.

- ✔ **3-on-0 passing drill:** This is a no-shot drill where the top three players pass the ball around, with the shooters taking the imaginary defender down and in, while the pointman steps to his pass.

COACH TIP

Attacking the 6-on-5 situation

In certain game situations, you have a chance to pull your goalie off the floor and send a sixth offensive player onto the floor. These situations usually occur on a delayed penalty, during the last ten seconds of a period, or at the end of the game when you're behind. Try these plays to take advantage of this type of power play:

🗸 **Bench play:** Just get the ball on the opposite side of the bench and run a player off the bench right through the zone defence. This can be an element-of-surprise to run even when the defence is not expecting you to pull your goalie.

🗸 **Regular play:** If the opposition plays a 2-1-2 zone, put a player in the middle of the zone and attack the zone as if in a power play.

🗸 **High play:** Against a 1-2-2 zone defence, place a man in the top middle of the zone. He can set a pick on the top defender for the pointman to get a shot.

🗸 **Low play:** Place a good scoring creaseman in the bottom middle of the zone. He looks to receive a pass in the middle, usually from a creaseman, for a shot.

Variation: Throw in reversal passes at random so that the shooters can work on getting the ball back to the point.

🗸 **3-on-0 shooting drill:** Pointman passes to one shooter, and on the return pass, he takes a shot. Then he passes to the other shooter, and on the return pass, he shoots. Switch to reversal passes (passes that go from shooter to shooter) with the shooters alternating shots.

🗸 **2-on-0 creaseman-shooting drill:** This drill has several options that your creasemen should work through in a progression.

- Creaseman receives a pass from the cornerman on the same side of the floor and steps around the imaginary defender and shoots.

- Creasemen pass back and forth a set number of times before one takes a quick catch-and-shoot shot.

- Creaseman receives a diagonal pass from the opposite shooter for a quick catch-and-shoot shot.

- Creaseman receives a direct diagonal pass from the pointman and shoots.

Playing defence on the power play

When the power-play unit is playing defence, it can double-team the ballcarrier to try to create a turnover, or it can play a 2-1-2 zone defence with some extra pressure on the ballcarrier. If a team double-teams the ballcarrier, the defenders cannot let the ballcarrier go between them because he'll head straight for the net. So the best double-team is to try to wedge the ballcarrier into the boards in a defensive stance and cross-checking only. If one defender goes for the stick, he *will* get beat.

The best way for the power-play unit to get the ball back quickly is to press the man-short players to force them to turn the ball over or to delay them for ten seconds from getting the ball over the centre line. The rule states that the offensive team has to get the ball over centre in ten seconds or lose possession of the ball. (See Chapter 4 for more about game violations.)

After a shot, the power-play unit does need to be prepared to play defence should the shot miss and the man short retrieves the rebound. On the shot, each player goes to a previously assigned defensive player.

✔ If the pointman shoots, he drops back, staying in the middle of the floor to take away any breakaway opportunities and to read the man-short players to try to anticipate their offensive plan. If one of his teammates needs help in denying a pass, he helps or he goes to double-team the ball. The two creasemen pick up the bottom two defenders on the man short to deny them an outlet pass from the goalie, and the two shooters pick up the top two defenders on the man short to deny them an outlet pass.

✔ If one of the shooters shoots the ball, the pointman backs the shooter up by picking up his defensive assignment. The shooter drops back and plays in the middle, reading the breaking-out man-short players.

✔ If a creaseman shoots, the shooter on his side of the floor picks up the creaseman's opponent, and the pointman slides over and picks up the shooter's check. The creaseman should stay in front of the goalie to delay and interfere with any passes he may try.

Defending at a Disadvantage: The Man-Short Defence

Maintaining discipline is even more critical for the man-short defence than for the power-play offence. If one of your man-short players ends up taking a retaliatory penalty or protests to a referee, you're going to soon find your team on the short end of a five-on-three power play.

To execute man-short defences, you need aggressive, quick, and smart players. Your decision to play a box or a diamond man-short formation should be based on where the power-play offence sets up its best shooters — and how many of their best shooters are on the floor. One very general concept is to play in a box if the power-play unit keeps working the ball to the sides; rotate into a diamond when the ball stays at the top of the zone.

Building your man-short defence

The two bottom defenders should be big and physical — all the better if they also have a long reach to deter passes and make that little slash on the offensive player's hands and arms. They should be good at getting loose balls in the corners and quick enough to get back into the play on any rotation by his defensive teammates.

The two top defenders are usually a little quicker than the bottom defenders; they need to be able to anticipate the results of a shot and use their quickness to explode down the floor for a breakaway pass. Though quicker, they still have to play aggressively and be physical on the man short; they should be smart enough to read who has the hot hand on the power play and overplay him a bit more. And if the two top defenders can score, the power-play unit may play more cautiously to avoid turning the ball over to the good scorers.

All your man-short defenders must stay active, both with their body movement and with their sticks. Because a power-play offence can involve a great deal of passing back and forth, you must guard against your defenders becoming bored and losing defensive focus.

Defending in a box: The man-short box formation

The box alignment is the common man-short defensive formation in lacrosse. Quite simply, the four defensive players play in a box formation, two players at the top of the zone, two players at the bottom (see Figure 16-5). The two top defenders play the three top offensive players, while the bottom defenders play the creasemen. From this formation, either of your two top defenders can easily break down the floor on a shot.

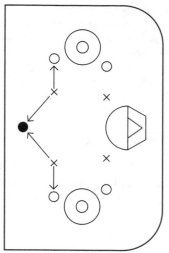

Figure 16-5:
The man-short box formation calls for the two top defenders playing against the three top offensive players.

In this formation, if the shooter on the power play cuts through the middle of the zone, the opposite-side bottom defender must leave his creaseman and cross-check the shooter with the ball.

Following are some variations to the man-short box defence:

- ✔ **Let the pointman shoot:** Against a poor-shooting pointman, you can assign your four defenders to stay with the shooters and creasemen, leaving the pointman alone to take (and hopefully miss) shots. The goalie moves out of his crease to play strictly the pointman. Because this set usually leads to long shots, your top defenders should be able to break away on a shot. If you're playing against a poor-shooting shooter, you may want to vary this set so that the shooter is left to shoot, and one of your top defenders covers the pointman.

- ✔ **Apply pressure on the first pass:** On the first pass to a shooter, one of your top defenders charges at the shooter. The other top defender plays between the other shooter and the pointman in this rotation.

- ✔ **Apply pressure before the first pass:** Charge at the pointman, preferably from the top defender on his blind side. The other top defender rotates to the middle to play between the two shooters.

In these alternative box defences, make sure that your players understand the difference between forcing the play and chasing the ball. If you're forcing the play, you're in control of the situation by maintaining pressure on the ball. If you're chasing the ball, you're not applying pressure on the ball and are getting sucked out of your positions.

Defending against a field offence advantage

If field lacrosse, *man-down defences* most often rely on a basic box-and-one scheme. One player follows the ball, while the other three or four play zone, reacting and sliding and trying to cover any holes as quickly as possible. As with man-up units, the best pure defensive players should play man-down. Lateral movement and take-away ability are more important than the speed to start a fast break. Once the defence gets the ball into the opposing offensive box, the penalty is released (unless it is a harsher non-releasable call). Teams can then push the ball toward goal, but it is usually advisable to pull the offence back and substitute your offensive players back in.

Diamonds are a defender's best friend: The man-short diamond formation

The diamond alignment of the man-short defence is just a box alignment turned on its corner. Three defenders (a point defender and two wing defenders) play against the three top players in the power-play alignment (see Figure 16-6). The fourth defender (the back defender) plays between the two creasemen in the middle of the zone, creating the fourth point on the diamond. Following are the roles of defenders in the diamond alignment:

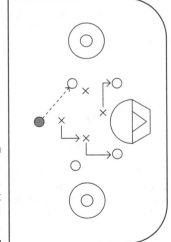

Figure 16-6:
The man-short diamond formation.

- ✔ **Point defender:** The point defender in the diamond plays the pointman whenever he has the ball to prevent any easy crease passes. His stick is always bothering the pointman's stick when he has the ball. If the pointman passes to either shooter, the point defender drops the opposite way to the pass to take away the cross-floor pass from shooter to shooter.

- ✔ **Ballside wing defender:** When the pass comes to a shooter, the wing defender on that side plays the shooter strong with both hands on the stick or tries to move him out while swinging the stick at him. If this shooter passes to the creaseman on his side, the ballside wing defender drops slightly into the middle to take away the diagonal pass to the pointman.

- ✔ **Off-ball wing defender:** If the pass from the pointman goes to the opposite shooter from this wing defender, he drops or slides down to take away the diagonal pass to the creaseman. If the ball is passed down to the opposite creaseman, the off-ball wing defender, now playing the back defender spot, takes the shooter if he cuts.

  If the ball is with the opposite shooter, either the off-ball wing defender or back defender plays the shooter-cutter or creaseman-cutter. When the ball is at the top, the two wing defenders must play their sticks into the middle of the floor with their inside hand to help to discourage any passes to the crease from the pointman. Wing defenders can pass their stick from hand to hand depending on where the ball is.

- ✔ **Back defender:** The back defender starts in the middle of the floor. If a pass goes to a shooter, he slides over to the creaseman on that side of the floor. On a pass to the creaseman on the shooter's side, he plays the creaseman or pressures him by getting his stick up to interfere with a possible cross-floor pass to the other creaseman.

- ✔ **Goalie:** In the diamond alignment, the goalie faces many shots from the creasemen, so he has to be ready to step back and over to the other side of the net. Some goalies sit right back into their net anticipating these close-in shots.

Rotating from box to diamond: The rotating man-short defence

This defence starts out in a box formation and then rotates into a diamond. The rotation allows your defenders to pressure the shooter with the top defender on his side. When the shooter returns the ball back to the pointman, you can attack him from the off-ball top defender side, hoping for a dropped ball or some panic.

This all-or-nothing type of man short does not sit back and react to the power play; it forces the power play to move the ball, by rotating to force passes and shots. The philosophy is that a forced pass or shot has a better chance of going awry.

The first key to the rotation is to put pressure on the shooter right after the first pass. Don't rotate unless you can apply pressure on the shooter, that is, bother him with a hard slash on his stick. If you're just going to give him a little tap, don't rotate.

The second key is to put pressure on the pointman after the return pass from a pressured shooter. The off-ball top defender comes out hard, or *blitzes* this second pass to the pointman. Throughout this whole rotation, you want to maintain pressure on the ballcarrier.

After the rotation has started, when the ball is at the top, the defensive players are in a diamond, when the ball is on the side, the defensive players have rotated to a box formation. The player who rotates must arrive at the receiver as he catches the ball, not after, because it will give him time to make a good play on the receiver.

Playing offence on the man short

Although the man short is definitely a defensive specialty team, a game will dictate times when you have to think offence with your defence. Your man-short defence will be a little stronger if you have players at the top who are a threat to score. The power-play offence won't play as recklessly if they know they may have to get back because of this scoring threat.

If the goalie stops a shot, he first looks to throw the long breakaway pass to one of the top players breaking or to a breaking player coming off the bench. A breakaway situation can also occur following a loose ball. In the chaos that accompanies recovering a loose ball, you may be able to beat the power-play unit down the floor. Look to pass the ball up the floor rather than run the ball up, as passing is the quickest way to move the ball.

If your man-short defence can't create a quick scoring opportunity on the breakout, your best offensive option is to slow the game down to run out the penalty. This strategy, called *ragging the ball*, involves passing the ball around the offensive zone, waiting for the last possible moment to take a shot. In the NLL, ragging the ball usually takes one of two forms: ragging for the duration

COACH TIP

Defending the 6-on-5

When a team replaces its goalie with an extra attacker because of a delayed penalty or as a set offensive play, the best way to play this 6-on-5 power play is to set up in a 2-1-2 zone defence, with the defender nearest to the ball applying pressure on the ballcarrier.

of the 30-second clock just to kill time, and ragging for about 20 seconds before looking to score. In minor lacrosse, you can rag the ball for a maximum of two minutes.

To rag the ball, the four offensive players form a box formation in their offensive zone and run picks on the off-ball side. The ballcarrier passes the ball across the floor when his teammate comes off the pick. If the defensive team double-teams this ballcarrier, the previous ballcarrier sets a pick for his teammate on his side of the floor to get him in the clear for a cross-floor pass. The players keep doing this until the defensive team breaks down and creates an opening for a clear shot.

Running man-short drills

In addition to running the following drills, your best man-short practice work will come out of game-like situations and scrimmages during practices.

- 4-on-0 rotation drill: Place cones where the power-play unit would stand. The defensive players rotate together for cohesion.
- 4-on-0 ragging-the-ball drill: In this drill, practise ragging the ball by constantly running down picks on the off-ball side and throwing cross-floor passes to the player coming off the pick.

Winning the Faceoff

In the NLL, the 30-second play clock leads to a high number of goals scored. The faceoff has become extremely important in the professional league because one takes place after every goal. However, the faceoff is also a critical component of the minor game. This section offers advice on how to prepare your players for the faceoff.

Setting up

Two players, called centremen, place their sticks back-to-back to fight for possession of the ball, by either directing the ball to a teammate or by picking it up. The referee places the ball between the two players' sticks, and the sticks must not touch the ball. When the referee blows his whistle, the two players must draw the ball, moving the sticks straight back while trying to clamp the ball under the stick's netting. In the NLL, all centremen are right-hand shots because they have to stay on their own side of the centre line. The centremen can grip only the shaft of the stick; they are not supposed to touch the plastic head of the stick. Centremen cannot move the stick prior to the whistle, and they can't trap or withhold the ball from play.

Taking the stance

Each centreman should be in a squat position, with the feet shoulder-width apart to get balance and power. Grip the stick with the top hand on or near the throat of the stick and the bottom hand about halfway up the shaft. This midpoint position of the hand offers more leverage, more strength, and more choices for countermoves.

Practising faceoff techniques

Each centreman likely has his own technique that works especially well for him. Here are a few examples, straight from the professionals, that you can share with players who need to establish or modify their own techniques.

✔ **Steve Fannell of the Ottawa Rebel says about the faceoff clamp method:** "If I can beat my opponent cleanly, I keep the ball above the centerline, the line drawn in middle of my stick's pocket, and clamp to win. My options are to clamp on the ball and pull back or rake forward, to clamp and spin my stick back around and knock the ball back, or to clamp the ball and try to get it between my legs where I try to pick it up.

"If I clamp to win, I put more pressure on the head of my stick, lean over more, and bend my wrist palm flat on the floor and turn it up and over on the clamp. My backhand is at mid-shaft for more power and flexibility.

"If I want to clamp or hold the ball to create a stalemate, I'll keep the ball lower on the pocket to the bottom, below the centreline. I usually position myself to clamp when my players are tired. After you trap, you can try to block your opponent out by stepping or turning your body in front of him so he can't see the ball.

"Other options with the clamp are to go under my opponent's stick and flip the ball back to a teammate or goalie, or trap the ball and turn your stick around and knock it back to your teammates."

✔ **Brad MacArthur of the Calgary Roughnecks says about the push-and pull-method:** "I put weight on my front hand and near the top of the head of the stick. I move the front hand up as far as I can even up onto the plastic until the referee tells me to move it back.

"Besides gripping the throat of the stick as close to the head as possible, I put the other hand at the centre of the stick rather than at the end of the stick. I find that I get more flexibility and more power in my draw.

"I push forward with my top hand on the front of my stick at about 45 degrees to stop my opponent from trapping the ball under his stick. I then pull the ball straight back down the centre of the floor to a teammate on the defensive line or I can push the ball straight ahead to another teammate on the offensive line."

✔ **Steve Toll of the Toronto Rock, one of the best draw men in the NLL, does a quick clamp, pulling toward him and scooping up the ball:** Steve stresses staying low, keeping your weight on your feet, and applying a bit of pressure on the stick, but not on your gloves. He places his feet along the centre line, with all his weight on his front foot. "This keeps your hands free and relaxed so that you can move quickly (no weight on the arms). You don't want to put pressure on your stick or on your hands for a fast stick action. It is important to be physically and mentally ready on the draw."

Steve Fannell says about drawing against someone you can't beat: "When playing a guy I can't beat, I just let them win and play ball pursuit. I keep clamping down and when I'm ready to go, I release my pressure, remembering that he is going to win it anyway and that he will go down to clamp over the ball. As he goes down, I'm on my way up already to pursue the ball. If I play ball pursuit, I put pressure on both hands so that I can stand up and go after the ball like a sprinter."

Getting the edge on the faceoff

During a faceoff, you need to out-loose-ball the other team, each player out-fighting the player beside him for possession. This may sound easy but it takes team effort, not just one good draw player. Here are some tips to help your team improve their faceoff success:

✔ **Get the jump on the opposition:** Try to anticipate when the referee will blow the whistle. You don't want to cheat — that is, leave early just before the whistle, even though refs don't call this violation much. But try to pick up on some of the referee's quirks, what he does just before he blows the whistle. Some players count from the time the referee leaves the small circle until he blows his whistle, hoping to pick up a pattern. Jim Veltman of the Toronto Rock says: "I watch the referee's mouth and anticipate their blowing the whistle to get an early jump on my opponent."

✔ **Attack all loose balls:** On most faceoffs, the ball comes loose, so your players better be ready to battle for the loose ball. You need tough players on the faceoff unit — quick, big, not afraid to get hit — and good ballhandlers who can pick up the ball in a crowd. If the opposition gets to the ball first, your players shouldn't back off. Play his stick hard to stop him from picking it up or bang him into the boards. Send two players after every loose ball.

✔ **Line up on the opponent's stick side:** If your players line up in this way, they can interfere with their opponent's stick.

✔ **Protect the ball:** You want your players to use their body to protect the ball and keep both hands on the stick. Don't pick up the ball with just one hand on an exposed stick.

✔ **Back each other up on loose balls:** On a loose ball, the defender on the ballside cheats in for the loose ball, while the other defender balances the floor by going back on defence. The offensive forward (creaseman) also cheats on the line and can be extra aggressive because they don't have to worry about being scored on while the off-ball forward (creaseman) goes back to the middle or even farther back depending on the situation to balance the floor defensively.

The concepts and strategy for faceoffs in field lacrosse are similar to those for the box game. The goal is for the player facing off to either *pull* the ball and collect it himself or *push* it toward a teammate. Players in the wing area should be the team's fastest players and the players most adept at picking up the ball off the ground.

Chapter 17

Preparing Your Players

· ·

· ·

*G*etting your players ready to play involves more than running a few set plays during practice, playing a few scrimmage games, and doing post-practice conditioning. The decisions you make even before the season starts about which players to include on your team also go a long way to preparing your players — you stand a better chance of getting your players ready to play in the way that you want them to play if you build your team accordingly.

This chapter discusses what you should look for in players while you're evaluating them or watching them play. You can assess much more than just the nuts and bolts of playing the game. I also offer some advice for evaluating the character of your players. And if you need tips on motivating the players you do select, and on building a strong team that works together, that's here too.

Selecting Your Players

When you're putting together a team, remember to tell your players what you're looking for during the training-camp selection process. You want them to show you their strengths; you don't necessarily want them to show you what you're looking for. If a player has quickness, he should show that. If that player's speed is so superior that you want him on your team regardless of your system, you need the resources to be able to decide that.

Here's a system that you may use for selecting the players for your team. This process helps you define player roles and evaluate how individual players would fit those roles.

- **Picking the top third players on the team:** If you have 15 players to select, usually your top 5 offensive players will do 80 percent of the scoring; in other words, these players are going to carry the team in scoring. These players also usually make up your power-play unit.

- **Picking the middle third players on the team:** The next group includes solid fundamental players who can play both ways, offence and defence, but the emphasis is on defence. These are your man-short players. They will play great defence, get the team a goal here and there, and do the dirty work. In this group, look for size, tenaciousness, toughness, aggressiveness, and quickness on defence and loose balls.

- **Picking the bottom third players on the team:** The last group is usually the toughest because your selection is based on a number of different qualities. Your best bets, however, are role players or great attitude players — both have great character and a great work ethic, if not a great deal of talent. Here you may want to pick a particular player to fulfill a specific job, such as centreman on the faceoff, or some so-called *in-between players,* good athletes that can play many positions.

Putting your team together

When putting a team together, ask yourself the following questions. The answers give you three criteria to judge your potential players.

- Do we need offensive or defensive players?
- Do we need big, tough players or fast, quick players?
- Do we need right-shots or left-shots?

When putting a team together, you also need good chemistry, so how players complement each other is extremely important. You need players who can play together; for example, on offence, you need outside long-ball shooters to complement the good ballhandlers who can play inside so that you can execute the pick-and-roll game. Or on defence, you need some good defenders with size to complement defenders who are fast and who can score.

Never underestimate the value of experience. Players who have worked their way up in your league may be quite valuable in helping you build the confidence of your younger players. Experienced players will probably come through for your team in pressure game situations. And the younger players can have the youth and enthusiasm you need to keep the team energized.

Don't forget your specialists — every team needs them. A player who can take the draw on the faceoff is very valuable, even if he can't do much else. A player who can shoot outside and score, but that's about it, may help you against zone defences. Or a player who can play great defence but is a terrible shooter can serve as your defensive stopper at the end of close games.

Finally, look for players who come out of winning programs and who are used to winning — they know what it takes to be successful.

Analyzing individual players

You definitely have to know what type of system you're running to know what type of player you're looking for. The player's ability and talent should complement the system. For example, if your system is a running, fast-break style, you'll want to look for speed, agility, and conditioning, because everything you do on offence and defence is based on speed and movement so that you wear the opposing players down.

Looking for athletic ability

You want players who play hard, run hard, and rely on their conditioning. You should look for athletic players who have quickness, strength, and endurance. For some, great athletic potential may outweigh poor stick-handling skills. I'm a big believer in going on instinct with a player, especially if he's well conditioned — if a player is not fit and tires, he stops thinking and quits.

Also, you may find a player who has limited talent and athletic ability, but when push comes to shove, he sure knows how to get the job done. You're going to love this type of player when you need someone to double-team your opponent's best offensive player or someone to harass a great-passing goalie.

The history of lacrosse is chock full of stories about players who were small, skinny, and clumsy, but who were cagey and possessed a certain fire for the game — they became greater players than the ones with the perfect lacrosse bodies.

Great moves — looking for skill or talent

Physical talent is relatively easy to spot and is one of the major keys to a team's success. Players who are fundamentally sound in lacrosse skills will succeed on offence, defence, or both. If a player lacks the sport's specialized skills, he can still be a solid role-player who is able to out-hit, out-hustle, out-loose a ball, and out-run his opponent.

One specialized skill that's great to have on your team is passing, and great passers, such as John Tavares of the NLL's Buffalo Bandits, have great vision of the floor. A great passer can see a play develop before it happens and, therefore, make quick decisions — knowing who to pass to, where to pass, how to pass, and when to pass.

Understand that a player's offensive skill is something that he's born with; you can always teach a player to be a better defender.

Great plays — looking for intelligence

Look for players who understand the game, who play focused and alert, who make smart plays, and who seem to be aware of everything that is happening on the floor, even to the point that they're one or two plays ahead of everyone else. These players anticipate well and read the floor well; they have a kind of sixth sense about what is going to happen next. They know exactly what to do in certain situations because of their feel for the game, their experience, and their hard work. They are typically the ones who are the first to arrive at practice and the last to leave, taking the extra time to work on the skills they need to succeed.

Great spirit — looking for character

When I'm building a team, I look for character as well as athletic ability and lacrosse skills. Character is the hardest thing to recognize during tryouts because players do not reveal their true character unless they are put into an adverse situation. In fact, many coaches look more for the desire to play and the capacity to learn than they do for physical skills.

To build a solid program, a coach has to have players for a few years to get to know them and find out what they are made of. Coaches use the first year with a new group or team to trim out the bad characters, players who cannot play at a particular level, and players who do not fit into the system.

Character is made up of the following characteristics that you can look for:

- **Heart:** Desire, heart, fire — whatever you want to call it, some players have a strong passion for the game of lacrosse. This passion comes out of an ongoing drive to improve. They play the game with fire in their eyes and with such energy and passion that you know they just love to play. Many talented players play with no heart or passion, and many less talented players play with a great deal of heart. But usually talent and passion go hand-in-hand.

- **Zealousness:** You want players who will out-play, out-hustle, and out-run their opponents all the time. This type of player plays with a kind of killer instinct, because they hate to lose and therefore hold nothing back.

- **Tenacity:** You should be interested in players who never quit, are persistent, and never give up. These players are tenacious, both in games and in practice, working hard all the time and giving second and third efforts. The tenacious players often end up making the great plays long after less enthusiastic players have given up on the skirmish.

✔ **Unselfishness:** The unselfish player stands out a bit more in a training-camp setting because players sometimes try to impress the coaches in the wrong way. They try to do everything by themselves, which is counter to what most coaches want. You want players who are willing to give the ball up to a better-positioned player for a more open shot.

The tough part is that players have to be selfish and unselfish at the same time. They have to show that they can play selfishly when necessary, for example, when they have the hot shooting hands and their team is behind. And they also have to show that they are unselfish — team players — giving up the ball at the right time.

✔ **Self-discipline:** In my opinion, self-discipline is all about cooperation, having the willingness and confidence to do what someone asks you. In lacrosse, the self-disciplined player is the one who can respond to a coach's request by getting something done — somehow, someway — so that the coach's request is fulfilled.

✔ **Self-control:** Look for players who are calm and composed when everyone else around them is out of control. These are the types of players who can keep their emotions under control. They'll be the least likely candidates to become frustrated by a bad call or by a teammate's (or their own) mistake. And they won't take too many retaliatory or stupid penalties.

✔ **Positive attitude:** During your tryouts, look for players who are enthusiastic, who love to play, who seem to be always smiling, and who are optimistic.

✔ **Poise under pressure:** One of the truest tests of any lacrosse player is how he reacts to pressure. Look for a player who gives signs that he can remain poised and composed in a pressure situation. The poised players shut out any distraction and devote total attention to the play at hand.

✔ **Self-confidence:** You know the look — not quite cocky, but definitely self-assured. Certain players just give off that aura of self-confidence: the way they hold their head up and their shoulders back, the way they look their opponent in the eye, and the way they walk. Their body language gives off extreme confidence: It borders on cockiness, but it's under control enough to be a great asset.

✔ **Coachable:** This player wants to learn, so he asks a lot of questions and he listens. He takes advice willingly. When he makes a mistake, he admits it, corrects it without excuses, learns from it, and moves on.

Selecting Your Team Leaders

Many coaches like to pick the team captain and assistant captains, as they know what they want from their leaders. Other coaches let the team vote on the team leaders, but this usually turns into a popularity contest. I recommend doing both.

Have the team vote on who they think should be the team leaders, after explaining that the vote will help the coaches understand how the players feel about their teammates. Then, you can sit down with your assistants and discuss the results, still retaining the right to select the team leaders using all the information gathered. Another option is to create some kind of weighted voting system, where your vote as the head coach counts for 50 percent of the tally, your assistants' votes count for 30 percent, and your players' votes count for 20 percent. Or use whatever breakdown suits your team's need.

Whatever process you use to select your team leaders, the rest of this section offers some helpful advice about how you and your team leaders can work together for the highest benefit to the team.

Working with your team leaders

Some players are natural leaders who just emerge as the year goes on. You'll discover that many of your players are looking up to this "natural" leader. Remember that a player doesn't have to be an elected captain to be a team leader. In fact, on the best teams, every player displays leadership qualities.

Nevertheless, on most teams, you'll find a core group of players who end up leading the team, either by election or by example. As coach, you must work with this group of players in order to gain their confidence and trust in how you manage the team. Tell them what type of system you plan for the team and ask for their feedback. If you can convince and sell this core group on certain subjects throughout the year, they'll make it easier for you to get the rest of the team on your side.

Establishing guidelines for your team leaders

I give my team leaders some guidelines on what I expect of them. Most importantly, I want them to take charge in situations where I can't or shouldn't, for example, by leading the team in pre-game drills. I expect them to be dependable and always on time for team meetings, practices, and games. During a game, I want them to think and react as if they were the coach.

By expecting your team leaders to uphold the highest standards for themselves and the team, they will no doubt make everyone around them play a little bit better. Set ground rules for how your team leaders should lead. Some are more comfortable leading by example, that is, by the quality of their play and by their absolute respect for team rules. Other players prefer an in-your-face style of leadership, encouraging their teammates to achieve their highest potential. This verbal encouragement should come both on the practice floor and on the game floor.

Try to get your leaders to act like coaches, on and off the floor, even to the extent of taking younger players under wing to show them how to win and how to play the game. The team leaders can help create a kind of family atmosphere for the team in which no player feels like an outsider and every player is accepted.

And, of course, make sure that your team leaders represent the team with class, self-control, and politeness, especially in a game situation when seeking clarification about a referee's call.

Motivating Your Players

As coach, you're expected to motivate both your team and its individual players to play to their maximum potential. The greatest coaches are great motivators who know how to get their teams ready to play, no matter how important the game is, time and time again. One of those great coaches may be the local PeeWee coach who gets his team to play its best, week after week, even in the face of certain loss. And his players still find the season to be fun, enjoyable, and successful!

You can try all possible ways to motivate your players: gentle teaching, constant repetition, discipline with physical exercises, yelling, pats on the back or kicks in the rear, paying no attention at all, challenges, encouragement, praise or criticism, and most importantly, showing them you care. You can also make players aware of what self-motivation is, that internal motivation that comes from chasing a dream. Encouraging your players to set their own goals can help them to light their own competitive fire. This intrinsic motivation, which pushes players from the inside rather than the outside, is the best motivation.

Establishing outcome goals

The most direct way to motivate your players is to keep them focused on their future success by helping them set long-term team and personal goals. These goals help a team aim for something tangible that indicates they're getting better. This style of motivation has the added benefit of helping your team practise self-discipline: It's their choice to be successful or not:

This section discusses *outcome goals,* those goals that have an objective value that you can attach to them, such as hoped-for outcomes for the team for a season or a game.

Creating long-term outcome goals: It's not all about winning games and championships

Not every outcome goal for your team should be winning a championship. You need to be realistic about setting goals that your team has a decent chance to meet. You and your players would love to win a championship every year, but it just doesn't happen that way. Instead, aim for second place, or making the playoffs, or winning as many games as you lose. You may just end up improving enough throughout the year that you find yourself playing for the championship.

Keeping things interesting: Short-term outcome goals

Another type of outcome goal is more short-lived. These are goals that you set for your team that they try to meet at designated times throughout the season. These short-term goals can be as simple as winning your next game or as complex as forcing 100 turnovers over a 5-game period.

Reaching your short-term goals can help your team achieve its long-term goals. Short-term goals help your team focus on the immediacy of the game or the goal, whose success will lead to getting your desired long-term goal. These short-term goals also help to prevent the long season from becoming tedious. During a 20-game major lacrosse season, establishing short-term goals to achieve during, say, a 5-game stretch, will help your team keep focus at a time when they could look at the season as drudgery.

Devising outcome goals

In setting outcome goals, make them specific, realistic, and concrete so that players know exactly what they have to do. The goals should also be measurable and attainable. Players have to know that a goal can be achieved. For example, winning every game is an unrealistic goal, even when you have a pretty good chance to do so, because so many factors can make it impossible.

Post your outcome goals in the dressing room, along any relevant statistics to help your players to keep track of their progress. For example, if your long-term outcome goal is to finish in second place, post the league standings to let the players know where they are positioned.

Make sure that players know any deadlines associated with the goals; for example, by the end of the first quarter of the season the team should be able to play solid defence. Any time the team reaches a goal or even just a step toward the goal, reward them with a pizza party, a day off, or anything that you think will motivate them further.

Finally, let your players suggest new goals or revise existing goals. By involving them in setting goals, you'll create the enthusiasm, energy, and persistence to pursue them.

Setting performance goals

Performance goals are standards that you set that your team can aim for, which leads to improved play, or performance. Establishing these kinds of goals is somewhat like creating a grading system for evaluating the team's performance. What performance goals judge is not wins and losses, but how your players perform. If a team reaches its performance goals, winning will take care of itself.

Performance goals are the building blocks for the team's motivational system, and the statistics associated with these goals are the key to the team's success. By achieving or bettering these goals, the team will build confidence, motivation, and commitment.

Focusing on the process of reaching their performance goals, something they can control, makes players more relaxed and confident. Since they no longer feel they have to control the outcome of a game, they focus on playing and having fun.

Motivating with performance goals

The key to performance goals is that they help a team compete against itself. Players compare themselves to the standards set by the team, no matter who they are playing. Performance goals help a team perform as a group; a team will outperform a group of individuals every time.

Using performance-goal statistics

Keeping track of team statistics helps you figure out why you lost or won. After every game, you look at the statistic sheets to analyze, dissect, and break the game down. If the team did poorly on a particular performance goal, you can use this information to improve that area of play in the next practice or to reinforce and correct it to the team in a future team meeting. Even if you lost the game, you can always point out a few of the goals that your team improved on or actually reached.

Players have to know what quality is. Rather than telling your team that they had a good game, be specific. Performance goals give you the categories that include the specifics; game statistics provide the specifics. A good game means a 25-percent shooting percentage or getting 60 percent of the game's loose balls. With these real numbers that apply to real goals, your players will know where they excelled and how they can improve.

The following performance goals give you an idea of what you can create for your own team. When you post your team's performance goals, make sure to prioritize them. These goals will allow you to analyze a game to help your players figure out why you won or lost and to help plan the next practice and pre-game talk.

✔ Get 60 percent of offensive and defensive loose balls

✔ Win 60 percent of faceoffs

✔ Aim for a shooting percentage of 25 percent (40 percent for field lacrosse)

✔ Keep opposition to a shooting percentage under 20 percent (under 30 percent for the field game)

✔ Allow only one goal for every three chances on the man short

✔ Score at least one goal for every two chances on the power play

✔ Maintain possession of the ball for at least 60 percent of the game

✔ Keep offensive turnovers to 19 or fewer

✔ Force at least 19 defensive turnovers

✔ Restrict team penalties to 22 minutes

Devising performance goals

Make sure that performance goals are high and hard but also realistic and challenging so that you push your players to achieve them. If the performance goals are too easy, the players have little to challenge them. This leads to reduced effort and a situation ripe for a loss, not to mention the missed performance goals. If your team is easily and consistently reaching each goal, change them to make them harder and thereby more challenging.

However, goals that are too high or too unrealistic will set your team up for failure; the players will become overwhelmed and frustrated because they can't achieve them. Again, you need to monitor your players' success rate and change the goals if they're too difficult to reach.

As with outcome goals discussed earlier in this section, let your players help decide what goals and level of difficulty works for them.

Finding the right tone for your team: Behaviour goals

You also need a vision of how you want your team to act. Team-behaviour goals are principles or guidelines for acceptable behaviour that players must follow. These goals are not handed down by the coach, but are presented to the team for discussion. You definitely want your players to be involved in setting your team's behaviour goals. When you do, players are more inclined to meet or exceed them so that they don't let down their teammates.

Coaching is more than just showing kids how to play a game; coaching helps players learn how to behave properly and to make the right choices. You may teach, motivate, and relate to each player differently, but you apply the same basic standards of conduct to everybody.

COACH TIP

Correcting players for behaviour-goal missteps

If you fail to speak to a player about a mistake or about improper behaviour, he will probably repeat it. You will also send a message to the rest of the team that your team's behaviour goals are meaningless, that any poor performance or inappropriate conduct is acceptable.

Instead, tell players immediately what they did wrong and tell them how you feel about what they did. However, try to avoid doing so in front of their teammates. Have the conversation in private, and use the *sandwich* approach for feedback: Compliment a player, tell him what he did wrong, and then give him another compliment.

If the same player displays the same improper behaviour over and over again, you must discipline him. But don't discipline with punishment that you decide on. When you and your players create the team's list of behaviour goals, make sure that they also write a list of penalties. And don't let them go easy on themselves.

COACH TIP

My teams play under the umbrella of the following 12 behaviour goals. You'll notice that these goals are quite similar to the characteristics of character you should look for in players, which I discuss in "Great spirit — looking for character" earlier in this chapter.

These goals are designed to help improve level of play and attitude. They also work in the game of life. Use this list of goals as a starting point.

- ✔ **Play motivated and committed:** Play the game as if it were a marathon race, where the ending is determined by who wants it the most.

- ✔ **Play hard, play tough, and be aggressive:** Successful teams play hard right from the beginning of the game to the end and expect nobody to outwork them. Cut into the middle of the floor or dive for a loose ball, and expect to be hit. When you play hard, something good usually happens, and it usually happens near the end of the game.

- ✔ **Play together:** Keep your personal feelings in the locker room; bring an unselfish attitude to the floor. The team is always bigger than any of its parts. Unselfish players don't care who gets the credit as long as the team is successful.

- ✔ **Play smart:** And make your own decisions. Players grow when they can try new things, be creative, and take initiative knowing they may fall down in the process. Stress that failure is nothing more than learning how to do something correctly.

- ✔ **Play disciplined:** On a disciplined team, when you tell players to do something, they do it. Self-discipline comes into play when a player should do something, doesn't feel like doing it, but does it anyway.

- ✔ **Play with self-control:** There's no such thing as a perfect game. When you play lacrosse (or any game, for that matter), you're going to make mistakes. The key is to limit how you react to those mistakes.

- ✔ **Play totally focused:** As a coach, you want your players to keep their eyes on the game plan, not on how the opposition is bothering them, or how the officials are calling the game, or how the fans are responding to them. You want your players to stay focused in the present moment by blocking out all distractions that may take their minds off the game.

- ✔ **Play with enthusiasm, passion, and fun:** You must stress having fun. Players will then develop an attitude of enjoying the moment, and this reduces the pressure of winning or making mistakes.

- ✔ **Play with poise under pressure:** As a team, talk with your players and reinforce constantly their goals of controlling their emotions and keeping their composure in a crisis situation. You want your team to take pride in performing its best when it faces adversity.

- ✔ **Play with courage and mental toughness:** Aside from pure athletic ability, mental toughness is the greatest attribute that any lacrosse player can have. Mentally tough players play the same all the time no matter what. They do not get down on themselves after being scored on or after being beaten defensively.

- ✔ **Play with confidence:** You build confidence by believing in your players. Support them when they make mistakes just as strongly as when they do extremely well.

- ✔ **Play with a good attitude:** Keep your players' outlook positive, whether it's about mistakes, their opponents, or how they approach a big game.

Building Team Unity and Cohesion Goals

One of the most important abilities in coaching is *team building,* the ability to get players to think and act as one. The coach and players want a team with strong, sound values. And to help create this atmosphere, each team must have a code of conduct that plainly states how the players should view the team and treat each other. The coaches and players establish these principles together in a team meeting. These principles get everyone moving in the same direction — together they can accomplish much more than a group of individuals who work on their own.

- ✔ **Create a "team comes first" attitude:** Teamwork means working together. Team agendas replace individual agendas. When the team comes first, it doesn't matter who scores and it doesn't matter who gets the glory; what matters is the team's success.

The Toronto Rock has won three NLL titles without once having the league's leading scorer.

_____ **Chapter 17: Preparing Your Players** *305*

✔ **Commit to regular meetings:** Through team meetings as well as individual talks with players, you have the chance to talk frequently about your team approach.

✔ **Provide motivation for cohesion:** True motivation comes from a clear sense of shared goals and constantly comparing your team to its goals. See "Motivating Your Players" earlier in this chapter for more about setting goals.

✔ **Teach team skills:** When you combine a few individual skills, you create a team skill. And for a team to be successful, players must be able to execute these team skills and realize that the player who sets the pick or makes the pass is just as important as the player who comes off the pick and scores.

✔ **Reinforce consistency with the team:** Try to keep your lines together throughout the year; playing and practising together and getting used to each other all improve the performance and execution of the line.

✔ **Have fun together:** Make sure that you and your players do more than practise together. Make your pre-game and pre-practice stretches a required element. Have training-camp breakfast so that players can get to know one another.

✔ **Instill pride:** Foster team unity by creating an atmosphere that suggests "We are the best."

The result of a cohesive team is *synergy.* Synergy occurs when the total becomes more than the sum of the parts. Synergy is when you put together 20 disparate players and they end up playing as if there were 30 of them. Working together as a team, a smaller weaker team can overcome one that is bigger and stronger. Each player seems to gather strength and energy from each teammate to create this extra strength.

In field lacrosse, greater emphasis in practice is put on working with units, as opposed to the team as a whole. Because the field is larger and its restraining lines limit much of the action to six-on-six, the game features more elaborate set plays and two sets of lines that rotate in and out. It is important for the different units to work separately to gain cohesion and familiarity.

What Gives Your Team the Edge

Many coaching platitudes will tell you that when a team believes it will be successful, it can accomplish the impossible. Many teams may approach a season with the attitude that it's going to be successful, but few reach their sports ultimate pinnacle: a championship. To have an edge in any sport, you have to work for it. Here are a few practical and tangible tips that you can stress with your team to try to gain that edge:

✔ **Perfect your fundamentals:** Practise basic skills over and over again until your players can execute without thinking.

✔ **Strive for peak conditioning:** Your team's commitment and responsibility to training will require sacrifices, but it also gives it an edge.

✔ **Go full speed — always:** Whether during a game or a practice, in pre-game stretches or between-game training, give 100 percent.

✔ **Work to improve:** A good work ethic means little if you can't use it to strengthen your weaknesses.

✔ **Remember — no pain, no gain:** Sure it's another platitude, but if your players train harder and run faster and farther, even to the point of exhaustion, they'll be giant steps ahead of other teams.

✔ **Accept the hard road:** Players do not cut corners; they do not cheat on laps; they do not cheat by not touching the lines or the boards; they do not leave early on the whistle. That's the easy road to take.

Chapter 18

It's Game Time

*N*othing can really prepare you for your first time behind the bench as coach of a lacrosse team. Of course, you'll probably still feel totally unprepared for your 50th time behind the bench as coach of a lacrosse team. Believe me, even though I've coached lacrosse for 25 years, some games still leave me scratching my head, trying to figure out exactly what happened and how it all got to be that way.

Nevertheless, this chapter should help you at least formulate a plan for your first (or 50th) game as coach. With the advice in this chapter, you should be able to develop a strategy for an individual game, make sure that you prepare your players to match that strategy, and make coaching decisions during the game that support that strategy. And when all else fails, throw the game plan under the bench and let your players do what they do best — just play.

Preparing a Game Plan

When it comes to game plans, a good coach may be out-coached or out-worked on occasion, but he should never be out-prepared. Putting a game plan together takes an enormous amount of organization and time, but you need to put in that time so that you're prepared for whatever may happen in a game. Talent alone is not enough; hard work is not enough; strategy is not enough; and emotion is not enough. Preparation and execution are the primary factors for a team's success. A well-prepared team will approach every game in a state of total confidence and have a great chance of being successful as long as it plays hard, plays together, plays smart, and has fun.

✔ **You have to be organized and prepared — to a point:** The successful coach motivates his players for the game by having them prepared. It makes more sense to plan ahead for the game than to wait until the heat of the battle. You must believe in your game plan, but you must also be prepared for the unexpected. And you must have a plan B in case things don't go as you intended.

✔ **Put on the pressure:** Pressure may seem to be a bad thing, but pressure is necessary for players to play their best. Good pressure occurs when a team is prepared. Being prepared about the opposition is one way to combat stress. Good pressure is what players feel when they know what to expect and what to do. Preparation takes that pre-game pressure and changes it over to pre-game confidence. Bad pressure is stress, what players feel when they don't know what to expect and don't know what to do.

✔ **Know the opposition:** You give your team a tremendous advantage when you know what the opposition is thinking, what their tendencies are, and what their strengths and weaknesses are. Your confidence about your opposition research can motivate your team. You can gather the facts you need about the opposition through statistical analysis, live scouting reports about their best players and their goalie's weaknesses, game films and video analysis, and monitoring pre-game warm-ups.

✔ **Be specific:** If you know that a certain player is going to give your team some trouble, point him out, plaster his jersey number to your locker room walls, do whatever you have to do to make sure that your players remember this threat.

✔ **Base your game plan on your team's strengths:** After you understand the opposition, you can concentrate on your own team's strengths. In developing your plan, focus on what your team does best offensively, defensively, and on specialty teams. You, your staff, and your players must know exactly what you want to do and how you are going to get it done.

✔ **Remember your weaknesses:** If your team did poorly in a previous game, remind them. Stress that these areas need improvement in order for the team to be successful. Remind them of performance goals that are within reach (see Chapter 17 for more about setting goals).

✔ **Stress your team's behaviour goals:** Don't limit your game plan to only the *X*s and *O*s. Remind your players about the mental and physical toughness that they need to stay sharp and play well. Stress courtesy in dealing with the referees and sportsmanship with the opponents.

Before a game, write down (and keep with you) what you need to remember in certain game situations: what players to play; their backups; list of players on the three lines; list of power-play lines; list of man-short lines; and list of faceoff players.

Preparing the Team for the Big Game

The big game could be a game against your biggest rival, a game to move you up in the standings, or a playoff game. The players usually know which games are the big games without you saying a word. But here are some things that you can do to help them focus and stay sharp for the game.

- ✔ **Relax:** These big games can rattle your players' nerves and throw off their concentration; these games offer many more distractions than ordinary league games. As a coach, you have to explain to the players that they have to work at ignoring all the distractions, stay in the present moment, and focus on their performance. Encourage them to follow whatever mental preparation strategies they use to help them settle down (see Chapter 13 for some suggestions).

- ✔ **Minimize the moment:** Try to get your players to approach every big game in the same way as they do every other game. Encourage this approach with your team's normal and familiar routines. Don't do anything different in preparing for a big game than you would for a normal game. Remind your players that it's only one game in a multiple-game schedule.

- ✔ **Concentrate on your performance goals:** If your team feels that it has no chance of winning, your players will become anxious and lethargic. To counter this, use your team's performance goals to motivate team competition. Your team may go into the game feeling that they can achieve that goal, and they just may come out of there with a win. Chapter 17 discusses performance and other goals.

COACH TIP

Playing against an easy opponent

You probably know that you'll have a few challenges getting your team ready to play against a strong opponent or in a big game. But what about the so-called pushovers, the easy teams that you should beat every time out.

Getting your team to play hard against an easy opponent could be challenging. Your team is probably thinking that the game will be an easy one, your players may be looking past that game in anticipation of the next big game, and they may approach this easy game lethargic and unmotivated. If your team is not energized, chances are they'll play poorly, resulting in an upset.

In this situation, your team's performance goals may help (see Chapter 17 for more about team goals). The attempt to meet or better one or two team performance goals in a single game should energize and challenge your team, even in a game against an easy opponent. For example, you may remind your players of an area in which they performed poorly in a previous game and challenge them to achieve a greater success rate in that area. Do whatever you can to challenge your team to make what may seem like a boring game interesting, so your team will concentrate on what it has to do and play to its potential.

- ✔ **Add a new wrinkle to your game plan:** Come up with a strategy, a little wrinkle that will be a secret weapon to use to give your team an edge. Be careful, though; you still want to focus on the style of play with which you regularly achieve success.

- ✔ **Challenge your team and/or specific players:** When you play in a big game, you're usually playing against great players. Use this opportunity to challenge your best offensive players and your best defenders; make this a game in which they can gauge their personal progress.

- ✔ **Accentuate the positive; eliminate the negative:** In your pre-game talk, remind your players about all the ways in which they will be successful.

Preaching to the Converted: Pre-Game Speeches

When you walk into the dressing room to begin your pre-game speech to your team, you should walk with a posture of confidence and pause for a split second to announce your presence and to give everyone an opportunity to settle down. You want the players dressed and ready to go before you enter the room for your pre-game talk (you can ask your team captain to let you know when the players are ready).

One of the keys when you give your pre-game talk is your confidence, presence, and delivery. Sometimes a pre-game talk has to do with showmanship and dramatics; other times you want to deliver your message slowly and deliberately. Talk slowly to allow your players to absorb what you say, as well as to give you time to think things through before you speak. By slowing down, you give a sense of being relaxed, under control, calm, and confident. Conversely, talking too fast makes you appear nervous and not in control.

When appropriate, try to inject some humour into the course of your speech as a release from the tension of the pre-game jitters. And don't be afraid to make fun of yourself or laugh when a player says something funny.

You have to get to know your team so that you gauge your talk according to your player's body language. Sometimes you may decide to just let your team get ready on its own; other times you may have to give them a good pep talk because they seem to be down or flat.

Choosing your pre-game talk subject

You should keep your talk simple and to the point. Tell the team specifically what they need to do to be successful. Your pre-game talk is just basically giving the team any last-minute instructions or reminders; it's not for filling their heads with any new stuff that may confuse what you've worked on in practice. The following list offers a few suggestions for your pre-game talk:

- ✔ Review your game plan.
- ✔ Reiterate your opposition's strengths and weaknesses.
- ✔ Emphasize improvements from your previous game.
- ✔ Point out your opposition's weakest players.
- ✔ Assign defensive match-ups.
- ✔ Focus on one or two of your behaviour goals.

When you've finished speaking, give your players an opportunity to ask questions or seek clarification. And don't forget whatever pre-game cheers or rituals you may have. My players gather in a tight circle, each shoving a hand into the middle of the circle, and shout out a quick cheer before we leave the dressing room.

Understanding the point of a pre-game talk

The talk should make the team feel prepared, energized, confident, good about itself, relaxed, together, strong, and with a feeling that they will be successful. The talk helps gets the team to focus on their performance goals and behaviour goals — things that they can control — and focus less on winning, which they can't completely control. Primarily, though, your pre-game speech simply reinforces what you and your team have worked on in recent practices and throughout the season.

Some situations may call for a more specific pre-game talk. For example, during a losing streak, you should focus on building your players' confidence and reinforcing the value of your team's style of play and long-term goals. In fact, probably the best way to help your team get out of its losing doldrums is to get them to focus on some specific goals that they can easily achieve. Meeting goals can act as baby steps toward getting back on the winning track.

For just about any game situation, your pre-game talk should help get your players ready for the struggle ahead. You also may need to help them work up some emotion and intensity before going out to the playing surface. There's little you can do in the dressing room before a game to help your players improve their physical skills, but you can rile them up a bit, helping them prepare mentally for what lies ahead.

Speaking to your team between periods and after games

The pre-game speech is only one component of your game-day speaking itinerary. Remember to take advantage of the few minutes you have between periods to reinforce your team's focus for the game and offer a few minor adjustments for the upcoming period. And the post-game time with your team may give you your best teaching opportunity, when a game situation or a particular skill is fresh on your players' minds because of how it unfolded during the course of play.

Between periods, make sure that you give your players enough time for a bit of a break. They'll need to drink water, use the restroom, eat oranges, see the trainer, fix broken equipment, or just relax. Don't take this personal time from them so that you can have more time for your between-period speech. However, you should use the time to share your game observations with players as a group, making sure that they know what's happening during the game, changes that need to be made, and schemes the other team is using. A pre-game speech can only do so much; no coach can completely anticipate how a game is going to transpire. He needs to use any stoppage in play to check in with his team.

Performing a Little Game-Time Coaching

No matter how much preparation you put into getting your team ready to play in a particular game, events of the game will inevitably force you to make some game-time decisions or adjustments. Or you may find your players playing too tentatively or too aggressively and you will need to come up with something to change their mood. This section offers some tips for what you can do to help your team after they've left the dressing room.

Emphasizing your pre-game warm-up

Warming up for the action after you've left the dressing room can be more than just helping your players break a sweat and get loose. You can use the time to present your team to the opponent as an example of solidarity and cohesion. Get your team to run onto the floor together — leave no stragglers behind in the dressing room, not even the goalie with all his bulky equipment. Have your players run every warm-up drill with the same emotion and intensity that they'll use during the game. Warm up in every way as if it's a game situation — every pass is thrown on target, every shot challenges your goalie. And encourage your players *not* to look at the opposition, which may suggest some intimidation; you want the opposition to look at your team, to be intimidated by your team.

Making decisions during the game

Coaching consists of recruiting or selecting the right players, teaching and practising the skills, and game coaching. All three areas are important, but to be successful as a coach, you must know how to *game coach*. Without question, a coach's primary responsibilities during a game are calling line changes; changing players on the floor; and calling plays for the offence, defence, and specialty teams. To do all this, you cannot get caught up in watching the game like a spectator; you must stay focused on the game to get a feel for the game and to think one play ahead of everybody else. You must concentrate not only on what your team is doing but also on what the opposition is doing so that if you see a weakness, you must be ready to take advantage of it. Many games progress as you planned them, but when the roof starts to fall in on your game plan, you have to adapt or adjust to minimize or contain the damage.

Just as important as calling plays and dealing with line changes is adjusting to the game at hand. You need to observe the other team and the way your players are playing to pick up advantages and disadvantages, what to exploit and what to protect. A crucial part of any sport is dissecting a game on the fly and tactically using interpretations to your team's benefit.

Some coaches take notes during the game so that they'll remember which good plays and mistakes to talk about with players after the game or during the following practice. They also find that taking notes during the game helps them to pay better attention to the game.

Matching up

Game coaching is matching lines against lines and being aware of the better offensive players on the other team when they are on the floor and matching up with them with your team's better defensive players. Your best defender should defend their best offensive player every time. Calling for these match-ups is the most critical decision you make as a coach, putting the best defender on their best scorer and trying to take away what he most likes to do.

A coach certainly has an impact on the outcome of the game because he is constantly putting players in and out of the game. You need to substitute players wisely, develop a certain pattern so that players get used to the rotation of the lines, and make sure that you never sit your best players too long.

Managing line changes

You also need to recognize when your lines are ready for a change. You should know before the game how long a particularly line can stay on the floor and still be effective, and anticipate your line changes accordingly. But you should also be able to pick up warning signs from your players that show fatigue, such as lapses of concentration, signs of lazy play, increased turnovers, or needless penalties. Be ready to pull the plug on a line when you see these signs.

To change lines efficiently, have your players line up at the door closest to your offensive zone so that when your offensive players enter the field of play, they can become an instant offensive scoring threat. Conversely, every player coming off the floor should enter the bench through the door closest to your defensive zone. With this arrangement, you'll prevent pushing and shoving among your players trying to get on or off the floor.

Try to keep the same lines playing together throughout the game. By keeping lines together, you'll get better execution and timing, more cohesiveness, and extra consistency in their play as players get to know each other's tendencies.

Showing something different

When game coaching, you want to avoid offering exactly the same thing defensively all the time against every team. You have to maintain your defensive rules, which are based on your players' strengths, but against certain teams and players, you should make minor adjustments to take away a unique element of the opponent's offensive game plan. Plus, it's always nice to have a few tricks up your sleeve so that you can make the opposition think you are going to do one thing defensively while you are actually doing something else. You want to do anything you can to create confusion and indecision on your opposition's bench.

Practising your own behavioural goals: Be a good role model

You have to set a good example of the behaviour you want to see in your players. Give encouragement and praise from the bench, but be selective when handing out these compliments, and offer that encouragement or positive feedback as soon as possible. And don't forget to praise effort as much as you praise results; remember to praise the player who made the pass or set the pick in addition to the player who scored the goal.

And don't forget your defence: Never let a great defensive play go unrewarded. Because defence is so important to the success of your team, here are a few defensive reminders to keep in mind during a game:

- ✔ Play your best defenders no matter what their offensive skills are like.
- ✔ Compliment and reinforce defensive players for their hustle and hard work.
- ✔ Reward good defensive play by letting these defensive starts play a little bit on offence. Even defensive players know that the most fun part of the game is scoring.

After a mistake, keep your cool; with the right timing, when the player is receptive, give corrective feedback about the mistake. Try not to show a player that you are upset by raising your voice. If the mistake is inappropriate behaviour and that behaviour continues over time, you'll have no choice but to bench the player.

Maintaining order on your bench

To be a good game coach, you have to maintain some semblance of order on your own bench, and I don't mean baby-sitting your players (although you may have to do some of that too). You want your players sitting in an order on the bench that is most efficient for rotating line changes. If you have specialty-team players who play only on the power play, the man short, or the faceoff, you need to keep them out of the way so that your regular position players can easily run on and off the bench.

You also need to have someone assigned to the bench door. "Huh?" you say. Well, I say that the person who is opening and closing the bench door for your players is extremely important. He must be someone who can anticipate line changes and not be a spectator. He has to always be mentally in the game. He must know beforehand which player is going on the floor and which one is coming off the floor. He must make sure the right players are up at the door and ready to go on.

Of course, the field lacrosse playing area doesn't include a bench door; the field has sidelines, not sideboards. But the substitution area is still called a box. Careful organization of players coming into and out of the box is extremely important. No player can substitute into a game before he is in the box. And any confusion about who is going in and who is coming out can create big-time match-up mistakes if the wrong players are on the field.

Letting them play

You will have to shout some playing instructions to your players from the bench during a game. But you also have to strike a balance between maintaining some control over them by making sure they play in the system — in other words, give instructions — and allowing your players the freedom to react to the game as it unfolds — in other words, shut up. If you constantly yell instructions to your players during the game, you're not giving them the room they need to focus on the game, because they'll be paying attention to you.

Anticipating the comeback

Coming from behind is an art. You must show your team and your opponent that you absolutely believe you can make up any deficit and win the game.

What can you do when you get behind in a game? You just have to get your players to step it up, play harder, and make super hustle plays. Coming from behind requires nothing fancier than just old-fashioned hard work. Your players have to win every loose ball and faceoff, they have to run to get the quick goals, and they have to play a full-floor press.

But most importantly, you have to continue to play within the foundations that you've built as a team. When losing, players often try to make up any deficit on their own and they stop playing within the team structure. In other words, they panic and forget how they've been playing all season long. Remind them that lacrosse is a game of emotion and momentum; once your team shaves off an opponent's lead by two or three goals, the opponent will probably start to panic and forget how they've been playing all game long.

Chapter 19

Coaching Kids — and Having Your Kids Coached

*W*ith nearly 300,000 active players in North America, your neighbourhood is bound to have a lacrosse league or two for your children to join, especially if you live in Canada or the northeastern U.S. Whether it's at the local arena that hosts a junior-level box lacrosse organization, at the local high school where your son lines up against players from other schools, or the local park that features girls' field lacrosse competition, several options exist for kids who want to play lacrosse. This chapter helps you to prepare for that inevitability.

Or you may be one of the many parents or community leaders who have been asked to take on a lacrosse team as its coach. After the requisite panic, take a look through this chapter for some helpful hints on coaching a kids' lacrosse team.

Coaching Philosophy about Dealing with Youths

Many parents start coaching in minor lacrosse because one of their children wants to play the game and they want to be involved with them. Other parents coach because they love the game, because they were involved in lacrosse themselves when they were younger, or simply because they love to coach and they need to keep busy until hockey season. Whatever the reason to coach, this section explains why young players do some of the things that they do.

Understanding why young people participate in sports

The number one reason kids play lacrosse is for fun. Competing is what matters the most! When you ask kids whether they would rather be on a winning team and not play much or be on a losing team and play often, most just want to play; it doesn't matter whether they are on a winning or a losing team. The fun of playing is more important than the satisfaction kids get from winning.

Kids play lacrosse to develop and improve their skills; if they can pass and catch and are good at lacrosse, they have more fun. By being good at lacrosse, they will have more success, and that leads to more confidence and more satisfaction.

Youth field lacrosse

Historically, field lacrosse in the U.S. has been caged in the northeast, with New York and Maryland serving as joint capitals of the sport. The sport has been most popular in regions around New York City; Baltimore, Maryland; Philadelphia, Pennsylvania; Syracuse, New York; and Washington, D.C. Beginning in the 1980s and rapidly fast-forwarding into the 1990s, field lacrosse began to spread into the U.S. midwest, southeast, and west, to states such as Ohio, Illinois, Florida, Texas, Colorado, California, Arizona, Utah, and Washington.

According to numbers released by U.S. Lacrosse, some 250,000 people were playing lacrosse in the U.S. in 2001. Most of the game's growth can be seen at the youth level (67 percent of U.S. Lacrosse's membership in 2001), as the number of NCAA Division I colleges playing lacrosse hovered around 55 teams throughout the late 1990s. Youth leagues start boys and girls playing as young as five years old. They progress to junior high school and high school teams, and many players aspire to play college lacrosse.

Some growth has also been seen in the men and women's division levels of the U.S. Lacrosse Intercollegiate Associates (USLIA). The USLIA is an organized league consisting of about 160 men's club teams at U.S. colleges and universities (many of which are among the country's largest and most prominent schools) that do not sponsor varsity programs. The women's division sponsors about a hundred teams, some of which are at schools with varsity programs. The National Collegiate Lacrosse League (NCLL) sponsors an estimated 75 men's teams, many at varsity schools.

Having fun, however, is just one reason why young people want to play lacrosse. Here are a few others:

- **Motivation:** Many kids want to improve their skills because they are driven to be the best.

- **Camaraderie:** Kids like to play and compete because they love to play any sport, they enjoy being with their friends and being part of a team, and they compete because they like the action. If you ever listen to former professional athletes talk about their careers after they are finished playing, the one thing that nearly all of them miss the most is the companionship of their teammates.

- **Competition:** Some kids like the thrill and excitement of competing against other kids. Although they should be playing to compete with themselves rather than another person, they love the challenges involved in sport.

- **Staying active:** Some kids play to keep themselves in shape for other sports, such as hockey.

- **Fame:** And some kids like the recognition they get from playing.

I have found through years of coaching minor players that winning is one of the least likely reasons for kids to want to play. So, keep this in mind when you plan practices and make them fun, not gruelling. When you give your pre-game talk, fill them in about the other team and focus on improving performance rather than stressing the need to win. When you talk about winning, remind your team that the effort, doing one's best, is more important than beating your opponent.

Knowing why kids quit sports

Besides recognizing why kids want to play, it helps minor coaches to understand why kids leave a sport. This section offers some of the reasons behind a kid's decision to stop playing. It may help you keep some of them in the game.

- The sport was not challenging or exciting; it was just plain boring.

- The sport was all work and no fun.

- The kids didn't like the coach.

- The kids found other interests. They just wanted more free time to do other things, such as have a social life, play on the Internet, and so on.

- The kids didn't get to play a lot and, with the lack of playing time, became discouraged and frustrated.

When to start kids in lacrosse

Parents often ask when the right time is to start their children in lacrosse. It's never too early — kids love to play with balls (bouncing, kicking, or throwing), but if the player isn't ready, don't push him. If he wants to play, he will tell you so. It is always best to start him off in a house league to let him grow into the sport.

Also, if he isn't a big person, he may be intimidated by the size of the other kids until he figures

out what his assets are, which may be speed, quickness, ball handling, or intelligence.

Naturally, the time to start will differ from kid to kid, and pushing your child to start an activity before she is ready may hinder her performance. Remember that many great players (of any sport) started late in life and were still very successful. Early is not necessarily better.

✔ The kids felt they were being treated unfairly. They became discouraged because they were lied to and promised things that never happened.

✔ The kids were not happy with the way they were playing.

By trying to understand all the reasons behind why kids quit lacrosse, you may be able to use this awareness to help your players stay tuned to the game. In doing so, you can work on not doing the same things that other coaches do to turn kids off from lacrosse.

Knowing your responsibilities as a minor coach

One of your main roles as coach is to help kids learn to love the game, and the best way to do this is to make sure that all the kids on your team have fun. However, while having fun, here are a few other things to keep in mind as coach:

✔ **Focus on the fundamentals.** As a youth coach, you are responsible to make sure that all the kids learn the basic skills as well as some team-play skills. Keep the team strategy simple so that players don't become frustrated.

✔ **Everyone plays.** A youth coach is responsible to make sure that all kids have maximum participation during practice and games.

There's a natural tendency to pay more attention to the better kids on the team in practice because they will probably be the ones you rely on in the crunch. But it is amazing how the weaker kids are often put into pressure situations in a game because of injuries or penalties, so you — and they — better be ready for that too. The bottom line is to work with the less skilled kids as much or more as with the skilled players.

✔ **Effort trumps winning.** As a youth coach, you are responsible to keep "winning" in the proper perspective and to stress to kids to strive to be the best they can be and not be concerned about winning. The two quotes I like for kids are these: "Giving all it seems to me is not so far from victory" and "Success is not being the best, but doing one's best."

✔ **Keep them safe.** Finally, as a youth coach, you are responsible to make sure that all the kids are well protected by their equipment and to teach them how not to get hurt.

A youth coach is also responsible to make sure that all kids have as equal playing time as possible. For more discussion on this critical topic, see the section "All things being equal — playing time, that is" later in this chapter.

Motivation tips for minor coaches

Minor coaches in any sport have different demands on them than junior or major coaches. Here are some points to keep in mind:

✔ **Treat your players as you would your own children.** Be yourself; you are really a surrogate parent for the kids you coach. Sometimes you may be hard on them, but you should counteract this by offering praise.

✔ **Stay composed.** Having patience is a great asset for a youth coach because kids make a lot of mistakes and you cannot get upset every time they either don't do something, forget to do something, or can't do something technically. And how you react to all these mistakes tells a lot about how your team plays the game.

✔ **Be a good role model.** Stay cool in front of your kids. Being a good role model also means not swearing, smoking, or drinking alcohol in front of the kids.

✔ **Stick to the basics.** When teaching young kids, remember the K.I.S.S. theory — Keep It Simple, Stupid — regarding fundamentals and team strategy. Coaches have a tendency to talk too much when explaining skills and may lose the kids' attention.

Instead, make sure that you get them practising and moving around, which will help them learn more and have more fun. Talk and reinforce as much as you can about what you want them to do. Explain it carefully and with a visual demonstration. You may find out that some kids listen better than others, and those who don't will need to be told over and over again. Remember to be willing to listen to suggestions from the kids.

✔ **Set objectives.** Motivate kids by giving them short-term goals that they have a good chance of reaching immediately. A simple thing such as concentrating on catching the ball can be a major accomplishment. And remember when running drills that it is not the drill that teaches the skill but the feedback a coach gives as the players do it.

✔ **Promote values.** One of your main roles as a minor coach is to help the child grow and develop certain values, such as independence and responsibility. From the beginning of the season, you can gradually give your players lessons in responsibility by giving them the power to make their own decisions on the floor or by asking for their input on major decisions about the team. This process results in independence.

As a minor coach, you should leave the wins and losses to the pros; your job is to teach skills to your players and to make sure that they have fun. As one coach told me, "In watching minor sports as a coach, I learned more about what not to do rather than what to do!"

Keeping Your Coaching Head in the Game

In minor lacrosse, you find that lots of parents coach their own kid's team. The question is whether that's a good thing. If a coach knows how to balance coaching his son (or daughter) and treating him (or her) the same as everybody, it should not be a problem. However, keep in mind that it is tough to coach your child when you are truly trying to make decisions that positively affect your team and not your child's playing time.

Giving up the ball

The two biggest coaching challenges with minor lacrosse teams are players who don't want to pass the ball and players who lack discipline and take bad penalties or mouth off at the referee or the opposition.

Minor coaches should be able to instruct and sell their players on when it is best to pass the ball and when to carry the ball. Some minor coaches encourage their best players to be totally selfish, minimize passing, and try to do it all by themselves. Instead, minor coaches should stress team play and unselfishness to the players.

A lacrosse team is not a "team" if five players are not playing as one. When the team is not playing together, the ball carrier is usually not looking to make a play, but rather to go one-on-one or to shoot. On most underachieving teams, you'll find players who are selfish individuals and a coach who does nothing about it or doesn't know what to do about it. (See Chapter 17 for tips on motivating your players.)

A good way to promote team passing and unselfish play is to run a lot of team passing drills where players *have* to give up the ball in order for the drill to work. If they don't pass the ball, you should reinforce over and over the necessity to pass the ball. Chapter 8 includes a number of team passing drills for you to try.

Taking bad penalties

When kids take bad penalties, the coach has a responsibility to discourage this behaviour. If the coach does nothing about actions that incur penalties, he gives out the message that these types of penalties are okay to take.

One way to deter bad penalties is to bench players and take away their playing time. Players should be benched for lack of discipline. This not only helps the team but also helps kids down the road of life. (See Chapter 17 for more about motivation.)

Managing the intimidation factor in lacrosse

Many coaches teach "intimidation lacrosse," thinking that they can beat teams by playing "dirty." Now, you may be able to beat the weak teams this way, but not the good teams — a good team is tough and disciplined and can't be intimidated. Trying to intimidate teams by taking stupid penalties based on this style of play eventually catches up with a team. To be successful against the good teams, one thing trumps all others — discipline. In a close game between two evenly matched teams, the difference is discipline: A bad penalty can cost the undisciplined team the game.

Intimidation applies not only to style of play but also to style of coaching. A coach should never embarrass or intimidate his players by constantly yelling at them and criticizing them. The minor coach should learn to *talk* to his players rather than yell at them. Out of control yelling shows that the coach is losing his cool. Of course, sometimes coaches have to yell instructions or constructive criticism to players, but that is not the same as yelling constant criticism. It's not what you say, but how you say it that's the really important thing. Sure, you want to correct and teach, but if you yell at your players, they're not likely to listen. The best thing is to take a player aside and explain the mistake he made.

Coaches must be careful not to let negative emotions interfere with their coaching. Some coaches just watch the game and do no coaching when they feel angry at their players. But players need a coach who is enthusiastic and positive, especially when they are behind in a game.

Players want a coach who is a disciplinarian. In a disciplined system, players do what they are supposed to do, and if they don't, they pay the consequences for being undisciplined. Players want a coach who is demanding — one who will not accept mediocrity and who strives for perfection. A good minor coach demands three important things to build a successful team: play hard, play together, and play smart. A disciplinarian coach can work wonders with an underachieving team with these goals in mind.

An underachieving team is also known as a *front-running team*. If the team is winning, everything is okay. But if the team gets behind in a game, players seem to quit, choosing instead to just go through the motions.

Addressing your minor lacrosse team

You can say any number of positive things to motivate your team to play well, to practise well, and even to get along with each other (see Figure 19-1). I discuss many of these motivational techniques in Chapter 17. More important, however, is the damage you can do to your team by saying the wrong things. Here are a few tips to help you avoid sending the wrong message:

- ✓ **Don't deflect blame.** Some minor coaches love to say that their team lost because of the refereeing, which gives the kids an excuse for losing. As a coach, you should never give players excuses for losing.

- ✓ **Don't deflect blame, part 2.** Coaches may blame the players for not playing well rather than looking at what the coaching staff may have done poorly. If you are frustrated because the team is not playing well, you must still take responsibility for it. Look for ways that you can improve how to communicate to your players.

- ✓ **Don't compound a loss with a scolding.** Some coaches tell the team after a loss that they lost because they played terribly. Your team may occasionally play poorly, but reminding them that they've done so soon after a loss only serves to add insult to injury. Your players know when they don't play well. Instead, remind them of the positive aspects of that loss, giving yourself the opportunity to build your players' confidence in upcoming practices.

- ✓ **Don't humiliate your players.** I've seen some coaches actually tell their players, "You embarrassed me." Remember that your players are playing for the team and for themselves, not for you. Instead, try telling your players that you were surprised by some of the things that happened during the game — they are things to work on at the next practice.

Figure 19-1:
Keep the lines of communication open with your players.

- ✓ **Don't delegate learning.** After a loss or a poor practice, some coaches have a tendency to ask the players for their opinion about what went wrong. You're the coach. You're the authority figure for these kids. They expect you to tell them where they can improve.

- ✓ **Don't go ballistic.** Don't become so enraged that you swear, rant, and rave at your players. In doing so, you're less likely to give a logical explanation to your players as to why you're so upset; you just come across as ticked off. Remember to maintain self-control, especially during adversity and losses.

Some coaches tell their players, "What is said in the change room, stays in the change room," that is, don't tell your parents. Even though you say that, most kids are going to tell their parents what's going on with the team, including what you say to them. Be aware of what happens in the change room, including what you say and do, because most parents will find out about it.

All things being equal — playing time, that is

This section discusses a major concern in minor lacrosse, especially as players advance to the prominent and successful teams, such as *rep teams* (teams that represent their league in all-star or travelling schedules). In dealing with your players to achieve equal playing time, remember that you're also probably dealing with two sets of parents: parents who are happy because their kid gets equal floor time, even though the team may have lost as a result; and parents who are unhappy, even though everybody played, because the team lost.

Some parents want equal playing time at the more advanced levels. A coach can rotate the team's lines evenly, as he would in house-league lacrosse, but his team won't beat the good teams because they usually play only the two best lines or they rotate their two best players every other shift.

Because house leagues are less competitive, coaches of these teams usually make sure that every player has a chance to play. So, of course, parents do not usually complain about playing time at all. Yeah, right! If you give all kids equal playing time, some parents will still complain that you are not trying to win. If you don't give all players equal time, other parents will yell at you that it is only a house league.

Sometimes complicating matters more is a child's level of success in a game. A team can lose but parents are happy because their child scored a goal or played. Or a team can win and yet the parents are not happy because their child did not score a goal or did not play a lot. Parents may be happy, win or lose, because the coach did everything to win. Other parents may be unhappy even if they win because their child did not get equal playing time.

The bottom line for a minor coach is reflected in this saying: "I can't give you the formula for success, but I can give you the formula for failure — trying to please everybody." And in minor lacrosse, it is impossible to keep everybody happy, so don't try. As long as your decisions, right or wrong, are with good intentions, you can't go wrong. Coach to help make the team successful, not to please parents.

So the question is: Can a team be competitive and successful and still play everybody equally? The answer is no. Reality states that to play with the top teams, sometimes certain players have to sit, which is okay at the travelling team level. A coach has to do what he has to do to make the team successful, and if that means sitting players out in certain situations, so be it. A good rule of thumb is that the first two periods (in minor lacrosse, you play three periods) are the players' time and the coach plays everybody equally; the third period is the coach's time to do and play whoever will help the team be successful. If everything is going as planned and everybody is playing well, the coach can just rotate through the lines and everybody plays equally; if things aren't going well, the coach may have to shorten the bench to get back into a game or play certain players in key situations.

In lacrosse, equal playing time refers to a five-on-five situation. With any special game situation, such as after a penalty, coaches have certain players who specialize in the man-short on defence and certain players who play the power play on offence. Usually, the better players play on these specialty teams.

Remembering that there really is no "I" in "team"

Coaching develops players so that the *team* will be strong, not just certain players. Chances are that your players will develop quite well on their own as the season progresses. If you build your team around one player, you will get in trouble for a number of reasons, but mainly because your team philosophy should be to play as a team.

- ✔ **Injury happens.** Building your team around one player puts you at risk if that player gets hurt or doesn't play for some reason. When you lose your best player, your other players are going to lose confidence in their ability to run the team without the star.

  And often after losing their best player, coaches will then take out their frustration on their other players. For example, when another player isn't successful at something that the star player can do with ease, the coach can lower the other player's confidence further by reminding him why the star player always brings up the ball.

- ✔ **Sharing responsibility is good game strategy.** If one player runs the offence 90 percent of the time, you can't expect the opposition not to adapt and try to take that player out of the game, leaving you without your best player. Spreading play-calling and play-running around keeps your opponent guessing about which player to concentrate on during any offensive set.

Coaching Philosophy about Dealing with Parents

Being a coach at the minor or youth level is not easy. Why? Parental interference and just plain dealing with some of the common challenges of youth, such as testing their independence against authority figures, will test you.

As coach, you must work toe-to-toe with parents to help your team, and their children, become successful. This section refers mainly to parents of all-star, travelling, or rep players. The parents of a house-league player usually are low-key about their children playing — they want their kids to just have fun and develop. And these parents don't have any grandiose ideas about their children turning professional — yet.

Parental guidance: Working with the coach

A coach, of course, can't do it all. Parents can help their child's coach in many ways; this section offers a few suggestions. First, I like to stress to parents that they offer positive assistance in many aspects of games and practices. Parents can help take statistics during a game, manage the team, serve as assistant coaches on the floor, organize drills, and raise money through garage sales and bake sales.

In my experience, kids develop better with less parental interference, so I suggest that parents should try to just let their kids play and stay out of their way. I know one coach who suggested that if parents didn't tell him how to coach, he wouldn't tell them how to parent.

Another way that parents can help their child's coach is to reinforce, whenever possible, the coach's philosophy that players be unselfish, work hard, and play smart. "Coaching" by parents after the game on the way home in the car, has to reinforce what the coach is teaching. For example, telling your child not to pass when she has the ball goes against the team's philosophy. Parents should support the team concept, even if it means putting it ahead of their children — and this can be tough. Parents also should understand and support the notion that sometimes their son (or daughter) has to sit on the bench in favour of better players at certain times of the game, or even sit on the bench so that less talented players have a chance to play, which can also be tough.

Finally, here are a few other tips for helping your child's coach at the same time that you help your child develop:

- ✔ **Try to be reasonable when it comes to your child's playing time.** Minor coaches should be available to talk to parents at every practice and every game, but they must draw a line when a parent wants to complain about playing time.

- ✔ **Resist the common practice of paying your child for every goal he or she scores.** I've seen this too many times in my coaching days and it only reinforces selfishness, so I don't recommend it at all. If you insist on some kind of reward for good play, make sure that you reward your child not only for scoring a goal but also for making an assist, to reinforce that the team comes first over personal goals.

- ✔ **Remind your child about the benefits of working together with other players.** To be the best that you can be, you have to depend on other people. And certainly being part of a team, you do become better than you could individually.

> ✔ **Take responsibility for your actions and reactions during a game.**
> Coaches have too much on their plate during a game to take the time to
> manage a player's reaction to what he hears from his parents in the
> stands. (See "Rules for parents at games" in the next section.)
>
> ✔ **Make sure that your child gets plenty of sleep and eats a proper diet.**

It's a good idea to have weekly meetings with parents, to give you an
opportunity to just talk or help anticipate any problems. Keep in mind that
every team has problems over the course of the season; teams that have
parents and coaches who can work out their problems are successful and
have fun along the way.

Rules for parents at games

If you're a coach, make sure at the beginning of the season that you offer a
list of rules to parents on how they should conduct themselves at games. If
you're a parent, commit this section to memory.

> ✔ **Cheer positively for every child on the team.** Avoid yelling negative
> comments at the top of your lungs at the referee, opposition players,
> parents of the opposing team, or your own child and teammates.
>
> Many negative parents try to relive their own youth through their
> children. They do this by venting their anger and frustration by shouting
> and screaming at their children, the coach, the referee, or anybody who
> they feel is holding their kids back.
>
> ✔ **Do not yell instructions or criticism to your child from the stands.**
>
> ✔ **Do not encourage your child to look at you during the game for support
> or instructions because this can throw off her focus.** Participating in
> sports helps children to become independent by standing on their own
> two feet, especially when things are going wrong. They have to learn to
> fight through mistakes and adversity by themselves.
>
> ✔ **If possible, try to watch a game from the opposite side of the arena
> from where your child's bench is.** This simple trick may help you avoid
> interfering with coaching decisions and your child's play.
>
> ✔ **Do not interfere with your child's coach.**

It is the coach's responsibility to keep parents in line by reminding them to be
good examples for their children at games. If parents continue to complain, for
example, about their children's playing times, you can just remind them that
any coaching decisions are based on what benefits the team. The team comes
first, not the parents, not their children, and not the coach!

Parental Expectations of a Youth Coach

Just as parents need to know what is expected of them during the game from the coach, they should also know what is expected from the coach. During a parent meeting at the beginning of the season, the coach should present his philosophy so that parents know where he is coming from. Hopefully, what the coach will stress is a team environment that places the development of skills and character over winning. He should also talk about a coaching environment in which he is a good role model, his reasons for why he will bench players, and how all decisions will be based on how they affect the team. (If you're really fortunate, you may have a coach who will put all this in writing; see Appendix B for a sample coach's "contract" with parents.)

Dealing with negative parents

Parents as well as players need direction for their behaviour during a game. It is the coach's responsibility to make sure the parents act accordingly. I have seen games ended by the referee because of the way parents acted in the stands, which then gives the team and organization a bad reputation that could follow that team all season.

Yes, it is the coach's responsibility to see that the parents behave themselves, even to the point that if they act up, their children may be asked to leave the team, which no coach wants to do. But as a coach, you have to take the initiative. In your parent meeting at the beginning of the season, be up front with all parents about how you expect them to behave. You may want to hand out a list of behaviour expectations to them. Throughout the season, you'll find that you may have to remind certain parents about how they should act. If your reminders don't work, you may have to ask these parents not to come to games or risk having their children taken off the team. (Some coaches give a contract to parents; see Appendix B for one example.)

If you are going to coach, you are going to deal with all types of parents, even negative ones, so get ready. Here are a few of the types:

- **Disinterested parents:** They do not get involved with the team, which is sometimes okay. But these parents do some damage by their absence in not supporting their own child.

- **Politically motivated parents:** Parents who suck up to the coach to get more playing time for their child.

- **Overly critical parents:** These armchair coaches believe nobody can do anything right. They are never satisfied with either their child's performance or the coaching. These parents do damage by their presence. (Negative feedback from parents causes children to feel anxious.) Adults who continually find fault and give negative feedback often leave their children frustrated and anxious. The kids feel that they can never fully please their parent, and parental approval is extremely important to children.

When parents identify their children's mistakes with a view to correcting them for future performance, it often backfires. Kids develop responsibility by having the opportunity to judge themselves, not by someone else judging them, especially parents.

Coaches should explain to parents that being critical all the time causes stress in their children's play, hinders their performance, and takes the fun out of playing. Rather, praise and encouragement will make the sport much more fun for them.

✔ **Screaming parents:** They yell all the time: from the stands, at the coach, at their kids, and all the way home. You would think these parents would care about setting poor examples for their children, but usually parents who yell all the time don't care what anybody thinks. On game days, a normal, calm, intelligent parent can turn into a yelling maniac, standing in the stands shouting instructions to their child, criticizing him and yelling at the referee, the opposition, and anybody else who is against his son.

✔ **Meddling parents:** They are always sticking their nose into the coach's business, always wanting to know what is going on. These parents try to tell you how to coach, who to play in what positions, and what players are the best.

✔ **Overprotective parents:** Overprotective parents try to protect their children by making excuses for their mistakes. These parents are also so concerned about their children getting hurt when they play that they make their children overly cautious, and this affects their performance.

One of the values of sports is to help athletes become independent. Kids have to learn to take responsibility for their own actions. You cannot pamper them; you have to make them mentally tough by accepting their own decisions, right or wrong. Some overprotective parents never want their children to experience failure, to know disappointment, or feel pain or hurt of any kind. This is very unrealistic. Part of parenting is to let your child experience life, not avoid it.

Overprotected children are often called spoiled. They are used to getting their own way and getting things without working for them! These spoiled players make poor competitors because they truly can't tolerate the stresses of competition and the adversity they must face. They have to work for their success; it is not handed to them. Life has been too easy for them to build emotional strength and resiliency. Just like our muscles require stress to develop and grow, so do our emotions. Getting tougher for overprotected players means risking more — no more playing it safe!

✔ **High-expectation parents:** Parents, are you pushers or supporters? There is a fine line between the two. Is your child playing to please you or to please himself?

Mistakes are part of the game

Repeated failure generates anxiety, decreases motivation, and destroys feelings of self-worth. And lacrosse is a game where you fail more often than you succeed! As a parent, you should help your child to recognize the inevitability of making mistakes in this game, as well as help him to remember that these mistakes do not reflect on him as a person or how you feel about him.

Have you ever seen a perfect lacrosse game played where there were no mistakes? A lot of times kids think if they catch the ball or score a goal, their coach, teammates, and parents will like him. But if she drops a ball or misses the net,

in other words, makes a mistake, they won't like her. To become a better lacrosse player, you have to take risks with the possibility of making mistakes. If a young player fears failure because he is being criticized and put down for failures, he won't grow as an athlete. Fear of failure becomes the dominating force, and as a result, the game becomes too stressful. So the player never tries, plays conservatively, or avoids situations in which he might fail, robbing himself of the pleasure of playing all-out and being measured on his effort alone.

Some parents define their own self-worth in terms of their children's success and failures. Fathers are the main culprits here. They look at their sons as extensions of themselves: If the sons succeed, the fathers succeed. Fathers who push too much and live their own big dreams through their kids are the biggest problem in minor sports today, creating too much emotional stress for their children. Their expectations are so high that they feel they can stand in the stands and shout instruction and criticism to help their children do better. They feel their kids should be improving all the time, whether by working out on weights, running to get in shape, or taking shots. They feel that idle time is unproductive. The kids are pushed so much that they miss out on having fun along the way.

The proper outlook of parents should be that they want their children to succeed because they know it will make them happy. Parents must learn to put their own expectations second and their children's needs and enjoyment first. They must accept their children as they are! If expectations are too high, the children feel like failures because they can never please their parents. And all parents want their children to do well. This makes watching your own kid play one of the toughest things in the world to do. To help your child — and for your own stress level — create an atmosphere that emphasizes playing for the love of the game, growing as a person and player, and having fun.

Dealing with positive parents

Fortunately, minor coaches also have the pleasure of dealing with positive parents. Positive parents know that the primary objective of playing lacrosse is to strive to become a better player, physically, emotionally, socially, intellectually, and morally; the secondary objective is to win the game. Positive parents do not judge their children's success on wins and losses, but on how well they play. If parents emphasize that kids play their best, their children will never suffer from stress and not having fun. And kids will focus on their performance, playing well, and not on the outcome.

Kids should not feel that winning is good and losing is bad. They should feel that their satisfaction comes from playing a good game against a worthy opponent. Success is not being the best, but doing one's best. The journey, playing the game, is more important than the destination, winning the game. So let the kid have fun along the way.

Positive parents support but never push, as they don't want to put any more pressure on their children than the pressure that comes in a game. They want to help but they don't want to interfere. They perceive the game as just that, *a game,* trying not to take the game seriously. This attitude makes lacrosse much more fun for both parent and child.

Positive parents understand the real importance and priorities of their children playing. First, and most important, the child is involved in something constructive, and he's not hanging out on street corners; second, he is physically active (and improving lacrosse skills) and not lying around. Then look at all the other spin-off benefits: social (learning team values, such as interacting with others, getting along with people, and helping out others); emotional (learning to handle adversity and have fun); intellectual (learning strategies of the game); and moral (becoming a good sportsperson and building character).

Positive parents know that character, not talent, is the essential building block of being a good person. Positive parents let their children know that failure isn't a bad thing, as long as you learn from it. Parents give encouragement and support to their child more for their effort, helping them to relax when playing and not to worry about making mistakes. Failure is a natural part of learning and getting better. Kids should not feel that if they do not catch the ball every time, they are failures.

Positive parents offer a lot of cheering and applause. They feel that cheering is a way of to show support and to give their child a vote of confidence, especially when things are not going well. How many times have you cheered your team on to victory or so you thought? Cheering when your team is losing is even more important. Every time something happens, good or bad, positive parents find a way to say something positive. Children need support the most when they appear to deserve it the least! What does exuberant cheering and applause do? It increases adrenaline and gives the player the energy to go one more time.

How kids feel about themselves comes from their parents. Are their parents positive and always encouraging their children with a smile? Or are they negative and critical, demanding perfection and giving little or no encouragement? Parents who provide encouragement and positive feedback to their children raise the level of their children's self-esteem. It is a great feeling to play the game knowing their parents are behind them no matter how well they perform and knowing it is not the end of the world as long as they do their best. The bottom line is positive parents go to the games to enjoy them and to support their child through positive encouragement.

The ride home after a game

A parent can make the ride home after a game a pleasant time or a painful time. What do you ask your child after a game? Do you ask him who won the game? Do you ask her how she played? Do you ask him whether he had fun? Do you ask her what she learned in today's game?

By asking about who won, you're conveying to your child that winning is the only thing to be valued in sport. By asking about how she played, you get your child thinking about her own performance. It is not fair to compare your child with others who may just be better players. You should help your child focus not on winning but on playing to the best of his ability.

Fathers especially have a tendency to dissect the game with their sons after a game. Be careful here not to take the game too seriously. If you are having fun with your son, he will want to be with you; if you are critical all the time, he won't want to be around you. So after a bad game, after a loss, or after he makes a number of mistakes in a game, be supportive, be interested, and help him see the positive side of every dropped ball, missed check, and missed scoring opportunity.

And don't let your behaviour toward your child change after she plays a good game or after a win. You still need to support and encourage her. Emphasize that effort rather than winning is more important in the long run to being successful as a team or player.

Part V
The Part of Tens

The 5th Wave   By Rich Tennant

"I don't know who you are, kid, but goalie practice was over 2 hours ago! This is the NLL, kid! You can't show up late! Get in here! I'm not through with you!"

In this part . . .

This component of every . . . *For Dummies* book is fun and useful. You can find my personal all-time list of great National Lacrosse League players, as well as a few up-and-coming NLL stars. I share with you the elements about the game of lacrosse that I love the most, and I direct you to some online and traditional media resources that you can use to keep informed about lacrosse.

Take time to review the appendixes at the end of this part, where you'll find a glossary of standard lacrosse terms and some sample contracts for proper behaviour to be shared by coaches, players, and parents.

Chapter 20

Ten Reasons to Get Excited about Lacrosse

*T*he NLL may do many things (play loud music, run contests, send out a mascot) during a game to help entertain the game's fans, but the fact remains that the game itself provides the greatest entertainment. Lacrosse is an exciting game, played in an exciting atmosphere by men and women who love and respect the game. If these ten reasons to get excited about lacrosse don't do it for you, the rest of this book is sure to.

Lacrosse Is a Magical Game to Watch

You'll be amazed at the wizardry of the stick by professional players such as John Grant Jr., Gary Gait, Tom Marechek, and Kim Squire. From the best stick-handlers, you'll see fakes with the stick, behind-the-back shots and passes, pinpoint passes, no-look passes, and perfect simple passes. They even dazzle their opponents and the game's fans with such plays as the hidden ball trick, also called the ice-cone play, where players fake flipping the ball to a teammate and instead hang on to the ball. This trick still works against even the most experienced players who can be fooled when they're not paying attention to what is happening in the game.

Players and fans alike appreciate all this stick work, because they recognize how long and how hard these players worked to refine and execute these skills. And we also know that something more is at play with these players, they have an innate ability to perform magic with the stick and ball. Most of us could practise for hours and hours every day and never come close to what these great players can do.

Lacrosse Is Simple to Play but Hard to Learn

If you've never played the game, but appreciate lacrosse as a fan, get your hands on a stick and find out how hard and frustrating it is to pass or shoot the ball and hit a target. After a number of futile attempts, you'll appreciate even more the skill of passing and shooting.

However, after you have mastered the skills of the game so that you don't have to think too much about what you're doing but instead can just execute a game plan, lacrosse becomes easy. All you have to do is shoot the ball and put it into the opposition's goal. And if you don't have the ball, all you have to do is to stop the opposition from scoring. While you can still pick up a variety of methods to achieve those two simple goals, the game always comes down to scoring and not scoring.

Lacrosse Is a Fast-Paced Game

The tempo of the game makes it exciting. A game offers constant action up and down the floor. Players are running here and there. The ball is being fired quickly around the playing surface and at the goalie. The goalie gets in the action by passing the ball up the floor to a breaking teammate, quickening the pace of the game even more. And offences use plays such as the pick-and-roll or the screen to free up players so that they can attack — again, quickly — the goal.

Lacrosse Is a Contact Sport

Especially in box lacrosse, you'll see a great deal of hitting with the stick and body contact. Players battling with each other for a loose ball off a faceoff or after a missed shot look somewhat like rugby players in the midst of a scrum — except a rugby player never ends up with a stick up against his face.

Oh yes, and you'll see fights. Especially at the NLL level. Not so much at the minor level, where officials and coaches rightly work hard to ensure the safety of their young players. But you will see fights.

Lacrosse Has a Great Feel — Literally

One of the real reasons that players love to play the game is because of the tremendous feeling you can have by just throwing the ball and having it go where you want it to go. Players experience great exhilaration when the ball hits the twine of the net in goal. Players love a good old-fashioned cross-check that stops a ballcarrier from getting by. Goalies relish the challenge of stopping a player one-on-one. And players take great satisfaction from absorbing a hit yet still rolling past the player who is trying his hardest to prevent being beaten. These one-on-one battles really get the competitive juices flowing and provide a great feeling of gratification when you win the battle.

Lacrosse Is a Fair-Weather Friend

Especially in box lacrosse, the weather is always fine. You go to the arena on a rainy day and walk past soccer players getting drenched in the rain or baseball players shivering from the cold and think to yourself, "Boy, am I glad to be playing inside tonight."

And field lacrosse has its great-weather moments as well. There's not much to beat the atmosphere of the well-played contest on the soft green grass on a crisp sunny day in spring.

Lacrosse Is a Community Game

Lacrosse in small communities is much like a family gathering. Everyone involved in lacrosse pretty much knows everyone else who's involved in lacrosse. You see them all at games and at practices and at tournaments. You organize road trips together to playoff games. And when someone in the lacrosse community needs critical help, the lacrosse family pulls together and provides help. One such example occurred in 2002, when the young Orangeville, Ontario, native, Dustin Sanderson, was hit into the boards and became paralyzed. The lacrosse community rallied behind this fine young man and helped raise money for his rehabilitation.

And you can relate easily to the players as they are as likely as not to live right next door. For example, NLL players work in your community as teachers, policemen, firemen, or factory workers. They don't live in million-dollar homes. And they make themselves available to the fans before and after the game.

Lacrosse Welcomes the New Player

The lacrosse community is always willing to rally round, especially when it comes to helping new people become involved in the sport. Want to know where to buy a good lacrosse stick? Lacrosse people will point you in the right direction. Want to know how to play the game? Lacrosse people involved will give you direction and advice on what to do, including where to buy this book.

Lacrosse Breeds Respect

The true lacrosse player and fan holds the game in high regard. And this respect transfers to the players on the floor. Players respect each other because they know how tough you have to be to play this great game. No lacrosse fan — especially the NLL fan — is ever surprised to see players bruised up, bleeding, exhausted, sore, and fatigued from the game, who still take the time to shake hands with their opponent after the game. Grudges never last long after a game; maybe because if a player hits you hard, you know you'll have a chance to return the favour in the next game.

Lacrosse Creates Atmosphere

I love it when NLL players run around the arena after the game and wave or greet the fans.

I love how friendly and approachable the NLL players are in giving autographs when you ask.

I love the NLL cheerleaders.

I love catching one of the T-shirts an NLL team mascot shoots up into the crowd.

I love the familiar stinky smells of the arena.

Chapter 21

(Not Quite) Ten Resources for Discovering More about Lacrosse

. . . .

In This Chapter

▶ Staying in touch with the game

▶ Supporting the game's media exposure

▶ Finding places to outfit your kid

. . . .

*T*hough it's becoming a bit of a cliché to say "in the advent of the Internet," the Internet has helped to change the way lacrosse fans find information about the sport that they love. Teams have Web sites that include such items as team schedules and statistics. And some teams have fan clubs with their own Web sites devoted to their favourite players. This chapter directs you to the most popular and active lacrosse-related Web sites and also reminds you of a few other more traditional resources to go to for lacrosse tidbits.

Keeping Tuned to the Game on the Web

Yes, it's true. You can follow the game online. The National Lacrosse League's Web site (www.nll.com) features webcasts of selected games. Look for weekly previews of games that the league posts to find out which games are slated for an Internet broadcast each week.

Following the NLL Online

Go to www.nll.com to check out fan-friendly information about the NLL. The league posts up-to-date game results, standings, and player statistics; provides the season's schedule; and includes links to each individual team's Web site.

At the team Web sites, you can find even more information about your favourite team, including downloadable images to use as wallpaper on your computer screen, game photos, and information about tickets and seating at the arena. Follow the links from www.nll.com to get to your favourite team's site.

Finding Your Minor League's Web Site

Many lacrosse associations throughout Canada have Web sites that parents, players, and coaches can access. Typical content on these sites include registration information (and sometimes online registration), lacrosse rules and equipment requirements, directions to playing arenas (especially helpful for visiting teams), and schedules and standings. As with all Web sites, some are more sophisticated than others. Check with your local lacrosse association to find out whether they have or plan to create a Web site.

Most junior and major lacrosse teams in Canada — teams that compete for the Mann and Minto Cups — have Web sites that follow the local squads throughout the year. You can find player profiles, scores and schedules, player statistics, and sometimes even fan-club information and activities. The following lists a few of the club-based Web sites available:

- Brampton Excelsiors: www.excelsiors.com
- Brooklin Redmen: www.brooklinredmenlacrosse.com
- Coquitlam Adanacs: www.adanaclacrosse.com
- New Westminster Salmonbellies: www.salmonbellies.com
- Peterborough Lakers: www.ptbolakerslacrosse.net
- Victoria Shamrocks: www.rockslax.com

Keeping Up with the Game in the Media

Because live television coverage of lacrosse is not yet quite as sweeping as, say, the National Football League or the NCAA men's basketball championships, lacrosse fans still need to do a bit of digging to keep up with their favourite teams and players. But that task is infinitely easier with the Web resources available for finding lacrosse news and results.

You can scour the national newspapers' sports sections for NLL scores and standings, but you won't find too many stories and profiles about the teams' players. The local papers are more likely to include in-depth coverage of that area's lacrosse news, especially in the smaller communities that host junior and major lacrosse teams. The *Toronto Sun* (www.torontosun.com) and the *Calgary Sun* (www.calgarysun.com) typically offer the best Canadian lacrosse coverage, and you can also check out good Web coverage with the Canoe Internet news network at http://slam.canoe.ca/SlamLacrosse/home.html. The *Baltimore Sun* (www.sunspot.net), *Syracuse Post-Standard* (www.syracuse.com), *Newsday* (www.newsday.com), and *Washington Post* (www.washingtonpost.com) are the top U.S. papers that cover lacrosse — mostly high schools and college, but some professional news as well.

To keep up with the sport itself, as well as with scores, championship results, and player and team updates, your best bets are going to be found in magazines and online. The following list includes some of the best of these media for keeping up with the lacrosse Joneses:

- *Inside Lacrosse:* *Inside Lacrosse* was first published in 1997 as a weekly newspaper covering primarily NCAA men's lacrosse. It has since expanded to cover every portion of the game, from high schools and youth action to men's and women's college lacrosse to the professional outdoor and indoor leagues. *Inside Lacrosse* does an annual NLL Preview Issue and covers the NLL and Canadian lacrosse year-round with features and analysis. It is published 11 times a year. Insidelacrosse.com started in 2000 and has emerged as the top site for news and original commentary on lacrosse.

- *Lacrosse Magazine:* Published by US Lacrosse, this source for all things lacrosse covers every aspect of lacrosse, including the international scene. It recently celebrated its 25th anniversary. And while it is an amateur organization, the magazine does cover the NLL.

- **Total Lacrosse:** Started in 2002, this Web site (www.totallacrosse.com) is dedicated to Canadian box lacrosse. It gives extensive coverage to the NLL, the Ontario Lacrosse Association (OLA), and the Western Lacrosse Association (WLA), with breaking news and inside scoops not found elsewhere.

- **E-Lacrosse:** This exclusively online publication (www.e-lacrosse.com) offers news about high school, collegiate, and professional lacrosse culled from a pool of freelance writers and photographers across North America. The site also hosts an online store for lacrosse equipment, as well as its own branded products.

- *Face-Off Yearbook:* Started in 1994, this colour magazine is a must-have for college lacrosse fans, players, and coaches. It covers Divisions I, II, III, and junior college lacrosse, offering information on every team in the NCAA in addition to statistics, a full review of the previous year, coverage of the USLIA, and an academic reference guide for high schoolers looking to choose colleges. It is released in January and also holds the preseason All-Americans and team rankings for all divisions. It can be ordered through www.insidelacrosse.com.

- **YouthLacrosseUSA.com:** This Web site (www.youthlacrosseusa.com) includes instructional information for coaches and players as well as news about high school and college programs.

- **AllLacrosseAmerica.com:** With a Web directory–style design (think Yahoo!), this site offers news and scores for just about every skill level and style of play. Check out www.alllacrosseamerica.com.

- **USLaxcamps.com:** Lacrosse camps are a big part of a young player's development in the sport, and this site (www.uslaxcamps.com) is a good resource to research the process, including a comprehensive list of lacrosse camps that can be organized in a variety of categories — location, time, format, price, and so on.

Appreciating the History of the Sport

Lacrosse's organizing bodies noted in the following section are among the sport's repositories of its heritage, with resources to help you find out more about the roots of the game. The sport works hard to preserve its legacy, especially by honouring great players of the game, past and present, in a number of national and regional halls of fame, including the following:

- **National Lacrosse Hall of Fame:** In Baltimore, this hall of fame and museum is run by US Lacrosse, essentially the worldwide headquarters of the game, with an international membership of over 100,000. The hall of fame itself honours lacrosse players from the United States, with 293 inductees through 2002. This hall also supports a number of regional lacrosse halls of fame in the U.S.; check out www.uslacrosse.org/chapterfamers.html for details. You can get more information about the hall of fame from US Lacrosse at 113 West University Parkway, Baltimore, MD, 21210-3300 (phone: 410-235-6882).

- **Canadian Lacrosse Hall of Fame:** Opened in 1967 with an inaugural class of 48 inductees, this hall of fame is located in New Westminster, British Columbia. Through the 2002 class of inductees, the Canadian Lacrosse Hall of Fame honours 387 players, coaches, builders, and teams. For more information, contact the hall at 302 Royal Ave., New Westminster, BC, V3L 1H7 (phone: 604-527-4640).

- **Lock 3 Welland Canals Complex:** Located in St. Catharines, Ontario, this facility hosts an interactive exhibit on the history of the game and offers visitors a chance to try their hand at taking a shot on goal. The facility is at Lock 3, 1932 Government Road, St. Catharines, ON, L2R 7C2 (phone: 905-984-8880).

Supporting the Sport's Organizing Bodies

The national and regional organizations that help maintain the integrity and govern the rules of lacrosse can also be helpful for finding out more about the game in its various formats and levels. At these sites, you can find rules documentation and updates; information about the history of the game; and resources for coaches, players, parents, and media. Following are the primary organization Web sites in Canada and the United States:

- British Columbia Lacrosse Association: www.bclacrosse.com
- Canadian Lacrosse Association: www.lacrosse.ca
- NCAA Lacrosse: www.ncaa.org
- Ontario Lacrosse Association: www.ontariolacrosse.com
- United States Lacrosse Intercollegiate Associates: www.uslia.com
- US Lacrosse: www.lacrosse.org

Supporting Your Kid's Body: Buying Equipment

If you have a child who has signed up with your local lacrosse association for the upcoming minor lacrosse season, you need to get him or her outfitted for the game. Chapter 2 has more detail about the equipment required, but to actually buy the stuff, start with some of the manufacturers listed in this section. These Web sites may include only product information while others enable online purchasing. Or after you've completed your research, check out your local sporting goods store to purchase what your child needs.

- Brine Lacrosse: In the U.S., www.brine.com; in Canada, www.brinecanada.ca
- deBeer Lacrosse: www.debeerlacrosse.com
- Mohawk International Lacrosse (MIL): www.mohawkintlacrosse.com
- Proboss Lacrosse: www.probosslacrosse.com
- Rock Lacrosse Equipment: www.rocklacrosse.com
- STX Lacrosse: www.stxlacrosse.com
- Warrior Lacrosse: www.warriorlacrosse.com

Chapter 22

The Ten Greatest NLL Players

Most of these top ten players stand for longevity, endurance, and consistency, with an NLL career of ten years or more. Unlike other professional sports, what these top ten players have accomplished in so short a time is amazing both for its duration and their unparalleled proficiency in scoring.

Gary Gait

Gary is the greatest player to play in the NLL. Right from the beginning of his career in 1991, he started establishing records and winning awards, including Rookie of the Year in his first season with the Detroit Turbos. Known as a strong one-on-one player, he can score from anywhere on the floor. He has played in the league for 12 years (for Detroit, Philadelphia, Baltimore, Pittsburgh, Washington, and Colorado) and has been on the all-star team each year — an amazing accomplishment in any league. His teams have won three NLL championships: Detroit in 1991 and Philadelphia in 1994 and 1995. He has won the Most Valuable Player award in the league five times, and he is the all-time NLL leader in points with 820 (447 goals, 373 assists) through 2002.

John Tavares

John started playing for the Buffalo Bandits in 1993, and he's still there. He is known as a great scorer but considered an even better passer. He has also been a member of the all-star team every year that he's played in the league.

He has won two NLL championships with Buffalo, in 1993 and 1996. John has been named Most Valuable Player of the league three times, in 1994, 2000, and 2001, and stands in second place in the all-time points category with 749 (376 goals, 373 assists) through 2002.

Paul Gait

Paul started playing with the Detroit Turbos in 1991 alongside his brother Gary. Like his identical twin, Paul is a strong one-on-one player and can score consistently from inside and outside. Paul played in the league for 12 years and was selected to 10 all-star teams. A chronically bad back prevented Paul from reaching even greater heights, and he retired from competitive play after the 2002 season, a season that saw him earn his first Most Valuable Player award. Paul has won three NLL championships: Detroit in 1991, Philadelphia in 1994, and Rochester in 1997. He stands in third place for all-time points with 703 (404 goals, 299 assists) through 2002. Out of their 12 years in the league, Paul and Gary played together for 7 seasons.

Tom Marechek

Tom started in the NLL in 1994 and was named Rookie of the Year that year. He has played nine years in Philadelphia and been selected to the all-star team seven times. Tom has played on four NLL championship teams with Philadelphia. Tom is known for his wizardry with the stick and for running the pick-and-roll with his teammate, Jake Bergey — they're the best in the league at it. He is in fifth place for all-time scoring in the NLL with 536 points (290 goals, 246 assists) through 2002.

Kevin Finneran

Kevin started playing in 1991. His first year was with New England, his second with Detroit, and the rest of his career was with Philadelphia, before being traded to the Toronto Rock in 2002. He was known as a smart player who is good around the net. He played on four NLL championship teams with the Philadelphia Wings and was named to the NLL all-star team three times (1994, 1996, and 1998). Kevin stands in fourth place for all-time points in the NLL with 509 (210 goals, 299 assists) through 2002.

Duane Jacobs

Duane started playing in 1993 for the Detroit Turbos. After two seasons in Detroit, he went to Rochester and played for the Knighthawks for eight seasons. Prior to the 2002–03 season, Duane was traded to the Buffalo Bandits. Duane is known for his hard, accurate shot from the outside. He has been named to the NLL all-star team four times (1996, 1997, 1998, and 1999). He was a member of Rochester's only championship team in 1997. He stands in sixth place for all-time points in the NLL with 424 (206 goals, 218 assists) through 2002.

Ted Dowling

Now with the Colorado Mammoth, Ted entered the league in 1994 and has made his way nearly all the way around the league: from Detroit to Boston to Buffalo to Rochester to Albany to Montreal. Ted is known as a smart and great shooter, and was selected to the NLL all-star team in 1994. He stands in seventh place for all-time points in the NLL with 415 (241 goals, 174 assists) through 2002.

Mark Millon

Mark has played nine years in the NLL: four years with New York, two years with Baltimore, one year with Syracuse, and two years with Philadelphia. In 1999, he won the NLL championship with Philadelphia and was named to the all-star team for the fourth time (the others came in 1995, 1997, and 1998). Mark is known for his quick one-on-one moves that he backs up with a great long shot. He stands in eighth place for all-time total points in the NLL with 404 (212 goals, 192 assists) through 2002.

Jim Veltman

Jim started playing in 1992 with Buffalo and has played for 11 years in the NLL. He played for Buffalo (six years), for the Ontario Raiders (one year), and for the Toronto Rock (four years). He has been an all-star nine times and has won the NLL championship six times (three with Toronto and three with Buffalo). Jim is known as a great team leader and is one of the best two-way players in the NLL. He stands in ninth place for all-time points in the NLL with 388 (106 goals, 282 assists) through 2002.

Jake Bergey

Jake started playing in 1998 with Philadelphia and has played every year of his career with the Wings. Jake has played on two NLL championship teams (1998 and 2002) and has been on the all-start team twice. Jake is a big and strong player who, with Tom Marechek, runs the best pick-and-roll in the league. He stands in tenth place for all-time points in the NLL with 316 (152 goals, 164 assists) through 2002. He's reached this pinnacle after only five years in the league.

Others to Watch

Not quite making the cut in my top ten list are some players with very strong NLL careers. But I just single out a few of them here: Darris Kilgour, Matt Panetta, Shawn Williams, Dan Stroup, Chris Gill, Troy Cordingley, and Colin Doyle.

And a few players didn't make the cut because they lack the established careers of the players in my list. But watch out for these players in the next ten-year list: John Grant Jr., Gavin Prout, Tracey Kelusky, Josh Sanderson, and Gary Rosyski.

Appendix A

Glossary

● ●

Assist: A player receives a point when he passes the ball to a teammate who scores.

Attackmen: The primary offensive players in field lacrosse, they generally play behind the goal and provide most of a team's offence. Three attackmen stay in their own offensive half of the field at all times.

Back over: Violation where the offending team loses possession of the ball when on offence the ball goes back over the offensive line.

Backdoor cut: When a player cuts not in front of a defender but behind him for a pass.

Behind-the-back pass or shot: Another name is over-the-shoulder pass or shot. The ballcarrier brings the stick up behind his back and passes or shoots the ball.

Body fake: A move in which an offensive player pretends to go one way and then goes the other way in order to beat his defender. This move can be executed with or without the ball.

Box formation: A defensive formation on the man short.

Boxla: Shortened form of box lacrosse.

Break out: Getting the ball out of the defensive end either by running it or passing it up the floor.

Breakaway: A defensive player who breaks out from his own end or an offensive player who runs out of the bench door and gets behind the new defenders.

Bull dodge: This is an offensive move in which you lean into a defender while cradling the stick on the opposite side and use your size and strength to create room to pass or shoot.

Butt-end penalty: Player used the butt of his handle to jab an opposing player.

Centreman: The position name for the player who takes the faceoff.

Change area: Rectangular boxes in front of both benches where players coming off the floor must step before other players can replace them on the floor.

Charging penalty: Running at someone from a distance in an aggressive manner.

Checking-from-behind penalty: This very dangerous hit, which occurs when a player hits or cross-checks an opponent from behind, is an automatic five-minute penalty.

Chest protector: A heavy padding for the goalie to protect his chest and to help him stop the ball.

Circling or cycling: When on offence, the team just keeps cutting over and over again from the off-ball side.

Clamp method: A method of winning the faceoff in which the centreman traps the ball under his netting and pulls it back.

Cornerman: This player plays behind the creaseman on his side and is usually a good long-ball shooter.

Cradling: Cradling is when a player swings the stick in a sweeping arc, locking the ball into the middle of the pocket and setting it up for a quick shot, dodge, or pass.

Crease: In box lacrosse, the crease is the semicircular area in front of the net. The crease in field lacrosse is a full circle with a 9-foot radius. An offensive player is not allowed in the crease.

Creaseman: This is a position on the offensive floor. The player plays at the front of any fast break and usually starts his offence low in the corner area. Most of his scoring is around the crease.

Cross pick-and-roll play: A creaseman comes up the floor in the offensive end and sets a pick by cross-checking or planting the stick on the inside of his teammate's defender's body. The ballcarrier is now sent into the clear with the option of shooting or passing to the picker.

Cross-check penalty: It is usually called when cross-checking the off-ball opponent vigorously.

Cross-checking: A defensive tactic to stop a ballcarrier from scoring by keeping both hands on the stick, a shoulder's-width apart, and thrusting the arms out to jar or hit the ballcarrier.

Defensive zone: When the other team is on offence, the area between the restraining line and the end boards.

Delayed penalty: When the defensive team gets a penalty while the offensive team has possession of the ball. The referee keeps his arm up until the offensive team loses possession, usually on a shot.

Diamond formation: A defensive man-short formation that is used to take away the scoring threat of the three top players in a power-play offence.

Dodge: An offensive move in which a player jukes a defender.

Down pick-and-roll play: In this offensive set, the cornerman moves down the offensive zone to set a pick for a creaseman who has a ball. After the creaseman goes by him, the cornerman rolls toward the net for a pass.

Down screen play: An offensive play where the cornerman interferes or blocks out his own defender so that the creaseman or ballcarrier can cut inside and rub his defender off the screen created by his teammate and his defender.

Draw method: A method of winning the faceoff by drawing the ball straight back while clamping the ball.

Face dodge: An offensive move in field lacrosse in which the player runs at a defender and pulls his stick across his face to the opposite side of the body while running by.

Faceoff: Two players, called centremen, place their sticks back-to-back to fight for possession of the ball by directing the ball to a teammate or by picking it up.

Faceoff circle: The area in the centre of the arena where only the two centremen can go before the ball comes out of the circle. Minor lacrosse playing surfaces have two additional faceoff circles on each end of the floor.

Fast break: The defensive team obtains possession of the ball and quickly tries to get the ball up the floor either by running it or passing it up to breaking teammate off the bench.

Five-minute major penalty: Penalties are given for spearing and butt-ending, both using the stick; kicking; boarding; checking from behind; and fighting.

Five-second count: After stopping a shot in the crease, the goaltender has five seconds to get the ball out of his crease or lose possession of the ball.

Give-and-go: When the ballcarrier passes the ball to a teammate and then cuts to get a return pass back for a scoring opportunity.

Goal: Also called nets, when the ball goes into the net.

Goaltender: His main job is to keep the ball from entering the net. He carries the stick with the biggest pocket.

Hand ball: When a player touches the ball with his hand, his team loses possession of the ball. This is the first and oldest rule in lacrosse.

High-sticking penalty: Given when a player hits an opponent in the neck or head area.

Holding penalty: The act of using the arms to wrap around an opponent or grab an opponent's sweater to impede his progress.

Indian pickup: A specialized method of picking up a loose ball that requires whipping the stick over the ball and quickly flipping it into the pocket.

Inside-slide move: An offensive move where the ballcarrier goes one-on-one against his defender by leaning into him and trying to slide past him into the middle of the offensive zone.

Inside spin: An offensive move where the ballcarrier fakes as if he's cutting outside and instead goes down the sideboards to take a cross-check, and then spins and cuts into the middle of the zone for a shot.

Interference penalty: Making body contact with an opponent who does not have possession of the ball.

Kidney pads: An important piece of equipment to protect the kidneys. Players often turn their backs to their opponents, leaving themselves vulnerable for a hit in the kidney area.

Left-shot: A box lacrosse term for an offensive player who carries the stick over his left shoulder, but plays on the right side of the playing floor.

Line change: After a player comes off the floor, another player can go on.

Lob pass: A short, soft arcing pass thrown by the ballcarrier at the end of the pick-and-roll play.

Long stick: Held by defensive players in field lacrosse, these sticks can measure up to 72 inches long.

Loose ball: A ball that becomes loose where neither team has possession. These are the real battles in lacrosse. Balls can become loose off a shot, off the faceoff, or off a bad pass.

Man-down: When a field lacrosse team gets a penalty, it plays only five defensive players against six offensive players.

Man short: When a box lacrosse team gets a penalty, it plays only four players against its opponents five players.

Man-up: The field lacrosse offence that faces a penalized defence with a one-player advantage.

Mann Cup: This Canadian major lacrosse championship cup is awarded to the winner of a best four-out-of-seven series between the champions of the Ontario Lacrosse Association and the Western Lacrosse Association.

Man-to-man defence: A type of defence in which each player is responsible for guarding one player on the opposing team.

Man-to-man offence: A type of offence that is run when the defensive team plays man-to-man defence.

Match penalty: Match penalties are given when a deliberate intent to injure is involved, including biting, spitting, pulling hair, and so on. The dirtiest of all penalties, players are ejected from the game, and a subsequent hearing decides how many games they are suspended from participating in.

Middie: A midfielder in field lacrosse. These players play both ends of the field, offensively and defensively, and are crucial in transition play.

Minto Cup: This Canadian junior A lacrosse championship cup is awarded to the winner of a best four-out-of-seven series between the champions of the Ontario Lacrosse Association and the British Columbia Lacrosse Association.

Misconduct penalty: A ten-minute penalty for unsportsmanlike behaviour or becoming the third man in a fight.

Motion offence: All five players pass and cut looking for the open man in the best scoring position.

Neutral zone: The neutral zone is the central area of the lacrosse floor that lies between the two restraining lines.

No-look pass: An attempted pass in which the passer deliberately does not make eye contact with his intended receiver.

Non-releasable: A penalty in field lacrosse that does not end when the offence scores.

Offensive zone: The area below the restraining line to the end boards where the offence is run.

One-on-one or penetration: An offensive tactic in which the ballcarrier tries to score by beating his defender.

Outlet pass: The pass that triggers the fast break. On the breakout, the goalie makes a short pass to a teammate waiting around one of the side faceoff circles.

Outside-slide move: An offensive move to beat a defender where the ballcarrier cuts to the outside by leaning into his defender to overpower and slide past him.

Outside spin: An offensive move to beat a defender where the ballcarrier cuts into the middle of the floor and then changes his direction by spinning back and cutting outside.

Overhand pass or shot: A pass or shot where the stick is held straight up and down and follows through straight ahead.

Penalty: The result of an infraction of the rules by a player that results in the removal of the offending player for a specified time, such as 2 minutes, 5 minutes, or 10 minutes in box lacrosse, and 30 seconds, 1 minute or 3 minutes in field lacrosse.

Penalty box: Where the penalized player sits for the duration of a penalty.

Pick-and-roll: An offensive play where a player blocks or interferes with his teammate's defender to free him for a shot or pass. The picker then rolls to the net for a lob pass.

Pocket: The mesh area inside the frame of the lacrosse stick head. The pocket should be about the depth of a lacrosse ball.

Pointman: The offensive player that plays either on the strong side or at the top and in the middle of the offence.

Poke-check: Also called a can opener, a checking technique where the defender tries to get his stick in between the opponent's stick and his body to pry the ball loose or at least make him take a hand off the stick so that he is not a threat to score.

Power play: A team has more players on the floor than the opposition because of a penalty against the opposing team.

Push-and-pull method: A method of winning the ball on the faceoff.

Quick stick: Quick pass or shot where the player does not hesitate after the catch — the ball is in and out of the pocket.

Rake: A part of the faceoff in which a player pulls the ball toward himself or a teammate. On faceoffs, a player can either clamp the ball and then rake it or simply rake right off the whistle.

Rebound: A loose ball off the boards or off the goalie from a missed shot or missed pass.

Restraining lines: Also called offensive line and defensive line, the lines that run across the width of the floor on either side of the centre circle. These lines determine one end of the offensive and defensive

zones. In field lacrosse, these are the two lines, 35 yards from each endline, that separate the field into thirds.

Right-shot: A box lacrosse term for an offensive player who carries the stick over his right shoulder, but plays on the left side of the playing floor.

Scoop pickup: This is a shovelling motion to pick up a loose ball.

Screen: An offensive tactic where a player blocks his defender from switching to defend the ballcarrier.

Set play: An offensive strategy that usually involves a series of predetermined moves in which each player has an assigned task.

Shin guards: Leg guards to protect the goalie's legs and used for stopping shots.

Shooting strings: The strings stretched from the two widest parts of the head. Most sticks have between one and four shooting strings, and most are either nylon or hockey laces — or a combination of the two. They are used to create a smoother release of the ball from the pocket.

Sidearm pass or shot: A type of pass or shot in which the arm and stick movement is parallel to the floor.

Slashing: A form of defence to stop or dislodge the ball that is more prevalent in the game today because of the use of the plastic stick.

Slashing penalty: This box lacrosse penalty occurs when a player gets carried away with violent hitting of the stick on a player.

Specialty teams: A group of players used in specific situations, such as man short, power play, and faceoff.

Split dodge: This offensive move in field lacrosse involves running at a defender and switching the stick from one hand to the other and running by.

Stick-checking: A player tries to check his opponent's stick with his stick to try to dislodge the ball.

Stick fake: The ballcarrier fakes a pass or shot to get a reaction out of the defender and try to beat him.

Switch: When a pick is set and the defender on the ballcarrier gets blocked out of the play, the back defender calls "switch," and the two defenders exchange opponents.

Ten-second count: A violation that occurs when the offensive team cannot get the ball into their offensive end within ten seconds.

30-second rule: The box lacrosse offensive team must take a shot on net within 30 seconds or lose possession of the ball.

30-second shot clock: A clock that counts down the 30 seconds allotted to a box lacrosse offence to attempt a shot. With the exception of the 45-second clock in Major League Lacrosse, the outdoor professional league, field lacrosse has no shot clock.

Tripping: Using your leg to cause an opponent to fall.

Turnover: Losing possession of the ball without taking a shot, such as off a bad pass, when checked off the ball, or committing a violation.

Underhand pass or shot: A type of pass or shot in which the arm and stick movement comes from near the floor.

Up pick-and-roll play: An offensive play during which the creaseman moves up the zone to set a pick against the bottom leg of the defender on the ballcarrier. Ballcarrier cuts to the outside with the picker rolling into the middle of the floor going to the net.

Up screen or seal: An offensive play in which the creaseman moves up the zone to block or interfere with his own check so that the ballcarrier can cut outside and rub his defender off the screen created by his teammate and his defender.

Violation: An action that causes a team to lose possession of the ball.

Warding off: An act of pushing off the defender with the arm when a player has possession of the ball. If it is called, the ballcarrier loses possession.

Wings: These are the two lines parallel to the sidelines where one player from each team stands during faceoffs in field lacrosse. They are 20 yards from the faceoff X.

Wrap-check: Similar to a poke-check, but used when the defender has to go around the player's body to get to his stick.

Zone defence: Lacrosse features two common zone defences: 2-1-2 and 1-2-2. Teams play zone to change the pace of the game, to hide a weaker defensive player, or to enable players to be in position to breakaway on a shot.

Zone offence: An offence that is run when the opposition is playing a zone defence.

Appendix B

Contracts for Coaches, Parents, and Players

● ●

Although the following sample contracts are by no means meant to be legally binding, they should serve to let all participants in a lacrosse league — coaches, players, and parents — know just what's expected of them for the duration of the season.

Sample Coach-to-Player Contract

I, _____, agree to the following:

1. To remember that I chose you based on your skill, attitude, and character in tryouts, and I promise to develop your skill and proper behaviour through practice and games during the season. If I pick you, I play you!

2. To remember that I will be hard on you and push you to your limits. And I do this for your good and the good of the team.

3. To remember that you learn more through encouragement and reward than through criticism and punishment. I will at all times use the former, and resort to the latter only as a last resort and in extreme situations.

4. To play you fairly, remembering that winning is not the desired outcome of any game, but that your skill development and the team improvement is. I will bench you only as a consequence for behavioural problems, lack of effort, falling asleep on the floor, and lack of concentration.

5. To remember you will not be benched for making technical mistakes and game-playing mistakes. I might pull you off the floor to explain the mistake, and then try to put you right back out after it has been corrected.

6. To refrain from making deals with you or your parents regarding floor time, wearing the captaincy, or being on a specialty team. No special treatment will be afforded players related to the coaching staff, their friends, or the team sponsors.

7. To refrain from making promises or threats to you or your parents regarding a position on the team during the season or before tryouts.

8. To never encourage you to play dirty or to try to deliberately injure a player on the opposing team.

9. To never verbally, physically, or psychologically abuse you or players and coaches on the opposing team in a manner unbecoming a coach.

10. To discuss problems with you and your parents until we reach a solution acceptable to all of us. I'll also discuss team problems with the team.

Sample Player-to-Coach Contract

I, _____, agree to the following:

1. I will play because I want to, not because my dad or others want me to play. I know that playing lacrosse is about having fun, improving my skills, making friends, and doing my best, and not about just winning.

2. In preparation for a game and during a game I will concentrate on trying to play my best in order to help the team.

3. I agree that my coaches know more about lacrosse than I do. When a coach offers me advice or instruction, I will listen attentively and will accept their decisions and show them respect. If my initial reaction is to disagree with the advice, I will delay expressing that thought until I have had a chance to consider whether the coach might be correct. If I do not understand something, I will ask for an explanation.

4. I will not criticize my teammates and will acknowledge and cheer good plays by my teammates.

5. I will not complain or sulk during a game about the amount of playing time I am receiving.

6. If I have any problems concerning coaching decisions, my teammates' play or behaviour, or any other concern related to the team, I will discuss it with the coaches after the game . . . not during the game.

7. I will not carry on conversation, threaten, "yap," or say anything to opposing players before, during, or after the game. If an opponent says something to me, I will keep my mouth shut and move promptly to my position or to the bench. I will respect my opponent.

8. At the conclusion of a game, I will follow exactly and promptly the coaches' or referees' instructions concerning staying at the bench or proceeding to the dressing room without incident.

9. During the game I will control my temper. I will try to restrain from fighting and mouthing off.

10. I will sincerely try to avoid retaliation, fighting, and unsportsmanlike or misconduct penalties. I recognize that these types of penalties do not help the team and are selfish displays of temper or lack of discipline.

11. It is okay to be disappointed after a loss. It is unacceptable to display that disappointment by unsportsmanlike behaviour or lack of class.

12. I will play physical, and hard, and play not to hurt my opponents. I will play by the rules of lacrosse and in the spirit of the game.

13. During practices, I will listen attentively and promptly follow the coaches' instruction.

Sample Parent-to-Coach Contract

Parent/guardian of, _____, agrees to the following:

1. I will not yell instructions to my child during the game.

2. I will not criticize my child during the game.

3. I will not make derogatory comments to our players, the opposition players, the referee, and the parents of the opposing team.

4. I will reinforce the coach's philosophy. I will not meddle.

5. I know that my child will learn more through encouragement and reward than through criticism and punishment

6. I will be a good role model for my child. I will follow the high standards the team set for spectator behaviour.

Sample Coach-to-Parent Contract

I, _____, agree to the following:

1. My first priority is the development of my players' skills and character. I promise to develop the players' skill and character through practice and games throughout the season. I will teach players to play fairly and respect the rules, the officials and their opponents. I will coach my players like they are my own children.

2. I will teach them the basics of the game. I promise to develop the players' skills and make them aware of the strategy of the game and team concepts through practices and games throughout the season.

3. I will try to set a good example for the players. My behaviour and demeanour should be such that I am a credit to the team, the organization, and a good role model for the players. I will keep in mind that I am not perfect and that I will make mistakes. I am here to encourage and develop sportsmanship, skill, and a love of the game in all players.

4. I will positively reinforce the players. I know that players learn more through encouragement, support, and positive reward than through criticism and punishment. I will, at all times, use the former, and resort to the latter only as a last resort and only in extreme situations.

5. I will be fair with the players. I promise to play each player fairly, which doesn't mean "evenly," remembering that success is the result of skill development. I will bench a player only as discipline for behavioural problems. I will try to be firm and fair. I will treat everybody equally.

6. I will not bench players for making technical mistakes or mistakes in their play. I will call players to the bench to explain their mistake, and then put them back on the floor. I will be generous with praise to build their confidence. I could bench players as a consequence for being late for a game or practice, not hustling, sulking, showing negative emotions, getting upset and taking retaliatory penalties.

7. I will not coach politically by making deals. I will not make deals with players or parents regarding floor time, playing on special teams, or wearing the captaincy. No special treatment will be afforded players related to the coaching staff, their friends, or the team sponsors.

8. I will not make promises to players or parents regarding a position on the team during the season or before tryouts.

9. I will not threaten players about kicking them off the team because of their playing ability. The only way of being dismissed from the team is for continual bad behaviour.

10. I do not coach to hurt opposing players. I will never encourage our players to deliberately injure a player or players on the opposing team.

11. I will never verbally abuse my players or players and coaches of the opposing team. I do not believe in embarrassing players in front of teammates, parents, and fans.

12. I will discuss problems with the players and their parents until a solution can be reached acceptable to all parties.

Index

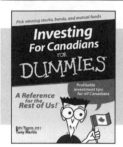

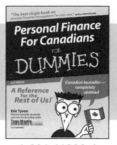

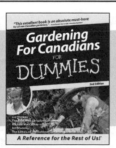

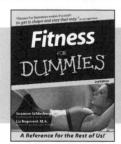

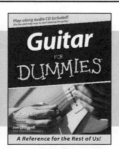

FOR DUMMIES®

A world of resources to help you grow

TRAVEL

0-7645-5453-0

0-7645-5438-7

0-7645-5444-1

Also available:

America's National Parks For Dummies
(0-7645-5493-X)

Caribbean For Dummies
(0-7645-5445-X)

Cruise Vacations For Dummies 2003
(0-7645-5459-X)

Europe For Dummies
(0-7645-5456-5)

Ireland For Dummies
(0-7645-5455-7)

France For Dummies
(0-7645-6292-4)

Las Vegas For Dummies
(0-7645-5448-4)

London For Dummies
(0-7645-5416-6)

Mexico's Beach Resorts
For Dummies
(0-7645-6262-2)

Paris For Dummies
(0-7645-5494-8)

RV Vacations For Dummies
(0-7645-5443-3)

EDUCATION & TEST PREPARATION

0-7645-5194-9

0-7645-5325-9

1-894-41319-9

Also available:

The ACT For Dummies
(0-7645-5474-3)

Chemistry For Dummies
(0-7645-5430-1)

English Grammar For Dummies
(0-7645-5322-4)

French For Dummies
(0-7645-5193-0)

GMAT For Dummies
(0-7645-5251-1)

Inglés Para Dummies
(0-7645-5427-1)

Italian For Dummies
(0-7645-5196-5)

Research Papers For Dummies
(0-7645-5426-3)

SAT I For Dummies
(0-7645-5472-7)

U.S. History For Dummies
(0-7645-5249-X)

World History For Dummies
(0-7645-5242-2)

HEALTH, SELF-HELP & SPIRITUALITY

0-7645-5154-X

0-7645-5302-X

0-7645-5418-2

Also available:

The Bible For Dummies
(0-7645-5296-1)

Controlling Cholesterol
For Dummies
(0-7645-5440-9)

Dating For Dummies
(0-7645-5072-1)

Dieting For Dummies
(0-7645-5126-4)

High Blood Pressure For
Dummies
(0-7645-5424-7)

Judaism For Dummies
(0-7645-5299-6)

Menopause For Dummies
(0-7645-5458-1)

Nutrition For Dummies
(0-7645-5180-9)

Potty Training For Dummies
(0-7645-5417-4)

Pregnancy For Dummies
(0-7645-5074-8)

Rekindling Romance For
Dummies
(0-7645-5303-8)

Religion For Dummies
(0-7645-5264-3)

Available wherever books are sold. Go to www.dummies.com or call 1-800-567-4797 to order direct